Humor i
Outdoors

JOHN SHUNNESON

MARY ELLEN SHUNNESON

JIM O'CONNOR

ISBN: 1535459026
ISBN-13: 978-1535459020

Visit us at:
humorinthegreatoutdoors.com

CONTENTS

Barry

Our friendship of YEARS
STARTING AS FISHERMEN
AND AS STUDENTS HAS
LASTED FOREVER. WE THANK
YOU FOR EVERY CHRISTMAS
WHEN YOU BRING US JOY.
MAY THIS BOOK BRING
YOU MANY LAUGHS AND
YOUR WONDERFUL WIFE
MAY GET A FEW TOO!
WE LOVE YOU, YOUR
FRIEND
John Skunneson
Sept-2016

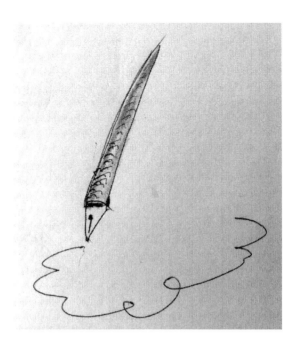

ACKNOWLEDGMENTS

The collection of stories making up this book actually began in the late 1980's. A good friend, Jim O'Connor and I started this book back at that time. Unfortunately, my good friend died in 1998 and that event ended all accomplishments. Due to earlier health limitations of my own in 2014 I picked up my pen once more to complete this book. I wish to offer an account of the other people and places that made this book possible.

First and foremost my Mother, Vi, my brother, Arlad and I lived on Grass Lake, Illinois. I can honestly say "on" as during spring floods our house was on and surrounded by the lake. At dryer times our home was located by three sides of the lake. The Fox River Dam at Wilmont, Wisconsin (Gander Mountain) flowed its water into Grass Lake. This lake was one of many that formed a chain in northern Illinois going partially into southern Wisconsin. The chain made a continuous circle that flowed back into the Fox River with the chain waterway ending at the McHenry, Illinois Dam.

All this water with its countless resorts would be the environment Lad and I would grow up in. The many outdoor and water sports were ours as young boys and what a dream it was in the 1950's and 60's. One true story, "Mud Hen Pusher" goes into detail about our life's there. At this point it should be said that all of my other stories within are fictional. The two stories by Mary Ellen and Jim are true stories.

My father's parents were Swedish and they owned a Grass Lake resort from 1914 until WWII. My father grew up at that resort and later operated his own on Channel Lake which was a part of the chain. He ran that resort from 1946 until his retirement in 1978. His entire life was in fishing and hunting resorts and he would pass this lifestyle down to his sons. Beyond the fun and outdoor knowledge he taught us there was plenty resort work for us as well. Barney was his name and he could take credit for teaching many children and adults the successful techniques of fishing. The Linder brothers of Minnesota started at Dad's resort and Buck Perry was a good friend that offered more for Dad to teach. In the winter his resort closed with ice up and then he went south to Florida to fish the Atlantic through the winter. Both my brother and I visited him and Florida during our high school days to learn about the ocean and alligators. Our parents were divorced while we were very young so we basically did not see him during the winter months. Dad had a good sense of humor and enjoyed clean jokes but told very few. He did own a great laugh but his main influences on his sons were the love of nature and respect for the outdoors. His story would be one of "How To" yet this book is one of humor.

The humor part then must be from my Mother VI, who lived to be 86. Her mom came from Norway while her father was of English descent. Now those two grandparents of mine knew humor. They could have taught anybody how to laugh and they did a good job of it with me. They gave that trait to my Mother who always could tell a funny joke and play one on you too. An example is once when I was six years old with her we were on our way to visit my grandparents. She was driving the car along and suddenly I had the great urge to pee. She told me, "Think about something calm, think about Niagara Falls!" With that I peed all over myself and in my pants. She laughed and laughed and mind you I was only six years old. The trick playing was with her all through her entire life. Every April 1st, Fool's Day Mom always had a trick for my brother and I without fail. She also loved to tell funny stories and what talent I have at it surely came from her.

A few times my brother and I pulled a few tricks on her as well. When Mom went bowling or on a date while we were young our babysitter was a family friend. He was Harry Novotny, a retired game warden that taught us many tricks. One was to put raw eggs in Mom's winter boots and another was to put live frogs in the kitchen's silverware drawer. It was all in great fun.

Mom was an outdoors' lady. She spent her married years with my Dad hunting ducks and pheasants while all through life she loved fishing. She went to Africa in her 70's with my brother the avid hunter and many years fishing with me. We went to Minnesota once where the perch were hitting and even at dark I had a hard time getting her off the lake. In Nebraska in her 80's she caught by herself a 10lb Northern Pike. She also took her two boys camping in Wisconsin too many times to count. That was in tents by the way. Yes, Mom loved the outdoors and humor a great deal. I owe a lot to her on both those wonderful life events. Our Grass Lake home always was full of fishermen, hunters and more importantly love and laughter.

A great influence in my life was the Boy Scouts of America. I was a Cub, Boy and Explorer Scout that made the Life rank. The years of learning and camping in Wisconsin taught me a great wealth of knowledge totally due to Scouting and my Scout Masters. Hopefully you the reader will see some of it in my stories and I hope every young boy and girl has the opportunity to join the Scouts.

Next to be thanked is my brother, Arlad always known as Lad to his close friends and myself. As of this writing he is yet a worldwide trophy fishing and hunting outfitter. He has been around the world fishing and hunting more than once. His adventures have been from the Arctic to China and all parts in between and few if any have matched his outdoor endeavors it must be said. We started out in duck boats and floating duck blinds while today he is well known in Safari International. We have shared many wonderful trips together but more importantly his true stories have always left me in awe. He also is an attorney in Colorado that does not practice. He told me that profession is no good as all the people you meet are in trouble. He prefers outfitting. During my younger wilder days in Colorado I might add it was lucky to have a brother practicing law.

Real credit for this book goes to my beautiful wife Mary Ellen. She only surpasses her out side beauty with her inside beauty. She has added a true story to this collection for your enjoyment. Mary Ellen has spent countless hours preparing this book along with always loving fishing. She is extremely kind to hunting dogs as well as all domestic animals. There were many years we operated a waterfowl hunting business in Nebraska, which included her working from 4 AM till 10 at night. The long hours never tempered her humor and laughs to everyone's enjoyment.

Finally our son, Todd the computer whiz deserves huge credit in making this book a reality. In this day and age a good computer guy is mandatory and he is that and more. Through life I have had the honor of passing down the outdoors' experienced to him. Our trips in nature have made my life complete in so many ways only a father understands. He has a great laugh and wonderful sense of humor most likely passed down from his Grandmother Vi.

Well, there you have it. This book of humor in many ways is my family's history. The goal of it is you have some chuckles and hopefully some good belly laughs too. Then this book is a roaring success.

Illustrations By: Dr. Les Coldfoot

A CAMPING WE WILL GO!

The vast majority of us on the planet today feel the natural need to connect with nature through the great experience of camping in the outdoor world. Oh to set up your tent and sleep on a rock, there is nothing like it. To camp or not to camp most of us do it or have done it or will do it. Many of us by our own free will and the rest of us in the U.S. Army where it is so much fun they get to sleep on two rocks. It is one big slumber party of sorts.

Our passion for camping no doubt dates back to our earliest ancestors who had no choice on the matter. They not only slept on rocks they slept in rocks called home, they were the cavemen. In that our earliest ancestors had no television for home entertainment they solved the problem by having many caves and traveled about nature switching their outdoor views from time to time. They camped here and there long before the invention of the park sticker or designated spaces. Their needs were simple and practical, a cave and a fire with a roasted rodent would do them just fine. The camping evolution from this earliest of times to our modern era is a story to be told.

Most of us started out camping where else but in our own backyards. The freeway with all its traffic buzzing away close to us or a few miles away did not exist in our world as we were pioneers in our own safe and sound vast campgrounds. We stretched a rope from our back door's corner as tight as we could to a backyard tree. The freeway with all its traffic zooming away did not exist in our backyard world, as the sounds would just be muted out. The ropes may have had a little sag in them, but heck it seemed good enough for us.

Next, Mom would give us an old blanket perhaps with a hole or two in it here or there which we hung over the trusty rope to learn our ropes were too high or too low. Adjustments would have to be made until at last the proper heights were accomplished with yet maybe some sags present. We accomplished and overlooked them; hey remember we are only kids. Then we would drive stakes in the blanket's corners and presto we had our very first tent suitable for a King. Heck, we are the Kings!

With our tent set up next comes that all-important bedroll just like the cowboys always had. Here again Mom comes through and hands out the nice warm blankets we can use, two of them to be exact. No holes in them neither. Somehow we do sneak out our favorite pillow as you can only take this cowboy stuff so far let's face it. A King's tent, a bedroll, a favorite pillow, oh boy a camping we will go! Maybe some marshmallows would go good in this operation as well, so we got them, the whole bag.

To add to this great outdoor adventure Mom cooks hotdogs on the outside grill. How sweet it is that gas grill being our very first campfire of sorts. Somehow Dad isn't much into this pioneer stuff as he gets his hotdog all right and then proceeds into the house to his easy chair and the TV. It is safe to say he would not have been a very good caveman or cowboy by any accounts.

Then night comes, well almost night but rather the darkness that only city life lights permit. The yard lights and the street lamps prohibit real darkness as only the real country would and could. In the homemade pup tent there is great security from the outside world with the added protection of the yard's chain-link fence, which will surely keep out the nights imaginary wolves and bears. Since the tent's ends were wide open it was nice to know the heavy duty chain link fence would surely keep such wild animals at bay. The open ends allowed the city lights to shine in just like sleeping under the stars if there ever happened to be any bright enough to outcast all the modern man made lights. Ah yes, this is true camping at its best with only one more item on our agenda before crawling into the warm awaiting bed roll. That is attacking the big bag of marshmallows. Of course it is eaten and eaten as any emergency rations would be and then leaving three or four for later survival in this wild space of our own backyard. One never knows what the future could bring and maybe all this unsupervised eating is the cause of the now bellyache we gave ourselves. Only perhaps?

Next crawl under one blanket with the other underneath to hold back all the yard's bugs and perhaps worse a garter snake or two. Such thoughts do cross our minds, as this is our first adventure in the great wild outdoors. Now seemingly protected from the snakes, bugs, bears and wolves with a gentle breeze sweeping through our homemade cave we finally should have peace of mind. To sleep we shall go, but no, the bellyache throbs with one thing leading to another.

We hear a sound unlike no other known to mankind or to us for that matter. It sounds like a scratching noise on our domain. This brings to our mind the story told to us about the creepy one-handed man that stalks the night. He has a hook where his left hand should be, thus he is called the old one-handed hooked man. How creepy is this for he is after us on top of a bellyache. Yikes, the old one-handed hooked man is to get us we believe based upon the outside sounds we hear. No, to our delight we learn the scratching is not the old one-handed hooked man but just Fido our dog. He just wanted to join us in our tent so we happily let him in. We were just using the best of the seat of our pants wisdom thinking it was the old one-handed hooked man.

Next to make things worse, sure enough we set our home right up over one of the yard's automatic sprinkler systems. As luck would have it the time to go off is any minute. This was poor planning, but heck remember once again we are kids with no Einstein reasoning abilities. It is 10 o'clock and the sprinklers activate with the one under us hissing like a wild animal in quicksand. The sprinkler spraying results in our bottom blanket now soaked with no let up in sight. Lucky enough it is a warm night with the warm breeze sweeping through the open ends of the shelter we proudly built. The only options we face are to call it quits and return inside to our own dry warm bed or stick it out here in nature? Pondering the options it is decided to stay and simply pretend we are just sleeping on a huge waterbed. Maybe it is a good thing, the wet bottom surely will keep the bugs and imaginary snakes away.

The bellyache finally lets up and we become accustom to the wet ground. Then Fido goes outside to lift his leg on our tent to do his business. Old faithful Fido made the one wall nice and wet and smelly. By 2 AM lightning and thunder is in the heavens headed directly to our humble campsite. It rains and it rains like cats and dogs even though nobody has ever seen those animals falling in the rain. We are now in a monsoon with everything wet and soaked. Fido is the smartest as he quickly leaves for higher and drier ground with our campsite a torrid mess we too decide to call it quits as Einstein himself surely would. Our initial solo camping experience has not been the best, however we enjoyed it enough to try it again in later life.

The next stage of us enjoying the great outdoors comes when we joined the Boy or Girl Scouts of America. They are great organizations with wonderful adult leaders. These leaders are called Scout Masters as they are masters of us, all of nature and the whole universe we believe. They teach us how to travel into the wilderness with all the proper equipment and the right way to conquer the outdoors. While some of us learned to start a fire with the old flint and steel method smarter scouts brought along a hidden Bic lighter. Oddly enough their campfires were the first going while others were striking away the flints. Then there was the scout that against all rules brought his canteen full of gasoline. This was totally unethical and illegal so that's exactly what he did making his fire erupt into an explosion ten feet high creating a light upon the entire camping area. Scout Masters of the world would go into a rage over this dangerous event, a far cry from the old flint and steel method. The Scout apologized and much later in life goes on to use his genius ways to invent the Internet. Come to think about it, maybe it was Bill Gates after all he was a Boy Scout.

The Scouts taught us a vast amount of outdoor knowledge that would endure us our entire lifetimes. We learned about animals, plants and trees with all below and above them. We learned about poison ivy and poison oak the hard way by walking straight into it. Then pink calamine lotion for two weeks to cure it. Those affected would be covered from head to toe in pink so we knew who the stupid ones were. The really stupid one was those who used the ivy leaves to wipe their butts when nature called. They really ended up with painful pink butts.

Next we were taught to use trees beyond their fire use. Just like Native Americans you could simply make a canoe from birch bark we were told. Good luck on that one as no canoe has ever been seen of birch bark to this very day. However, trees did make great rafts, which were fun and useful. In later life you might find yourself on one of those cruise ships that broke down in the Pacific Ocean. You could swim to an island and presto make a raft and what a hero you would be! Also trees of course make houses and so many other items in our daily lives. As Scouts we did not make a log cabin, however we did whittle out a spoon or two as a start.

Then there were animals to learn about. Survival skills would be needed perhaps someday in your distant future with animals providing you with food. A simple trap could be constructed with some mesh wire like that of a rabbit cage, an old tin can and a mousetrap. The idea is a chipmunk goes into the can after some bait and triggers the trap, which flips up the wire, and presto you have your meal. Doesn't roast chipmunk sound like a gourmet entrée as it did back then? By the way you used peanut butter for bait, so why wouldn't you just eat the peanut butter as your meal one Scout asked? No answer was ever given by the Master. Next, in your survival skills you have to now learn about animals you could eat if you had neither bait nor trap. The answer came that you find a porcupine as it was told this animal is a ground one which could be approached with ease. You simply approached it, clubbed it with a mighty stick and roasted it on your open flame. What was never taught was how do you skin one of these critters in that they have a zillion sharp arrows protecting them. Thus it must be said the scouting experience did teach many of us a great wealth of nature's habits and an enduring love of the outdoors.

Next, the day comes when we are adults and wealthy ones at that. Our love of the outdoors continued from those old caveman days, so a camping we will go once more. Ah, to explore our beautiful national parks is as easy as driving there to set up our tents and RVs. We arrived at the parks with expectations of being in the wilderness where the antelope roam. Our dream is broken when we are directed to a designated area where our "campsite" is a space 12x15 feet marked off with fluorescent red paint on asphalt. So much for the old Boy Scout wilderness. Okay, we get to our asphalt space in our $60,000 RV and the space has one lonely pine tree next to the white and green trash barrel. Worst, there are fifty more asphalt spaces each with a RV in them making this National Park look exactly as any big city suburb. Is this what Teddy Roosevelt had in mind you ask yourself? Oh well, you pull into your designated space and be happy your drive here is over. Next, set up your jacks then push the button that springs out your extra room off your used $60,000 RV. Could it get worse? Yes, night comes and a zillion cute little strings of lights come to life set up from the trees to the fifty RVs. Some of the lights have Santa's and others have green-lighted trees. Is this Christmas or what? Well, we rough it and tuck ourselves in for a good night's sleep except our neighbors three feet away have different ideas. A group of them gather singing off key to a guitar not tuned through all hours of the night. Then there are many generators making their loud mechanical and exhaust sounds. These monsters power the poor souls that did not get electrical hookups as you have. Oh what fun!

But at least you know no self-respecting bear or for that matter even a chipmunk would wander into this modern-day concept of nature lovers.

Morning comes with cooking a hearty breakfast in your self contained RV's kitchen just like the fifty other families here are doing. You decide a nice long hike is on your agenda. The friendly park ranger in a military type uniform gives you a map with marked trails to insure you do not get lost or find yourself in a poison ivy patch. You remember from your scouting days of how dangerous poison ivy can be and also that ugly pink lotion cure. Maybe marked trails are a good idea after all. Now you and Junior will take off into the wilds. The women opt out to stay at camp to watch satellite TV and check on grandma back home with their cell phones. Camping surely ain't what it used to be!

Off Junior and you head out to the designated trail marked "LONE WOLF TRAIL" which sounds a lot safer than the one marked "BEARS DELIGHT." After all we don't want Junior to be eaten on his first nature journey trek. So it is "LONE WOLF TRAIL" to find and take after getting out of the maze of 50 asphalt RV spaces. Once found the trail is clearly marked as well as signs reading "DON'T FEED THE ANIMALS" and "KEEP OF THE GRASS." Are we in the city or what? Nonetheless we hike along the well-trotted path that at least one hundred others have also done this season. After a mile or so you can see less and less have made it this far. Probably old retired people, as the markings of canes are no longer in the ground. They most likely have returned to the safety of their homes away from home where no bears or wolves roam. They never got too far away from the asphalt jungle to see the lone wolf you guess. A good thing as now you can tell junior about the old days when you were a Boy Scout and how things used to be. Junior kind of listens to you while playing a game on his iPod as you explain trees, leaves and animal tracks that you see which you call wolf tracks that are really only raccoon tracks. Old age has fogged your memory it seems. Hiking along he asks, "Dad, what is this?" as he points to the ground. You look down and sure enough it's a used prophylactic. All you can say is, "It's a medical device for use with a bad thumb." The kid by now not interested in nature goes back to his iPod. All you can think is now you know why this is called, "The LONE WOLF TRAIL."

Back to camp with one more night of off key singing and all those generators humming along to give you one more restless night. The weekend is over the next day so you push the button to have the extended room retracted and then pack up the rest of your campsite. You need to pick up the folding chairs, the firewood you purchased at the convenience store although due to a high fire warning no fires were allowed, a beer can someone threw into your space and the hammock you could not use since you only had the one trash can tree. Your asphalt "campsite" is now clean as a whistle, which means a pleasant drive back home is anticipated. At last back on the road with at least thirty other campers making up the caravan headed for home. Yes, one more weekend of nature and modern-day camping is gone until another day. The blankets in the backyard days are gone forever, yet with fondness you recall them to yourself and to yourself alone.

THE HIKING STORY

This is the story on why and how I wrote this story. First, the why I wrote this story requires the background of myself, Tommy Welch. I am a student in my junior year at the South Dakota School Of Mines located in Rapid City. In order to help finance my education I work part-time during the evening shift flipping burgers at the local McDonald's. The manager, who of course is my boss, tells me he is writing an instructional book concerning the great outdoors. His name is Ricky Overton, age 32 and I doubt he is capable of writing a letter home to his mother. Now he tells me he is writing a book with the kicker being he wants me to write a story to put in the book. I'm sure he would take credit for the story. He is my boss so if I say, "No I won't write you a story," that probably ends up with no job for myself. This boss is the type you love to hate but I needed the job's money so it looked like I would be writing a story like it or not. I asked, "Okay, Ricky, what type of story do you want me to write?" He said, "Well since you go to that rock school you're outside most of the time. I want you to write a story on hiking and it better be good. Your future here is on the line." See how direct he made things? He went on, "It has to tell everyone how to do it, young, old, skinny, fat, rich, poor, black, white, men, women, and Vets with one leg too. I mean everybody! It has to have drama and adventure way beyond your one, two, three flipping a burger. You've got thirty days to do it or you'll be out the door." The only thing I could think of to ask him was, "Should it have a girl in a bikini in it too, that really sells?" He replied, "Yeah that's a good idea." Now you know why I wrote this story but I was left with how would I write such a story? To do this story I decided on enlisting my four buddies from the rock n roll band I am a part of. However, my plan was to keep it a secret from them as if they knew I thought for sure they would all act as clowns resulting in no true story. My secret writing space would be my old 67 Chevy pickup truck complete with a filing cabinet known as a glove box. The hard part would be to convince them all we should take up hiking.

Our band was one that played part-time on weekends for college dances and local small saloons. We are a five-piece band that did regular rock n roll with some country music now and then. Ivan is our drummer and a good one at that. He also goes to the School of Mines with the only goal of learning where diamonds rest in the earth's foundation. He is a rich kid from New York City that never has worked a day in his life. He is a lot of fun for having an eastern accent such as he never has ideas just idearrs. Then there is Donny our rhythm guitar player from Sioux Falls. He is skinny, clumsy, and speedy and never sits still; rather he is moving every minute. The best way to describe Donny is he would make a cup of coffee nervous. Next is Ira our lead guitar player and lead singer who is the best looking guy in the band. It seemed he had more girls chasing him than the hills have rocks. He is a big joker in the band with a lot going for him. His real job is he is a mortician and he claims he likes slow moving people. Next is Owen, our keyboard player that sings harmony. He grew up here in the Black Hills and he is a big guy, okay let's face it he's just fat. He goes to the School of Mines with an obsession regarding all dinosaurs. Given his size that fits him to a T as in T-Rex. Finally then there is me from Sturgis playing base and singing some when not flipping burgers. We consider ourselves interesting, somewhat talented guys and in the beginning we had to come up with a name for our band. We decided to use the letters of our first names, which spelled out "Idiots." So, we are "The Idiots." My goal was to get the Idiots to go on a hike in order that I could write a story and keep my hamburger job. The problem was how do you get a bunch of idiots to do anything?

My only hiking experience was limited to one time when I was very young. Back then my family went camping in the Black Hills and we decided to hike up to the top of Mount Harney. This is the highest point in South Dakota. It was a hot August day and Dad decided he would stay at camp to snooze in his hammock. That left my Mom, older brother and myself going on this major hike. My brother and I were very excited about going to the top of our state. Our mother as the good sport she always was thought it would be great fun too. Mom packed up needed emergency rations of candy, potato chips and liquids. It seemed we had enough for a small army. Away the three of us went on that hot afternoon which only got hotter. In the hike's beginning the path looked like a real army had marched up the mountain. One-third the way up the beaten easy path turned into hard going and then only huge rocks were there with no path. My brother and I declared, "Let's go Mom, it'll be a lot of fun," and Mom naturally agreed. It became over two hours of climbing huge rocks up, down and around in the heat of the day. My brother and I had a blast doing the big rocks while Mom puffed and sweated in the 90 plus-degree day. Eventually we did arrive at the summit to find ourselves all alone as the brutal heat continued. To our surprise in an effort to cool down Mom took off her blouse exposing herself with only her bra. To see our mother only in a bra was a shock and actually embarrassing for us young boys. As Mom attempted to cool down she told us, "Boys I'm 50 years old and I want you to remember this hike. When you both reach fifty I want you to come back here and repeat this climb with your children and make sure it is a 90° day too." That is the only hike I can recall, one I will never forget.

Running through the Black Hills is a nature path going many miles from Spearfish to Hot Springs. This was a railroad route in the days of old while in modern times the tracks and ties were removed to create a hiking and nature trail. In the autumn of each year wealthy business companies promote the trail by hiding six separate $1,000 prizes in one hundred dollar bills hidden within the route. The Rapid City Journal newspaper advertised that the cash prizes would be between Deadwood and Hill City during the year we were to go. The paper also gave out clues to the money's locations on the day before the actual event. The prize money was placed out during the proceeding night. My job was to convince the band members to go on a search for the money. Then I would have a good hiking story and let's face it I was dealing with four idiots. The band was in need of upgrading our sound system so I used that as a ploy to get the idiots interested in the money hunt. Only our full figured guy, Owen was reluctant as his concept of a big hike was from his couch to the refrigerator. The other three idiots convinced Owen it would be good for him and they promised they would bring a full box of Snicker's candy bars just for him. Finally with all in agreement to go find the money I'd have a story and surely would keep my burger-flipping job.

The day of the money hunt was September 15th and it was a beautifully warm autumn morning that would begin the search for the hidden treasures. The basic rules were you could start from either town but you had to check in between 6 AM and 8 AM. We paid the fifty-dollar entry fee and checked in at the Deadwood starting point. The sponsors estimated that 1500 people would participate but I thought double that number showed up. We had our newspaper with its clues and we all had our red T-shirts on that proclaimed in huge white block letters, "I'm An Idiot." That made people wonder why we would be on any hunt I'm sure. Our plan was to search for eight hours and then walk out to Highway 385 where Ira would get on his cell phone to call one of his girlfriends who would pick us up. With our backpacks full of food, candy bars and liquids we were off to find the money.

My hiking story adventure now was becoming a reality. It actually was 7 AM when we left the Deadwood starting point headed for the second prize location. We figured the first would have been discovered by the time we had arrived there. Well this group of idiots was wrong as when we reached that point at least 800 people were yet searching that area. I said, "Better for us as this will mean less where we are going." Owen was lagging behind and Ira yelled back at him, "You have to keep up with us, we're going to go faster now." Owen muttered back, "This is too much for me, I'm going back so give me a couple of Snickers." Donny, the speedy guy remarked to Owen, "Holy Macaroni Molly, big buffet boy you afraid of losing your baby fat?" I added, "Come on Owen, we've only hiked a mile or so and you won't find any money or dinosaur bones if you go home now." Owen looked at me and said, "That's too bad, you guys can look for me. I'm beat carrying around 200 extra pounds than you guys. Besides, with luck I can get back in time for the Pizza Hut's noon all-you-can-eat buffet." With that Owen quit the hike and went back to Deadwood our starting point. We were now one less idiot. The three remaining idiots and I hiked on towards stash #2 on the route. The clue read, "Treasure #2 from Deadwood. Hike 2 ½ miles down the trail to a creek. Once there look for a dead cottonwood tree and there is a hole with the money in it. Good luck!" I said, "We have about one mile to go to reach that point." Then I asked, "How will we know when we get there? None of us have a pedometer or any way of knowing our distance traveled, boy are we stupid." Ira responded, "We're not stupid, we're idiots. A creek, a dead tree and I'll bet one hundred people will be there. If they are there that's good as then the money will be there." I said, "You are right Ira, I'm looking through binocs and there are a lot of people hunting there. The cottonwood has no branches for at least fifteen feet up, it's a big old tree and I see about four guys trying to scale the fifteen feet. One guy is on top of another's shoulders trying but it looks like they all are pushing each other to the ground. Then there is a huge crowd on the ground watching all this. But I don't see any hole in the tree, must be on the other side of it." Ira responded, "Well let's get going before somebody finds the money," and the group picked up the pace until reaching the crowd gathered by the old dead tree. Ira spoke first, "Man there's five of 'em trying to get up that tree and none of them are making it up. If one even gets close to a branch the others pull him off and down. I don't see how we are going to do this." Ivan responded, "I have to rest up from that last jog we made, let me think about this." I was just thinking about how we might be able to get up the tree too while Donny was running around like his pants were on fire. He was by the small creek that was so small anyone could easily jump across it. Not clumsy Donny though as when he went to jump his one foot fell into a hole. A hole! He pulled out his foot and then a bag. He yelled out for all to hear, "I got it, Holy Macaroni Molly I got the money!" Sure enough the waterproof bag had ten $100 bills in it and someone in the crowd yelled out, "The idiot got it!" Apparently they had read the big letters on his red shirt.

The four of us gathered together happy as the day is long that Donny had found the money. Somebody in the crowd muttered, "Look there's four idiots." Yes, there were four very happy idiots. After a few snacks we decided to go look for the next $1,000. I got out the newspaper to read about the next hidden money; it read "Clue #3 from Deadwood go 1¾ miles from the dead tree of #2 towards Hill city. Once there you will cross a bridge, then go five hundred yards to the rocks on your right. Treasure #3 is in the town of rocks. Good luck!" Happily as can be the four of us started on our march to the rocks and of course the entire crowd hiked forward as well. The nature path seemed more like a LA freeway at rush hour than any place even a chipmunk would be. As we were going along Ivan and Ira were talking about this and that. I was thinking to myself on how lucky we were to find the money and how I had put no effort into a story about hiking. I had no real information about hiking clothes; shoes or gear so figured Ricky was not going to like my story about us idiots. Worst, I surely had no way of adding a girl in a bikini for him. I put myself to rest by thinking maybe with no job I could just borrow more money for school if need be. Then I overheard Ira and Ivan talking about money. Ivan said, "You know when I finish school I'm going to Australia to find diamonds. I'll have my degree and go to work for a big outfit to become a fat cat." Ira made the point, "You know Ivan had you saved all the money you have spent on women you would be a fat cat already." Ira simply responded, "You know what I'd do if I had all that money I spent on women? I'd take that money and spend it on more women." As they talked on Donny was ten steps ahead of us all saying, "Come on, Come on, let's get going to the rocks as they could be full of diamonds and women plus we know there's money in them for sure." He motivated us to keep going even though it was lunchtime. We never thought about stopping for lunch nor did any of the crowd we were a part of. Everyone kept hiking like it was gold fever in the Black Hills once more. It was about one in the afternoon when we crossed the bridge to arrive at the rocks. Yes there were rocks, thousands upon thousands of them. An ancient glacier had created a bed of rocks ¼ mile wide by ½ mile long. They varied in size from marbles to boulders and all in between. Already fifty or so hunters were in them searching for the thousand dollars upon our arrival. I, as well as many others looked at this site in total amazement and wondered how could anyone find a treasure hidden within it? It surely was the needle in the haystack situation I'd ever seen. This is going to be a time consuming effort with a lot of luck needed.

We all agreed upon a plan and that was we would walk through the field ten feet apart and in a row. This way we could comb the field in one direction then at the end turn around and do the same coming back. We started our march where we saw less people already in the vast rock field. To walk ½ a mile would only take twenty minutes but we were painstakingly searching. It took us over one hour to go from one end to the other in the huge rocks and boulders. Plus the dead trees made it all the more difficult for us. After our third pass through the rocks it was 4 o'clock in the afternoon. Ivan spoke out, "You know we are getting nowhere and nobody else has found the money either. Don't you guys think we should call it a day?" I agreed, "Yeah we do have $1000, let's finish this pass back to the bridge and then head for home. Once we get out of these rocks we have to go another ¼ mile to the highway." Ira was in agreement but Donny as usual was jumping around in the rocks paying no attention to the rest of us. As clumsy as he always was he fell down in the rocks were a dead tree was lying on the ground. He yelled out, "Holy Macaroni Molly, this old tree is hollow and there's something in it." Yes, as luck would have it Donny found another $1,000 treasure for us. I would have to say at that point we were the happiest four idiots in the world! The clumsiest of us, Donny had found both treasures to our amazement. I wished Owen could have been with us to share in our joy but that was not to be. Then I looked back at the clues on the treasure Donny or we had just found. It's said, "Treasure #3 will be in the town of rocks." Now the money was not found in the rocks at all, it was found inside a dead tree. The clue said, "town" and the dead tree was for the town of Deadwood. All we should have done is looked at the dead trees in the field of rocks. It was easy to understand that after-the-fact and I shared the idea with the others to only hear, "Oh yeah."

Next we hiked out to the highway where Ira called one of his girlfriends for our pickup. That done he called Owen to tell him the good news. On our trip we had found no diamonds or dinosaur bones but us idiots were $2,000 richer to put into our band. We eventually purchased bigger speakers and new idiot shirts with sparkling gold letters. I never wrote any story for Ricky and did lose my hamburger job. To protect him the reason he used was I was late to work several times which was true. I would just have to obtain more student loans and I surely would not miss Ricky. For many months the band members reminisced about that September day when Donny had found the two secret treasures. I always felt good about not having to use my old 67 Chevy pickup to write a different story. The glove box went empty. As time went on we did write a song about that autumn day. The final line was, "Not bad for a bunch of idiots!"

THE WRITER

Denny Hopkins is an outdoors writer for the monthly magazine "HAPPY OUTDOORS." This magazine is sold over-the-counter coast to coast and also has a subscription readership of 600,000. On the store magazine racks it seems it is always hidden amongst the ladies magazines, which is totally out of place. Why an outdoors' magazine would be among lady glamour ones baffled Denny a great deal for many years. One fall day Denny was in a convenience store along the interstate highway and sure enough his magazine was among the lady ones. Denny calmly asked the high school boy at the counter why "HAPPY OUTDOORS" was placed so wrongly on the rack? The young man replied, "HAPPY OUTDOORS" fits in with glamour as it tells the ladies on just how to make their yards and gardens look wonderful."

Needless to say Denny did not approve of the young man's answer. Denny next asked the boy, "Didn't you ever open the magazine up to see it is about hunting and fishing and has absolutely nothing to do with yards or garden improvements?" The young man taken back some replied, "No I don't read any of them, if I did my boss would fire me. I can't afford to lose my job as I'm saving my money for college in order that someday I'll be smart." Denny the writer by now is baffled by the entire situation. He is a writer all right, but he loves humor and jokes the most of all. Now is a situation where he thinks humor might get his magazines where they belong right next to "FIELD AND STREAM." He tells the young cashier," Smart uh, well yesterday I was smart when I was driving along and saw a small white styrofoam box along the side of the road. I stopped, got the box and opened it. Inside was a human toe wrapped in ice, yes a human toe. I decided the smart thing to do was take it to the hospital. When I got there they told me that they did not want it nor would they take it. Next, I decided to give it to the police and went to their station. Once there they also told me they did not want it nor would they take it. So you know what I did? I did the only smart thing I could do, I called a tow truck."

With that the young clerk laughed. Denny next asked if his "HAPPY OUTDOORS" could now be with the other outdoor ones? The young man did just that and then Denny figured he would have to tell thousands of jokes across America to have his outdoor magazine placed where it rightly belonged in thousands of convenience stores in our great country. A task perhaps even beyond his ability so he just decided to write his stories, maybe even with some yard and garden tales. "HAPPY OUTDOORS" is a man's magazine at heart with a staff of writers telling the readers serious stories of hunting or fishing depending upon the season. As with all of today's magazines one half are stories with the other half being advertisements. The focus was on men's products, everything from fishing poles to ford trucks to Viagra. Why you need Viagra to get your Ford truck running is anyone's guess, but there they were on glossy pages right next to each other. Denny's job was to write humor on his pages and he was indeed good at it. One of his autumn stories' goes like this.

"THE DUCK HUNTER"

Oh to enjoy the crisp fall weather by being a duck hunter which I am one. As an avid duck hunter along with millions of others one day I decided to scientifically examine the sport. It seems we will go to any and all lengths to shoot a bird one-sixth the size of a cleaned frozen turkey available at any local grocery store. My scientific study concluded that all duck hunters are either nuts or close to it. First, the duck hunter gets up at 4A.M. in total darkness with only the stars shinning in the heavens above. Why 4A.M., so he may trek out to his duck blind long before the sun will appear. Next, he loves the weather conditions to be at the worst possible. The wind blowing thirty miles an hour with the temperature freezing is ideal for him. With snow blowing in the howling wind much the better. This sportsman indeed loves the weather that any sane person would just turn off the alarm clock, roll over and go back to sleep. No golfer would consider such conditions making him a tad bit smarter or maybe a lot smarter by a long shot. More about the long shot later.

So the hunter gets up with little sleep and hopes for weather conditions not fit for man or beast. Right away this tips off any reader that there must be something amiss with any and all duck hunters. Why would anyone go for this sport is the question already? There is no answer as to why miserable conditions would attract any Homo sapiens to this outdoor event. Yet the duck hunter claims to be in his glory in such conditions. The frigid cold, windy, icy rain or snow he loves more than words can express.

On this cold windy day the hunter next places out his duck and goose decoys in a pattern of attraction. Of course all day he will change this pattern believing the new arrangement is a much better one. This activity continues all day for the perfect one is never found he thinks. He is doing all this in his trusty hip waders that always has a leak letting in the frigid water down to his leg. No need to complain as this is just part of the sport. Then there is the time while out arranging that he finds a hole where the boot goes way too deep and totally fills up with the cold water. He now is allowed to complain and retreats to his heated blind. Here he takes the boot off, empties the water and rings out his sock. The sock is hung above the burning cook stove to dry out. As luck would have it the sock often is too close to the flame that in turn burns nice holes in his sock. He puts the holey sock back on to once again brave the water to get the pattern just right.

The dog, every serious duck hunter has to have his faithful

Labrador retriever. At home this dog will play catch and retrieve seemingly one million times with the toy rubber ball. Now to have him bring back the dead duck is another story. Maybe he will, maybe he won't. If the faithful dog thinks it is his duck you are out of luck for he takes it were only he may have it. Then once free he might just take the entire day off far away from the icy cold water. He finds a nice warm spot in the weeds hiding until all the decoys are picked up at day's end. Sometimes he takes off into the heavy weeds to locate the worst, a skunk! Then he returns to the warm blind smelling, you guessed it, just like a skunk. Boy, oh boy you always love your Lab. If all this insanity has not deterred the hunter as of yet there is more, lots more. One duck flies over in range and three hunters get up and shoot at the unlucky bird. It falls down dead and all three hunters yell out in unison, "I Got Him." No one knows if all three or just one actually hit the bird which is a mute point. What counts is the yelling out of "I Got Him." This is the very first rule learned by every duck hunter regardless of creed, race or religion. Actually it is a religious dogma by itself.

Then there is the ridiculous face painting. Even though the blind has total weed camouflage the hunter must paint his face as though he is Rambo going into a war zone. He gets up at four to paint his face as if he is in Special Forces or maybe it is Halloween each and every day. In what other sport does this happen, count them, none. Next is the matter of the duck call. Duck calls come in all shapes, colors and materials making it a very big business for the call makers. This is only surpassed in making it a much more serious business for the duck hunter who believes he is the best caller of all times. A huge ego is necessary here for at best one out of one hundred really can use one to call a duck within shooting range. The other ninety-nine go quack, quack, quack sounding like an off key water pipe in your home. Nonetheless all believe they are the best but in most cases that good old howling wind drowns out the sick quacks meaning no harm has been done.

Now for the long shot. Duck hunters always hunt in pairs or a group proving the old saying that misery loves company. It just would be no fun to hunt alone as with most sporting activities competition is good. With one buddy or several buddies in the duck blind an unusual competition develops to see who may down his target at the longest possible distance. The Long Shot is Born! In the beginning of the season everyone starts out about even with similar guns and ammo. Accordingly, all bag their birds at the same equal range. But then the good old male ego kicks into gear. One guy gets a 3-inch gun and the next guy gets a 3 1/2 inch gun and the race is on. Each larger gun adds distance to the long shot where compliments are offered. In truth the losers are actually thinking of how can I out do this guy? In the meantime the poor dog is thinking, what's with these guys, now I have to go forty more yards in this ice-cold water to get their stupid duck! It would seem the dog is ego free. Then it finally happens as one guy shows up with a 10 gauge. Yes, a 10 gauge which makes all the other guns equal to peashooters. This gun wins out as the long shot of the year. The dog shrugs as all the hunters conclude that next year they will all have 10 gauges too. Then they all will make the long shot, receive compliments and have their egos restored.

Back to the scientific study only one factor remains and that being the cost of this great sport. Remember the grocery store turkey that cost $25 or so, well that is chump change compared to the duck hunters cost.

LET'S EXAMINE THE COSTS:

Hunting license – 28.00
Duck stamp – 16.00
Loud alarm clock – 19.00
Camo face paint – 7.49
Camo face paint remover – 6.79
Hunting clothes – 211.17
Hip boots – 82.49
Decoys – 24.62
More decoys – 48.92
Duck blind – 301.12
A lot more decoys – 128.32
Camo material – 49.99
Cook stove – 69.99
Heat stove – 52.48

Boat and motor – 1,120.00
Dog – 300.00
Dog food – 600.00
Dog training – 800.00
Gun – 850.00
A lot more guns – 2,400.00
Ammo – 250.00
Many duck calls – 180.00
Many goose calls – 160.00
More and more calls – 300.00

TOTAL COST – $7,820.37

We know now that the duck hunter spends $7,820.37 to go into the most miserable weather possible to enjoy his sport. Let's say he brings home twenty ducks during the entire season, as he had to share the total numbers with his fellow hunters. Therefore, each duck cost him a mere $3,970.85. Now at the grocery store let's again say the average cleaned turkey costs $25. Given that number he could have had 158.83 turkeys. Also there was no need to arise at 4AM nor face any other discomforts.

The End

Denny had a contract to write one story for each month that "HAPPY OUTDOORS" was issued each year. His duck hunter's story received mixed reviews by the readers as most stories tend to, (please only respond to this one if it is positive). His story was meant to demonstrate humor and entertainment but sometimes any story can end up in the wrong hands. His did. The country's duck hunter population would forever be minus one.

A subscriber sent him a very sad note. It seems his copy of "HAPPY OUTDOORS" found it's way into his wife's hands. She read Denny's story all right, in fact over and over. Her keen eyes spent seemingly days and days looking at the financial costs while thinking about turkeys. Next, she banned the poor fellow from his favorite sport and made him take up golf. Little did she know what that sport could cost, but from Denny's story she at least knew it would be a gentleman's sport. When the next summer came the wife created the worst possible nightmare scenario to any duck hunter. She held a yard sale selling all the poor chaps hunting equipment for pennies on the dollar. At the end of the two-day sale all his equipment, even his leaky boots and favorite 10 gauges were gone forever. However, the hunter's friends noticed not one of the wife's pots or pans were put out to be sold. The note to Denny had teardrop stains combined with the lost forever duck hunter's note made him somewhat guilty and very sad. Denny wrote back to the fellow and did advise him to write Ann Landers regarding the situation. He really wanted to say get a divorce, buy another 10 gauge, in fact buy two and kick the old bag out the door but his professional position would not allow him to offer such honest advice.

THE REAL END

BAIT

On November 11th at 11 o'clock in the year 1918 the treaty was signed to end the war to end all wars. Unfortunately, it did not work for more wars would follow. Then a new era and experiment in America designed to improve most of mankind's ills followed too. It was prohibition of the 1920's making alcohol products illegal in the entire nation, but it did not work either. What it did do is in the larger cities create private nightclubs where alcohol flowed like water. The clubs were called speakeasies where for the first time both men and women would drink, dance and listen to jazz music into all hours of the night. Prior to the speakeasy men only would gather in saloons while women would not. This new American era would forever be known as "The Roaring 20's."

In the rural northwestern Wisconsin area the only things roaring were a few corn whiskey stills and winter heating fires. Here there were no speakeasies, roads, automobiles or even electricity. A few local travelers brought back stories of the Roaring 20's going on in Milwaukee and Chicago but this was strictly lumberjack country where no speakeasy would ever be seen. Men had their Men Only Clubs with women restricted to wedding celebrations that did have modest drinking and music.

Outside of weddings and holidays in this northern society only hard work existed on a daily basis. This area had no Roaring 20's, fancy glamour or even a paved road. There were old worn wagon tracks made by oxen before the newer logging trucks came to haul their loads to the river. Once there they unloaded the logs so they might float down the river to the local sawmill. All day the trucks rambled through the town of BIWABAMISHINAM MENAWAH on the dirt streets to the water's edge. The town originally was a Chippewa settlement and the English translation meant, "Come see us again." Only the Chippewa and Ojibwe could pronounce such a native name so the whites called their town Bibambam. The town was over 2,000 with the whites making up over three-fourths the inhabitants with the economy dependent only upon the logging industry. The town offered; a blacksmith shop, general store and the all-important Men Only Club where men could get their drinks as they always had done. It might be roaring with a fistfight or two on a late Saturday night but here there was neither jazz music nor any women to dance with. The club was not hidden and men needed no password to enter the unlocked door. It was where alcohol did flow, some of it good Canadian whiskey but most of it white lightning corn whiskey. Then home brew was always there too.

The County Sheriff was well aware of the doings and was known to visit for a drink or two himself. He considered it wrong to take a drink away from hard-working people by a bunch of fancy politicians that had never worked a day in their lives from far away in Washington D.C. Yes, the Men Only Club operated as it always had and always would. Other town services included an undertaker, one community church, schools and one doctor that tended to both mankind and animals alike. A mail boat came up and down the river once a week to give and take the same. In this North Country,

Bibambam was a complete town having all those services and others as well.

Houses for the most part were simple log cabins with a few board and shingle structures owned by the wealthy or lumberjack bigwigs. The bigwigs were those that pushed pencils and the ones that never picked up an axe. All of the homes had the narrow tall buildings in back used for human necessity. Most also had a cabin like structure used for horses and other animals behind their homes. A few inhabitants had their own wells, mostly the bigwigs, but others used the community well for water. The water of Bibambam was said to be the best for hundreds of miles around as it had such a sweet refreshing taste and was crystal clear.

The Chippewa population yet living in Bibambam lived in the Northwest section along the river. The whites called this section the Indian town or Red town. The Chippewa were not allowed into the Men Only Club and aside from this one discrimination all in the town did coexist well. The Chippewa men worked as lumberjacks with their specialty riding the logs down the river. The Chippewa women taught the Anglo women a wealth of knowledge making this relationship a very good one. The Indian section of town had very few log cabins, no lumber homes and no narrow tall buildings. They preferred to live in their traditional teepees and lean-to structures with large animal skins making up the walls and inside a fire pit sat in the center to provide their heating needs. They used the river for their water source.

Chippewa paychecks were equal to that of the whites. This situation was settled 10 years earlier when whites had been paid over double the rate of the Indians. The Chippewa rebelled at that time with bloodshed taking place on both sides. The bigwigs saw nothing was being accomplished in the lumber industry as a result of the conflict so they wisely put into place an equal pay policy in order to get the mills back running. The Chippewa with the white man's wages improved their lives greatly. Their first purchases would always be a horse or two followed by general improvements; blankets, pots and pans, guns, knives, axes, traps, beads, sewing needs, fishing supplies, canned goods and even candy for the children filled out their list.

The Chippewa would come down the dirt streets of town to purchase goods but the whites seldom ventured into the Indian section, as there was no reason for them to visit there. Along the red and white border of Bibambam many families did live. On the Indian side there was a 10-year-old boy named Oden. Oden's father honored his long time fur buyer by giving his son this Scandinavian name. Oden did have a traditional Chippewa name as well but it was another two-part word that in English meant, "let's do lunch" and was seldom used and if used lunches never occurred. Oden was a typical young boy living on the border allowing him to enjoy both cultures and have many white friends. Living on the white side of the border was a ten-year-old boy named Adam and he too was a typical youth of the times. Then there was Louise an eleven-year-old girl living on the white side with her family. She was a tomboy type that always preferred boy's events plus Louise was very smart in all ways.

All three children went to the same small school called Grassy Lake where Miss Biggermouth was the teacher. The children would call her Miss Big Butt from Bibambam when she was not around. To be caught using that name would result in grave punishment and the children knew this. The Grassy Lake School was a one-room cabin with three windows and naturally a narrow tall building in the back. The log school proudly announced, "GRASSY LAKE SCHOOL," in big carved letters right over the one and only doorway. Inside large wood logs cut to length provided both seats and writing tables. In the yard there were swings hung from trees and even a wooden teeter-totter toy. A bell was fashioned from an old tin can that was rung by the large metal spoon that hung along the can. Many ages and subjects were instructed to 23 students during full attendance, which rarely occurred. Most of the time 18 or so did show up with the others out helping their families.

Being neighbors along with going to Grassy Lake the three children became good friends. In fact their friendship would endure their entire lifetimes. Along with other schoolchildren they played hide and seek and kick the can down the road. The road of course was nothing more than a wagon track packed down by the logging trucks. Above all the three loved going fishing the best and went as often as possible.

Bibambam's North West edge was Red town where the Sweet Water River ran from north to south all the way down to the Mississippi. At Bibambam the river was one-fourth of one mile wide with a very strong current making it ideal to float the long heavy logs to the sawmill down the river. When settling the town the whites saw all the trail dust created by the oxen and log wagons so decided to build their cabins away from the Sweet Water. The Chippewa having no wells needed the river water and therefore kept their settlement along the river as they always had.

Minnesota is known as the land of 10,000 Lakes but the truth is Wisconsin has more lakes, many more. Two such lakes were located on the eastern edge of Bibambam where the whites lived. Both lakes had always been plentiful in the fish species of walleyes, pike, bass, bluegills and other pan fish. The fish provided food for all during both the summer and winter months. The smaller lake the whites named Gull Lake and the bigger was named Pelican Lake based upon the birds they saw there. If there were Chippewa names for the lakes they were lost in time. The three children would fish the lakes and river with Gull Lake being their favorite. Here they could sit amongst the sweet smelling pine trees and always catch fish. They had factory made hooks and line fastened to their willow branch poles along with their homemade pine bobbers. They would sit by drop-offs to put their lines in and always catch big fish for it was the ideal fishing lake. Pelican Lake was much bigger and harder to fish as weed beds surrounded the open water. If the wind was blowing huge waves developed making it even harder to put a line in. That meant Pelican Lake was one fished by the three only in the winter when ice covered it. The river had catfish and big ones at that. The Chippewa men would have fifty hook set lines placed upriver from where the logs were dumped into the river. One day they caught a forty-two pound cat yet most were in the ten to twenty pound range. The Chippewa would smoke the fish and there was none better as table fare.

In the summer when not playing games with other children the three friends would fish the river and Gull Lake as often as they could. In mid-June Louise asked her friends, "You guys want to go to

Gull Lake today? Heard the fish are biting over there more than the mosquitoes are. Henry Toefoot caught a twenty-seven pound pike there yesterday. I'm not sure where on Gull but you know we always catch fish there, maybe a big one like his? I sure want to go." Adam replied, "Yea I can go, Dad's at work and all my chores are done." Oden added, "Yep, I can go too. You really think Henry caught one that big out of Gull? I know lots of big ones come out of Pelican. I'll bring some bread along, can you get any jam Louise?" Louise answered, "I'm sure Henry did catch the big one out of Gull and yes I can bring some wild grape and Adam can you bring along a shovel to get the bait?" Adam replied, "Sure, let's all meet at the trail going there as fast as we can."

In a very short time they all did meet at the trail and with it yet being morning the trio would enjoy a pleasant day of both weather and fishing. Louise was the first to talk, "Let's go dig halfway down where there aren't as many trees as we always do. Onward." Once at the digging location Adam pushed his shovel deep into the dark black soil. Oden cried out, "There is a big crawler, got him, keep going there might be more big ones. Ah, no more big ones but might as well keep all these earthworms." Adam picked up over two-dozen small worms to go with the big one. He put them all in a can he had brought along as he had that job whenever they went. Louise looking at the worms crawling in the can said, "You know we have used night crawlers, earthworms, red worms, grubs, frogs and minnows. The minnows have been all sizes and in the winter we have used wax worms and weed worms too. In the River we use that smelly bait Oden makes up. I think we have used every bait God has ever made that we know about. I'm going to start taking notes on what fish we catch on what bait at which lake with the time of day we catch them. That will be fun and maybe we will learn something? I have no paper now, but I'll put down the facts tonight. Today we're stuck with these worms, let's draw straws to see who gets the big one." Oden and Adam agreed with Louise's idea, as they both knew from being with her and her schoolwork she was the smartest.

They arrived at Gull Lake, laid down their poles and drew straws for the big worm. Louise announced, "You won Adam, guess you brought the shovel so it's only fair today you get the crawler. Next time we come let's dig worms a day ahead of time so we all get big ones, lots of them." Oden said, "Yes that's a good idea, hey look there's a guy over there fishing one of our other good spots. Lucky he didn't get this one as I think this is a better one, don't you?" Adam answered, "Louise all your book taking is a good idea, do you guys know who that man is?" Louise now answered, "I've seen him around town, but I don't know his name, he's a bigwig, look at those nice clothes he has on and Oden I do think this is a better spot." With that the three got their poles ready and put their lines in the water. Adam had the night crawler and the other two had regular worms on as bait. Their fishing went on with a big 4-pound bass on the big worm and a mess of nice bluegills from the smaller worms. They put their fish on a strong long string and tied one end to a stout little tree with the fish placed in the lake. The trio kept on fishing to add more bluegills and some perch to their catch. The bigwig man seemed to be catching nothing and he walked over to the three friends.

The man said, "You guys are doing good, all that's been biting my way are the damn mosquitoes. What are you lucky guys using for bait, all I've got is a few dead minnows." Louise answered the man, "Dead minnows are good for Pike sometimes and we're using worms to catch bass and pan fish." The man asked, "Would you sell me some?" Adam said, "Oh we'll give you some if you have any way to keep them from crawling away. Wait, we have some paper from our bread cover we can put some in." Oden gave him a dozen or so saying they had enough. With that everyone introduced themselves to the man whose name was Mr. James Herter. James took the worms and dug into his pocket, "Here you guys go two nice shiny pennies. I really appreciate you helping me out as I'm new to these parts from Minneapolis where I never did fish." Louise said, "No, you can just have the worms free." The man said, "I can afford that two cents and you kids need to learn if you're going to run with the big dogs you got to pay up or you have to go sit on the bench." With that the man left returning to his fishing spot. Oden said, "Wow two pennies, you guys know how rich we are? We can buy a bunch of penny candy or maybe enough for all of us to get some new hooks or even both." Louise added, "I don't feel so good about taking the bigwig's money. Wonder what he meant about dogs and benches? I never saw any dog sit on any bench. Never heard anything like that before, I'm going to think about it and maybe ask Miss Biggermouth what he meant."

The bigwig Mr. Herter was at his spot and sure enough was catching a lot of bluegills. He had no stringer and just threw the fish on the ground to watch a few flop away back into the water. It seemed that did not bother him as he was catching fish and very happy about this new event. At one point he walked back to the trio and asked another question. "Do you young folks have any extra string I could use to carry my fish back home? Thanks a lot for the worms, they really work. I can come back fishing here next week on Thursday. If you three can bring me a bunch of worms then I'll give you two bits." As Louise was cutting some extra string off of their string she answered, "Here Mr. Herter you can have this string, just run it through their mouths to their gills. Yes, all of us or some of us can be here next Thursday and we'll be here early." The bigwig took the string and added, "Thanks for all, I'll see you next Thursday then." With that he went back to his spot and fished. Adam looked at his friends to declare, "Two bits that's fifty cents, I've never had that much money in my life, what could we do with all that money?" Louise answered, "Me neither, Wow two bits that's two quarters, I'd have to figure out how much that is each. We had better tell our parents about this, as they would want to know how we got so much money. Better not tell anybody else about this or we might lose this deal." Oden took his turn, "Wow, I think that is one half of what my dad makes all day chopping down trees, wonder if he will believe me? Anyways let's go digging on Tuesday to make sure we get enough for him and us. Better find a bunch of big old night crawlers for Mr. Herter too. What a deal!"

The three of them with that loaded up their fish and went for home skipping most of the way. They had totally forgotten to eat any of the bread with jam because they were so excited. The days and nights until the next Tuesday seemed like an eternity to them. They all told their parents what had happened and showed them the shiny two pennies. Their parents were very happy for them but said chores still had to be done before digging or fishing. None of them had any idea of what the dog and the bench could possibly mean. The three kids had very little sleep through the week leading up until Tuesday. That much money gave them too much anxiety wondering what they could buy with so much money. Oden thought they could buy out the whole candy store while Adam had dreams of being the richest guy in Grassy Lake School. Louise had her dreams too but thought they should save most of the money and have fun with the rest. She always had the most mature ideas although all of them wondered what the others were thinking. Tuesday came and with chores done they met to go digging for Mr. Herter's worms with the extra day to make sure they obtained plenty worms. Fifty-cents worth! Louise started, "You know guys the best place to dig is by the stable the blacksmith uses. There always are big crawlers in the manure piles plus we need to turn over all the dead big tree branches in the woods were the crawlers live. Did you bring two cans Oden?" Oden answered, "Yep, I got one for us and one for moneybags. Let's go to the stables and get to it." They went to the stables and asked the blacksmith about digging worms in the manure piles. He said, "Sure and if you find any diamonds they belong to me. Horses eat everything and anything you know? Who knows maybe one got into Mrs. Snodnose's jewelry box, say hi to all your parents for me will you?" Mr. Whitestuff, the blacksmith was always joking around making it hard to tell what was true that he would say. True or false the three were going to dig his piles and if they found a diamond the odds were a million to one. There would be night crawlers in the piles, many of them and big ones too. After an hour or so Adam declared, "I'm tired of smelling this stuff, we must have over one hundred of em, so do we need more?" Oden added, "Me too." Louise was tired also but said, "This is a gold mine that is going to make us rich. We need a lot more for Mr. Herter as then maybe in a week or two he will want more once he sees how good we are at getting them. I'll bet he will ask us again, not somebody else. With all of the crawlers here we won't have to go into the woods looking under branches and be eaten up by the mosquitoes." Adam fired back, "Sure, but all the zillion flies here are mighty bad too. Some of them bite, the big black ones you guys must know. This smell is making me sick and my hands are full of this poop. None of this has anything to do with benches or dogs unless he was talking about the rear end of a dog. I'm saying we get fifty more and we call it quits." Oden agreed, "I'm for that. It will take a long time to clean up our

hands and shoes because I for one can't go home smelling like this."
Louise got angry with her friends and reminded them once again,
"Yes we will go clean up at the river, so let's get another fifty at least.
We will receive more money than any one of us has ever seen in our
lives. Sure the flies are bad but if we went into the woods looking we
might get poison ivy as you guys have both dealt with before,
remember that? Let's dig in that pile over there where we haven't
been yet. We can get fifty in no time and then go to the river. We'd
better use one of those pennies and get some soap at the general
store on the way. Maybe use the other one for candy?"

Louise's motivational speech worked on the boys, especially the
part about the candy. They all did dig more than fifty worms, headed
to the soap and finally to the river to smell like roses. Louise was the
keeper of the night crawlers for safety and she put them in her
family's narrow tall little building behind their house. She figured
nobody would notice any smell of the worms there and she was right.
She did wonder what Mr. Herter might think if they did let off too
much of an odor. To fix that she changed all the "dirt" to clean loose
black real dirt she obtained along the river. The smell did go down
quite a bit and now to wait for Thursday. The friends had agreed to
meet as always at the trail leading to Gull Lake early in the day. The
anticipation of earning all that money kept all three friends in great
moods yet they slept little for two nights mind racing about the fun
to come plus they would be fishing too. Only Louise kept thinking
about the dog and the bench wondering what the big wig meant by it.

Thursday finally came at a snail's pace and the three friends met at
the trail to arrive at the lake by eight o'clock. Louise started, "Well he
isn't here yet, we may as well fish after all we have big crawlers for all
of us this week. We are at the same spot as last week so he will find
us." Adam talked, "What if he does not come?" Oden answered, "He
will be here it's plenty early yet. I'm going to get fishing." Adam now
said, "Okay let's fish. Do you guys want to bet a penny today on who
catches the biggest fish since we will all have lots of em, pennies I
mean." Louise said, "No, I don't like to bet on fishing as it doesn't
seem like the thing to do." Oden answered, "No I never have bet on
anything and I never will, sorry." The three commenced to fish for an
hour or so and they caught perch and bluegills. An hour seemed like

eternity to them and no Mr. Herter had showed up. Tension was in the air as another hour crept by with no bigwig insight. The three continued to add pan fish to their stringer but not much fun seemed to be in this day yet. They all wondered if he was going to come or not?

Finally about 10:30 the bigwig came down the trail. They could hear his noisy walk for a long time and attitudes brightened as bright as the sun itself. Mr. Herter appeared, "Good Morning to you all, sure is a pleasant day. I expect you have been here early but I am a gentleman fisherman so never would think about the sunrise to sunset ordeal of fishing. For me a late start is good enough. Any luck on the worms?" Louise answered his question, "Oh yes we have them in a special can for you plus giving you a nice stringer for all the fish surely you will catch. That can has a top with holes for air. You should keep the can in a cool dark spot and once a week put some damp leaves or grass on the top of the inside dirt. That will keep your big night crawlers for weeks to come. We have about 80 in here for you." Mr. Herter took the can with delight and talked to the trio, "You guys have thought of everything and I appreciate it greatly. Here are the two bits and I think you have given me enough to last a few weeks. When I need more I'll catch you down here on a Thursday and let you know a week in advance, now to go try them out." "Well Mr. Herter you may fish right here if you would like, this is a good spot with room for all of us," Louise advised. He said, "That's a good idea I'll do just that." The four of them got out their poles with Mr. Herter naturally having the best equipment money could buy compared to the humble willow poles the kids had. None the less all day everyone did catch plenty of fish. Mr. Herter by three o'clock had landed the biggest fish, that being a six-pound largemouth Bass. He beamed with pride over landing the largest fish. At different times the three kids had all caught larger Bass but said nothing about those facts. It was better to have their customer be the day's champion. At that hour all had enough fish and decided it was a great day and homebound they went.

Once away from Mr. Herter Louise the smartest of the three proposed, "We should go into the bait business. We now have made two bits, a fortune to us and maybe there are more bigwigs we could sell bait to? We could put up a little counter at the trail leading to both lakes. We would get our home chores done and take turns at the counter. We know about every bait and there aren't any other jobs we can get in Bibambam because of our ages. We don't have to do it every day just maybe weekends when the bigwigs are off work. I think we should try it, as it would not cost us anything. What do you guys think?" Adam and Oden were mind racing over the two bits of this day and how easy it was to make such a large sum of money so they eagerly both agreed to the idea. Then they divided up the fifty cents by getting change and candy at the General Store. They received sixteen cents each with two cents left over for candy, which bought a lot back in the 1920's.

After their home chores were finished during the final days of June the three worked on their "Bait Shop." Along with a saw and axe they constructed a stand like structure complete with a counter, a cigar box for money, a pencil with paper to figure sale totals, some wood box containers to hold different baits and old tin cans which would be used for customer sales. Then they put up a big sign held up in the air by two poles. It read their initials, "AOL BAIT CO." What remained was to gather the bait and have a price list for all to see. They knew two bits for night crawlers would be a one-time event and their prices had to be reasonable. Louise wrote out the list:

RED WORMS – 2 cents per dozen
EARTH WORMS – 2 cents per dozen
NIGHT CRAWLERS – 5 cents per dozen
GRUB WORMS – 4 cents per dozen
WAX WORMS – 2 cents per dozen
WEED WORMS – 2 cents per dozen
FROGS – 4 cents each
JUNE BUGS – 2 cents per dozen
BEETLE BUGS – 2 cents per dozen
MINNOWS – 2 cents per dozen
BIG MINNOWS – 4 cents per dozen
STINK BAIT – 5 cents per bottle

Through trial and error the three friends learned it was necessary to have the AOL BAIT CO. open on all days. On Sunday mornings

Adam and Louise would go with their families to the community church were they prayed and sang hymns. Oden did not go to the white man's church as the Chippewa had their own celebrations in the evening time of day. So he would run the shop on Sunday mornings and then have the afternoons off. Generally he chose to stay the whole day to be with his friends and sell bait too. They decided it was most important to be open when the bigwigs were off work. The lumberjacks and other people always got their own bait as the three had expected. Mr. Herter was one customer that came every two weeks and told many people about the AOL BAIT CO. He became a good friend and was a walking billboard of sorts for their company. The summer months averaged $2.32 a month in sales it was learned later after the summer was over. This made the three rich for kids in the 1920's.

Louise was always thinking of ways to increase the business while the two boys kept very busy collecting the baits. She addressed the problem of selling minnows with a creative method used to this day. The problem the bait stand had was minnows required fresh water or oxygen constantly added into their water. Their stand had no means to do either so Louise came up with a plan. That if a customer wanted minnows they would need to order them in advance. Then the boys would deliver the minnows directly to the customer the next day or any required future date. Today the pizza delivery system uses this idea as you order your selection and it is home delivered.

One day a fellow came to the stand specifically to talk with Louise about her sale's methods. This man was dressed much nicer than the town's bigwigs making his appearance curious to Louise. He told her, "I grew up in rural Wisconsin and now I am building a large department store in London, England. It is being constructed right now so I have a few months to visit my roots and here in Bibambam I'm visiting my cousin. I happened to see your advertisement posters nailed up to trees around town. That is a new idea, I might try that in England and it seems you do have more new ideas here at this stand. My name is Harry Selfridge and yours young lady?" "I am Louise," and with that Harry looked around the stand. He saw Louise's ideas in a series of signs that read; "THE CUSTOMER IS ALWAYS RIGHT, ONE AND ALL WELCOME HERE, MANAGER

SPECIAL ON LABOR DAY–ALL PRICES REDUCED" and on the Frog box another read, "BUY ONE–GET ONE FREE". Harry really liked the fresh beautiful wildflowers in vases at both ends of the counter only topped off with the narrow tall building located at the rear end of the stand. Then he noticed a mirror shining sunlight onto a blue colored paper and asked its meaning? Louise explained, "That's our blue light special which we can move to any store selection." This and all the ideas he had never seen anywhere astonished Harry. He told Louise, "Well young lady your business sure has been designed for your customer's every needs. The sale's ideas are fantastic. Have you any more yet to come?" Louise jokingly answered, "Well we were going to have a rent a worm program but decided not to as the poor worm would come back dead. Then we were going to sell snakes but decided they would scare too many people away. Maybe we will have other ideas once fall comes, who knows?" "Well Louise I am not a fisherman but I'll take a dozen of your night crawlers to give to my cousin. Here is a dime, keep the change, your ideas here are ones I may use in London" Mr. Selfridge then said, "Goodbye to you young lady" and when he returned to London he did adopt many of the bait shop's ideas right by his Bond Street department store. They were revolutionary in England as the first of their kind to be seen. There were no narrow tall buildings for necessary use in downtown London so Mr. Selfridge put water closets right inside his store. This was another first in the whole of England and Mr. Selfridge thought all the new ideas only cost him a dime.

The AOL BAIT CO. by August was known to most in Bibambam thanks mostly to the advertising signs posted on the trees and Mr. Herter relaying the information. The business was yet mainly dependent on bigwig customers with only a few lumberjacks buying some minnows now and then. Louise knew Labor Day was coming which meant a big celebration day and then back to school. After that they would only be able to be open on Saturdays and Sundays if the boys agreed. It turned out both Adam and Oden were in favor of keeping the business going even through the winter. No other kids were making the money they were and that was a great motivator. There became no demand for minnows and all the other baits were well stocked a few days before the September holiday. The boys took off two days and finally were able to go fishing on Gull Lake. Louise was happy to stay operating their store and wished her partners "good luck."

Business was slow now, which gave Louise more time to think about new store ideas. She printed out on paper and glued to container cans and jars an idea. She thought if more people knew where the bait was from it would increase business. The idea was a label that read, "AOL BAIT CO. AMERICANS ON LINE TO CATCH BIG FISH." Then Louise thought about all the money they were earning. If the boys agreed her idea was to put one half of it in the new State Bank of Bibambam to earn interest yet keep the other half to divide as usual. Then she wrote out coupons, which gave the customer a 10% discount if they spent over fifty cents in one month's time. She knew her partners would need to agree with this idea too.

The Monday of Labor Day came with a few bigwigs purchasing bait. The boys agreed to Louise's three plans and all thought since business had slowed it would only be necessary for one at a time to run the store this fall. They would take turns with the two off still available if needed. They had earned a fortune by kid standards the past summer resulting in all happy to keep the business as active as possible. The AOL BAIT CO. went on the weekend schedule as school now had started. The two boys were not eager for school, as they liked the summer store much better. Louise was very happy to be back in school as learning to her was like candy to the boys. The fall went on at the Grassy Lake School with Miss Biggermouth happy to be teaching her students once more. She had spent six summer weeks in Minneapolis and had stories to tell of that big city. She never did say a word about "the roaring 20s" or even speakeasies. The big city must have had those things but she told stories about a zoo, automobiles and how the big river there had a bridge over it. Here in Bibambam of course nothing like those things existed. Her best stories were all about the different zoo animals and she even brought in pictures of some of them.

In October Halloween came as the most favorite night all the children would enjoy. This was the night of the school party plus there would be candy gathering afterwards for all. Often a few pranks would also occur in the dark of night. Grassy Lake School's big party had kids dunking for apples, playing pin the tail on the donkey and the best costume contest. On this year a fifth grader won the contest by being a bum. Since Bibambam had no railroad a hobo was never seen so to see one was funny. The kid hobo was dressed in all-raggedy clothes with a bright red hanker chief hanging from his back pocket and his face was blackened and dirty. He was a funny sight resulting in winning the Halloween prize of apples with even an orange, which was a rare fruit in this northern area. Louise was dressed as an angel, Adam as a cowboy and Oden as an Indian chief. Since he was a Chippewa his dress was familiar to all the kids, as they had seen a real chief at various times. There were no cowboys in this north woods making Adam a favorite by many. Next children went door to door in order to collect treats and as much candy as the town's people could hand out. The three of AOL BAIT CO. always had money so had all the candy they ever wanted, yet they went door to door just the same. Then the three decided to give away all their "loot" to three children who were unable to go due to being very sick. It was very nice of them and made them feel very good, as the three kids had been sick for a very long time. After the party and candy gathering there was a huge bonfire located in the business section of Bibambam. This was always fun in the late October cool night and concluded all the activities for another year.

The next morning was a school day and walking to school the three saw that their business had been vandalized. Apparently some jealous youths had attacked their stand. The big overhead sign was on the ground, their narrow tall building was tipped over and the frogs were let loose. They were jumping around as frogs out of water plus the flower vases were gone to never be seen again. Louise suspected two older boys were the pranksters but had no way to ever prove it. Then in town some narrow tall buildings were also tipped over on their sides. This gave the entire town a stinking odor and an act that seemed to occur every Halloween. Louise said, "Well we will have to deal with this catastrophe after school, the frogs won't go too far." They went on to school where a crowd had gathered by the doorway. To enormous shock there were letters missing from Grassy Lake School. The G, R, Y and L were gone so now it read "ASS AKE

SCHOOL!" It was funny and sad at the same time. Everyone wondered what knuckleheads would do such a thing? Within a week new letters were made but no pranksters were ever found out.

Winter came with both Gull and Pelican Lakes frozen over tight enough that ice fishing was now going on. The bait shop sold some wax and weed worms on the Saturdays and Sundays, which were the only two days it was open. Total sales would only be four to six cents each weekend and they had to obtain an old fifty-gallon barrel to furnish a fire barrel. This way the one working on the slow long days would have heat. After one December weekend with no bigwigs and no sales Louise said, "Adam, Oden I don't think it is worth us dealing with this bitter cold and snow to sell as little as we are. I think we should close for the winter and open back up in late April. Then we all can go skating, sledding and fishing on our weekends plus not look for worms. We all should have enough money to coast through the winter and we have some in the bank too. The worst weather is to come next month and we are selling very little." Adam's weekend to sell was coming up so he eagerly agreed. Oden wanted to stay open but finally agreed with his partners that it would be better to wait for springtime. The AOL BAIT CO. was officially closed for the winter.

The three enjoyed the few warmer winter days mostly fishing Pelican Lake where the big pike lived. They yet had one minnow trap working in the river and that was the best pike bait. They caught quite a few pike but no real big ones and their families through the winter enjoyed the fresh fish. All in Bibambam were eager for springtime, as the winter was so cold they needed sweaters for their mouths! No one made any but it was a good idea just the same. Through this cold winter all of the trio would think about new ideas for the store. Adam thought they should sell products other than bait. Maybe they could buy candy from the general store at a discount if they bought a lot and then sell it at retail. Maybe other things too? Oden said he was tired of going fishing in the bitter cold and his idea was to make artificial lures on his weekends. He had an abundance of wild bird and chicken feathers to make flies with and he might whittle out some big lures too. He asked for money to buy hooks, thread and paint from the company money to do it. The other two thought his ideas were good ones and company money would be used for his projects. Louise said she had no ideas for right now but surely would have some later.

The spring of 1929 came with the roaring 20s yet going stronger except in Bibambam were only three kids seemed to be roaring in their own way. On Saturday, April 19th they opened the AOL BAIT CO. with as much bait as they could find after school that week. Adam was not sure about the candy yet or for that matter any other items to sell. Oden had made twenty-five flies he displayed on cardboard to sell at three cents each. He had made four wooden lures painted bright red and white with hooks attached. He had tried them out on a friend's fancy pole and since they were his first they were all somewhat lopsided and swam in a goofy way. He decided to call them Crazy Crawlers and would sell them for eight cents each. Louise finally had her idea and that was to have a sales box marked "BARGAIN BASEMENT" and put it on the ground. In the box they would put slow moving baits plus all the wax and weed worms from last winter. Everything in the box would be sold at cheaper prices and it might mean they would sell a lot more bait. The two boys thought this was an idea of a genius and they had never seen anything like it. The BARGAIN BASEMENT was born!

April sales were slow at best and they learned that the BARGAIN BASEMENT box was selling the most. In it all the wax and weed worms sold out at one cent per dozen and some frogs with only one leg sold at two cents each. They wondered why anyone would want a one legged frog? They could only swim in circles but maybe they would be good to put in Miss Biggermouth's desk drawer? It did demonstrate that the BARGAIN BASEMENT did very well and it was nice to be earning money again. They would put one half in the bank while dividing the rest amongst themselves to buy clothes, gifts for their families and of course candy. Adam finally came up with another product they could sell and that was fireworks. His father thought the idea a good one and was both willing to finance them and to go to Hayward to buy them. They would start selling the fun explosions in early June but it was April making bait and Oden's lures their products for now. Louise got out all her fishing notes she had made on the few days she was able to go fishing the past summer. It seemed her notes of when, where and what fish she had caught were too few to be much help in the bait shop for now. As her habit would have it she continued her fishing notes the rest of her life and had written on the inside cover "if you're going to run with the big dogs pay up or go sit on the bench." That is what she recalled Mr. Herter had said the year before and she wondered often just what this could mean to now a twelve year-old girl living in the north woods?

The April weekend sales were slow as the cool and rainy weather saw very few bigwigs interested in fishing with the lumberjacks only buying from the BARGAIN BASEMENT box. The water temperatures were yet cold so the fish were not biting much either. The boys took this slow time to build more minnow traps to use in the river and while at the Sweetwater they caught two more one-legged frogs. They figured that these poor guys would have to catch bugs that only went in circles too. Oden wondered if there were one-legged bugs also and if so it would be fun to watch a one legged frog catch a one legged bug. Then he really wondered how could a one legged frog hop? How could he go anywhere in life if all he did was go in circles? Frogs went hip pity-hop so these one legged ones must only go hip pity. Oden's father didn't like Republicans and always said they only talked in circles when it came to helping Indians. Maybe that meant these frogs were Republicans as they did croak a lot and only went in circles? Soon the boys went back to their bait shop and put the frogs into the BARGAIN BASEMENT box. Oden figured his dad would be happy that the Republican frogs were there.

The month of May finally came bringing warmer weather in turn making fishing much better for everyone. The gentleman bigwigs now were fishing bringing a boom to the AOL BAIT CO. sales. They always paid full price for their bait and never even looked at the box on the ground. Almost all of Oden's flies sold with reports that they were excellent in catching fish. However, his brightly colored wooden lures did not sell at all. He wanted to place them in the ground box but Louise convinced him not to do so as she said, "The long summer coming would surely have buyers for them." Oden agreed and said, "he would go try them once he could afford one of the fancy poles that you could cast out." That would have to wait for summer so in the meantime he decided to use a Republican frog. One Sunday morning while Adam and Louise were in church and Oden was alone running the shop Mr. Herter came by. He gave Mr. Herter one of his lures free of charge and said, "Please try one of these out to tell me if they catch any fish?" Mr. Herter took the lure and said he was happy to try it out and would report the results. Then he asked, "What do you call this lure Oden?" Oden told him, "Well I pulled one around in the water and it kind of goes goofy back and forth so I call it a Crazy Crawler." With that Mr. Herter was on his way with some worms, a Crazy Crawler and his fancy pole.

Soon summer would come and school would be over for another year. The trio of the AOL BAIT CO. really looked forward to them being open every day of the week once more. The idea of selling candy did not work out for them but they would have fireworks as Adam's father had bought them already. They knew sales would be good as Bibambam was as busy as ever in the spring of 1929. The demand for lumber was up and more lumberjacks along with bigwigs had come to town to work. A few of the bigwigs had even bought Ford Model T cars they drove around the town. The Men Only Club continued operating as usual despite talk that Federal Agents might show up. The Lumberjacks said if they did they would just change the name to "Dead Fed Speak Easy" and that should be enough to leave the club alone.

It was the night of June First and the sky of Bibambam lit up with huge explosions in the air. The kids were trying out the fireworks to see what they did along with telling everyone they now were selling them. There were some big fireworks that gave off brilliant and beautiful colors that lasted a long period of time. Then they also had M-80 firecrackers that sounded as if a war had taken place. Everyone in this town on this night knew fireworks had come to town long before the Fourth of July. The AOL kids had a great fun time but maybe all the dogs howling would not be loved by all? The night would end and the next day the bait shop opened with Adam bringing out their new products. They had built a counter to display all the fireworks on earlier that week and it was a very large counter. On that very first day they sold five times the amount of the fireworks as they did their bait. All that money would go to Adam's father until he was paid in full and that was going to happen faster than they had thought. The bait money was kept separate and Louise would put one half of it in the State Bank and divide the other half. Louise explained it to her partners, "Well you see we take this half and divide it three ways, then we each get our share to do as we please with our money. Then the other half we put into the bank because they give us interest money for it. That is free money we don't even have to work for, I don't know how they do it but it is free money for us. We always own the money and can take it out any time we want but the longer it stays in we keep getting more free money on top of it. Every once in a while they tell us how many real dollar bills we have and how much free money we have made. So even though they have our money we can get our real dollar bills any time we ask for them." Adam and Oden did not understand the bank concepts but also knew Louise was smarter and they trusted her decisions on all matters. They both did wonder when they would get their real dollar bills as Oden wanted a fancy fishing pole and Adam wanted a bike.

The month of June continued on with the nights full of the beautiful colors and days sounding the loud explosions. No Federal Agents ever did come to Bibambam and life went on in the normal way. Everyone was catching fish this month and Mr. Herter came to give his report. "Well Oden, your lure is wonderful, I'll buy two more of them as a matter of fact. I have been catching both big bass and pike on them. I encourage you to make more of these lures and sell them at a higher price." Oden was real happy to learn this and then they visited on how nice both the fishing and weather had been. Now there was only one Crazy Crawler left and Oden took it for himself. He knew soon he would be able to buy a casting pole because the fireworks were selling so fast. In fact by mid-June Adam's father went back to Hayward to purchase more for the upcoming July celebration. In earlier years the weekly mail boat would bring some fireworks but now that people could buy them right in town it seemed everyone wanted them. Then when they came for fireworks they would buy some bait too. So much that the boys had to go back to the dreaded manure piles for night crawlers.

The first four days of July brought huge crowds to the AOL BAIT

CO. to purchase fireworks. Every night and all through the nights the brilliant colors filled the sky. Bibambam had never seen a time like this making the kids heroes with an extremely successful business. It was a great time in this small Wisconsin lumber town. Soon the Fourth was over and it was back to just the bait business as the people went back to their regular routines and the demand for fireworks also was over. Oden was able to buy a fancy fishing pole and Adam got his bike. Louise for now did not care to buy herself anything special. July fishing was good at both lakes and because there were more bigwigs in town the bait sales continued to do very well. The trio made more money this month than they could have ever dreamed of.

Fishing slowed down in August with the mosquitoes equally deterring the fisherman. The bigwigs especially avoided the woods and lakes due to the numerous biting bugs, which in turn slowed down the bait business. The stink baits made by Odem did sell well because fishing along the river was good for catfish and the bugs were not as bad there. It was all the other baits that had little demand. Then summer was over and school started which meant back to the shop open on weekends only. September brought on hunting seasons and even a smaller demand for any fishing baits. The trio looked back and greatly appreciated Adam's idea of the fireworks with all the success they had brought them. They decided to close the AOL BAIT C0 on October First for the year.

Little did they know that in fact it would be the end of their little bait company forever. October 1929 was the crash of Wall Street, the beginning of the Great Depression and the end of the roaring 20s. At Bibambam the first effects were no demands for lumber, which in turn meant no jobs. Most all of the bigwigs left town and many of the lumberjacks as well. Many businesses had to close their doors forever including of course the bait shop. Most people could not understand how something in faraway New York was affecting them in Wisconsin. Then the worst happened. The State Bank closed its doors and boarded up the windows to never open again. The bank was gone and with that the people's money. Louise could not understand any of it although she tried. She was told her money in the bank was put into a bigger bank and that bank put the money into stocks and bonds which had become worthless so the money was gone forever. Louise could not understand were did the real money go, as the real paper dollar bills could not vanish into thin air. Somebody has to have the real dollar bills, but who? The adults of Bibambam had the same thoughts as Louise but the bank with their money was gone forever. This created a lot of poor people with no money and no jobs. The government did send up quantities of various foods each week on the mail boat. This food was distributed free and the town's men hunted game and fished which insured that all would eat throughout the depression years. By 1935 the boys were old enough to join FDR's Conservation Corps and they went off to work and sent money home, which was mandatory. Louise was able to find part time employment in the library and she loved her job. It was a difficult time for all although perhaps much better in the country over the big eastern cities. In 1933 prohibition ended which never affected the Men's Only Club before or after.

The 1940's did finally improve the nation's economy along with the lumber industry. Adam and Oden both went to work as lumbermen and Louise went full time at the library. The war to end all wars didn't work as now a big war in Europe had begun once more. Louise wondered how Mr. Selfridges was doing in London as a result and then Pearl Harbor brought the United States into the war. Oden joined the Navy and fought in the Pacific while Adam was in Europe as a Marine. During the war years Louise got married and moved to Eau Claire with her husband. There they started a bus company called Black Hound Bus Company, which ran from Milwaukee to Minneapolis. One day she sat on a bench, which was in her beautiful flower and vegetable garden. She thought back to Mr. Herter's words and decided now she really knew what he meant. She had Black Hound Buses running and she could sit on a bench anytime she wanted to. Louise concluded this must be the answer.

In 1945 the terrible war ended and the two boys now men returned to Wisconsin. They both knew that working in the woods was not for them and they teamed up in Madison with plans of starting a retail store. Even though Madison had many lakes their business would not be in bait but rather in furniture. With all the GI's coming home to start families they felt this would be a much better choice over digging worms. They leased a large building for their future business but had to wait two weeks before they could move into it. They decided to take a Black Hound bus up to Eau Claire to visit Louise and her husband with some of this free time. It would be enjoyable to talk about old times as well as to meet Louise's husband for the first time. The plan was they all would meet at a restaurant called the Hook Nook as their arrival time was at noon.

Adam and Oden arrived at Eau Claire on schedule and caught a cab to take them to the designated restaurant. The cab took them eight blocks and they arrived at the Hook Nook. Louise and her husband, Bill, were there and upon arrival everyone gave hugs and handshakes. It was great that the friends were together once again. They went in and sat at a table to begin their conversation. Adams started, "A bus company and a good one at that. We took one up here as you know, sure a nice ride." Louise spoke next, "Yes we started at the right time but had to go to the bank to borrow back some real dollar bills to get it going. I think they were the same dollar bills they took from us in the 20's. So what are you guys up to in Madison?" Oden explained, "We are going into the furniture business and now waiting to get into a building we have leased. We are set up with a Chicago wholesaler to buy our products and of course had to go to a bank also. This time we are getting their dollar bills instead of giving them ours. Anyways we will be selling beds, mattresses, chairs, tables, couches, easy chairs, sofas and everything else for the home. We have most everything in place but have not yet figured out a name for our store." Louise helped out, "You should call it The Lazy Boys!"

A NEBRASKA SANDHILLER FINDS THE GULF STREAM

The story you are about to read is a true story. It is an experience turned into the story by my good friend Jim. He and I spent countless hours fishing and in the outdoors during the 1980's and 1990's. His dry wit was with him every day and I sure hope you enjoy the same in this next story.

Outside of our outdoor days he and I also greatly enjoyed attending the local horse races. Our plans always included the doubling of our meager funds. That seldom worked out but the first time we went together was a time I shall never forget. I picked him up at his house to find him wearing the loudest and wildest sport coat ever made on this green earth. It was screaming red, white and stop sign yellow plaids making it possible to spot him easily at a mile's distance. It was great! He explained to me that it was necessary to dress up and look your best when going to such a wonderful event. I might add he would wear this coat on all further trips to the track.

This book owes its being to Jim. In the late 1980's we started writing stories with the ultimate goal of having a book published. The stories written back then were all true stories and even included some "How To" one's. Jim and I continued writing into the late 1990's but sadly Jim died of cancer in 1998. With his death came the end of our book's conclusion and dreams.

In the year 2014 I would pick up the torch and finally work on completing the book we had started all those years ago. I knew the book could never be completed without one of Jim's stories. This next story is one Jim left us with and I do hope you enjoy it. I also hope in heaven every day there is a horse race. If I should get up there I know I'll spot him in his wild coat at any distance.

A NEBRASKA SANDHILLER FINDS THE GULF STREAM

We all have experiences in nature which we love to recall. Perhaps in the mountains, ocean, brook or on the flat lands certain events occurred that stay with us forever. They are memories, treasured memories and in this instance I disagree with Thoreau who wrote: "He is blessed over all mortals who loses no moment of the passing life in remembering the past." I firmly believe that life should be lived for the day and I practice it too but I also believe that blessed is he among mortals that can look back on his lifetime's adventures on field and stream to remember them and relive them. I also enjoy other people's adventures: Robert Ruark, Edison Marshall, and Hemingway's "Green Hills of Africa." Other people's memories of places will never be my own. Not a thing wrong with remembering the past if it makes you feel good.

By way of introduction and it won't be long. I was born and raised in the North Loup River Valley in north central Nebraska between the sand hills to the north and the hard hills to the south. A long way from an ocean. We weren't even close to the Big Muddy. In 1949 or '50 I first saw a print of the famous painting "Gulf Stream." I was about 10 years old and the effect on me was immediate and visceral. I was entranced. The man, the boat, the sharks and the sea with the richness of its images were so powerful and compelling to an imaginative 10-year-old boy on the edge of the hills that to this day it is my favorite painting. I studied it for hours. I could feel it and I was there! When I was 12 I discovered "Moby Dick" and read it with the fascination and perseverance of a child eating a box of chocolates. That and a worn copy of Masefield's "Salt Water Ballads" did it. The mystery, the power and the romance of the sea had me in its grip.

I spent nearly 2 years in the Army at Ft. Ord, California and the Presidio in San Francisco. My most vivid memories are not of marching or drilling or cleaning rifles. They are of standing on a cliff top in Marin County watching sharks schooling far below. Also as I was lying on the beach with my fishing line far out in the surf while dreaming and watching the dim line of the Farallones out at sea. Then days spent studying the creatures of the sea at the fish market on Fisherman's Wharf and other days spent on the Embarcadero gazing at the ships.

But it was the Gulf Stream still that had caught the farthest reaches of my imagination. The Gulf Stream of warm waters, palm trees, long sandy beaches and islets along with sharks and Pirates. The Gulf Stream of the painting. In 1966 I spent a week in Houston and Galveston. I had my first taste of the Gulf Coast and then went back to Nebraska to my job, to pheasant hunting and fishing for catfish in small muddy rivers.

In 1972 I was living and working in Kansas City and was given a large territory that included Houston, Corpus Christie and New Orleans. It had been a long time since 1949 but I was coming to the Gulf Stream at last. I lived there nine years and although I moved back to the Valley of the Loup again at times I still yearned powerfully for the blue water. I yet missed the hot wet cotton-wool wind, the smell of wet sand, the water's salt, the ocean fish and tidal mud, meaning I supposed someday I'd go back.

I remember my first trip to Corpus Christie; I came from Dallas on the old Texas International on Thursday night. I was to work the area the next week. The weekend was mine. It was early evening and the sun was still out when I stepped off the plane and felt I could squeeze the water out of the air with my fist as it was that thick and wet. I saw palm trees moving in the wind that nearly always blows there. Two young Mexican-Americans approached me that worked for our store and they had brought me out a company car with directions to my motel and to the store. They helped me carry my bags to the car and I was on my own. They had made me a reservation at the Ramada Inn, Portland that was actually on the causeway between Portland and Corpus Christi. I found the cross town Expressway to take 181 N. and went over the Harbor Bridge at full dark with the lights of the city and Corpus Christi spread out around me. A sight I never grew tired of in all the years to come. Then I went through North Beach and on a highway surrounded by Corpus Christi Bay that was all around me. The shallows sprinkled with the lights of boats. I caught the smell of seaweed, salt, marsh and fish, the smell I've never tired of. I found my motel on the causeway with water all around it and checked in. All my surroundings were new and exciting ones with the sites, sounds and smells. I unpacked in a ground floor room and went to the bar. Windows looked out on the dark Bay now except for riding lights. Two young men sat at a table drinking beer in ragged clothes and long hair. I caught a whiff of salt and fish as I passed them and sat at the bar. A pretty but plump girl brought me a beer in a frosted schooner. As I drained the beer I saw small green objects rolling in the bottom of the glass. "Miss" I said, "Bring me another beer in a clean glass. I'm not Bob Hope." The reference to Bob Hope's famous movie scene was lost on her. She peered into the depths of my schooner. "That's just olives," she said. "I put them in there. We always have olives in our beer. It's called beertininis." She looked up from the offending glass and peered at me in turn. "You're not from around here are you?" No, I wasn't from around there but I already wanted to be, as I liked it just fine.

I ate and went back to my room and peeled back the blind and looked out the window towards the inland side of the Causeway. A concrete pier stretched into the night. Lampposts dotted it and a group of black men were busy at the side of the pier. Indeterminate shapes littered the pier at their feet. I went out. The men were fishing and one of them pulled in a long struggling narrow shape. I watched in my ignorance thinking it was an eel at first. Then I saw the pier was sprinkled with long narrow ugly fish. The strangest fish I'd ever seen. What they were I didn't know and I asked? "Gar," came the answer. They didn't look to me like something you would put in your mouth. "What do you do with them?" "Eat em." The fishermen were an affable lot and showed me the hooks and tackle they used. I don't remember what they used for bait but they were catching gar right and left. I watched for a long time fascinated by the lamp-lit pier in the blackness of the Bay heavy with the mixture of scents and sights. Nothing like that in the Midwest. I went to bed and dreamed of giant gar eating olives from frosted glasses.

I hadn't met the store manager before so we had arranged to meet for breakfast at 7a.m. at a restaurant called Price's Chef at Six Points. Corpus Christi is not a hard town to navigate so I got across town and got off on Staples Street to find Price's Chef. Once inside just as he had described it, a big red-faced man in his sixties with a white Stetson hat was the cook. Neither of us talked about business. We had all day for that. "It's all set up for Saturday," he said. He took his knife and fork and cut up his eggs, pancakes and grits and next stirred the mess with a fork and covered it all with hot sauce. "Charles will go with you. He's a nice young guy and likes to fish. He'll show you the ropes. I can't go; I'm too old for the boats anymore. Frenzel is down in the valley and won't be back till next week." Frenzel was an ex-employee that was now a boat captain and a friend of mine from a month long management school in Kansas four years earlier. "I think we'll just have Charles pick you up at the motel and go to Aransas from there. That's Port Aransas on the Island. You'll go out on the Thunder Ball for Red Snapper. The Thunder Ball is a good boat that used to be the fastest on the coast. The snapper should be biting as they were catching over a thousand pounds a trip last week. You may catch other fish too for you can catch anything in the Gulf but you'll be going to the snapper banks and fishing for them. If you like to fish you'll have a good time, if you don't get seasick. What you do is get some Dramamine that you can get at the motel. Take two pills at night before you go to bed and two more first thing when you get up in the morning. Don't pay attention to what it says on the bottle and drink lots of beer. Drink beer and take Dramamine and you won't get sick. Real simple. You'd better do it because if you don't and you get sick you'll be sick all day and it'll be a horrible day." I think my face must have paled a little as my perverse mind pictured what seasickness might do to that awful mess he was swallowing. "Don't worry," he said. "Just do as I say and you'll be fine."

Later that day I met Charles at the store. He was a mild mannered young guy, single and about six and a half feet tall. He was eager to go fishing. "It's always fun" he said. "Sometimes you catch so many fish the decks are full. You ever been out before?" I told him no, I hadn't and I asked him about the seasick remedy Clark had proposed. He agreed, "That'll work fine. Keep your stomach settled down. Getting sick would spoil your day for sure. I never use anything myself as I have never been sick in my life on a boat and I don't like beer. But that'll fix you up fine. Old Clark knows what he's talking about."

I had trouble sleeping that night. I was going out on a fishing boat fifty miles out in the Gulf waters full of large savage fish and strange creatures of all sorts. Fabled creatures. I might see flying fish, sail fish and sharks! I had Dramamine with my beertininis that night. Might as well get off on the right foot I thought. At four o'clock in the morning Charles knocked at my door and I was ready. It was dark and there was no moon. "Overcast," said Charles, "But it'll clear up by nine o'clock. We'll have a fine day." We drove through Portland and across to Aransas Pass and over to the ferry that crossed over to Port Aransas on the tip of Mustang Island. "In the daytime you can see dolphins following the ferry," said Charles. In the coming years I was to watch the graceful swimmers and divers many times never tiring of them. My first sight of the fishing and tourist town of Port Aransas was slight as it was still dark. We went directly to the Deep Sea Headquarters and got our tickets. I think at that time it was $20.00 for the all-day trip but it is much more now.

The Thunder Ball was tied up at the pier amid a profusion of boats of all kinds, big and little, powerboats and sailboats. The

Thunder Ball was not big as party boats go but it was the biggest boat I'd ever been on. It probably could have fished 75 or 80 people but we had a light crowd this morning. "The water's rough this morning," said Charles. "That's why there aren't more people." The crowd ranged from veteran Coastal dwellers to raw visitors like myself. Everyone was friendly and eager to go fishing.

Charles introduced me to the Captain. Captain Jimmy was the only name I ever knew him by. He was a small figure in clean pressed whites and his eyes were blue and lively in a still brown face. "This is a friend of Dick Frenzel's from Kansas City," said Charles to the Captain. "Dick said for you to treat him right." Captain Jimmy shook my hand. "We'll go out to the snapper banks now and find some fish. Come up to the wheel house whenever you want to." He turned back, "Better drink some beer, the water's going to be rough."

For the next six or seven years I went out on the party boats and faithfully followed that prescription. I never got sick. Some years later at a time when I was not drinking alcohol I went out and got sick as a dog. I don't know if it was psychological or if the coastal mythology of lots of beer (with or without Dramamine) had a scientific foundation. It worked for me.

We backed away from the jetty and headed into the sea. Immediately we ran into a violent chop. The boat picked up speed and spray which promptly ran us all into the cabin. It was a long run out to the banks, which were peaks in the ocean bed around which snapper clustered. It took over two hours as I recall it. The water was so rough and the action so violent that shortly after we started people began to get sick. My companion and teacher was one of the first. We were trying to play gin but the cards kept sliding off the table with the boat pitching. There was nothing to see from the cabin save flying spray. Charles had been telling me about Gulf Coast fishing. He talked about flounder, sheep head, drum, redfish, sharks and men-of-war. It was interesting but he trailed off into silence and became uneasily quiet. His complexion changed from its normal healthy pink to a sickly pallor tinged in green. He got up and lurched for the head "NO! "NO!" chorused voices. "Outside!" He made it outside and I watched him hanging over the rail. It caught on fast this illness. A lady sitting with a man was evidently caught unaware and suddenly filled her husband or boyfriend's lap. Then other people joined in, as the railing outside was dotted with people mingling their fluids with the wind and spray. A terrible stench filled the cabin. Charles came back limp, deathly pale and crawled under a table. I got up and went up to the wheelhouse. I felt okay. "Thank you, Lord" I cautiously muttered "For Dramamine and beer if it works."

There was no sickness in the wheelhouse. Captain Jimmy was at the wheel talking with the deckhand. It was daylight and the bay water was murky in the wan light. From up here the waves looked small to cause all this up and down movement. The clouds looked only a little way overhead and the Captain observed that there were rainsqualls in the area. Soon after the clouds broke and the sun came out, we crossed into the Gulf Stream. It was like a line drawn on the water from the murky coastal water into deep beautiful blue. It was a miracle. Captain Jimmy explained that on the outer edge of the Gulf Stream where it blended into the Atlantic water mass the line was seldom, if ever, as clear and distinct. Usually it blended gradually into the great body of water in a diffuse and gradual fashion. From the wheel house the water looked very lively but not quite so impressive as on deck level. The bright sun on the blue water was so beautiful and strange to me I could have watched it all day. Blue jellyfish were riding the waves with their long tendrils dragging out behind them. "Men-of-war." said the deckhand. "If you get one of them tangled on your line or on your fish cut the line. We don't mess with them. They'll sting the hell out of you." One of the invalids hanging over the rail of the pitching deck began to yell and point. I looked down. I saw a fin, slicing through the water and a long dark shadow under. Shark! This was living! I was ready to fish. Captain Jimmy was looking at the screen on his fish finder, "This is it," he said. "We've found fish." He positioned the boat along the waves. "Time to fish," he said.

I went down to the lounge to find Charles. The lounge was a scene from hell as it was a charnel house. Fully half of the hopeful fishermen were sick with bodies everywhere. The stench was overpowering. Charles had gotten up off the floor and was slumped in a booth. His face was a more delicate green than it had been and his eyes had the stricken look of someone who had learned he was going to die in the next week. "Charles, its time to go fishing. How do you feel?" His head rolled on his shoulders as if it were too heavy for his neck. "What time is it?" He asked. "A little after seven," I answered. "Isn't it time to go home?" "The captain said we'd head for home about four or five and get in about seven. That's about 12 hours from now," I answered. "Oh God," he moaned. A deckhand touched my elbow, "Come to the deck and I'll help you get started. Your friend's out for the day, because when they're that bad they don't come out of it till they hit dry land." "Charles," I asked, "Can I help you in any way? How about some Dramamine and a nice cold beer? Fix you up." His eyes rolled up in his head, as it was obvious he was near death. "Oh, God," he said. He began retching weakly. "See you," I said and left that reeking pit as I put a beer in each hip pocket. If beer would keep me from being like that I'd damn well do my part.

On deck was a different world for the air was clean and heady and the surging waters excited me. People were rigging and some were fishing. There was plenty of room as the crowd had been small to begin with and half of the people were too sick to fish. "Does this happen every time?" I asked. The deckhand explained that always a few people got sick but today was very rough and very seldom did they fish when the waves were this high. If it becomes much worse we'd probably have to go home early but I think probably the wind will calm down. "Here's your rig," he said. "We use electric reels cause you're going to go down about two hundred feet. You've got two hooks on there and bait with this. This is cut squid. Just hook it on anyway the fish don't care. Don't try to cover your hook. If we get into them good you'll catch a lot of fish, however they aren't exciting fish to catch but they are the best eating on the Gulf. When they bite you'll just feel a little tap unless it's a big old sow so then reel up. They won't fight. Hold the line in your fingers like this or you may not even know you have a fish on. Got it?" Down, down, down went my line until eventually the line slackened. It was resting on the bottom and I tightened the line. I heard someone yell first fish and saw my neighbor reel in two of the most beautiful fish I'd ever seen, one on each hook. They were between a bright pink and a mild red and practically glowed. They were two or three pound fish. He unhooked them and they flopped on the deck. I examined them closely and even as I did their color began to fade.

The boat heeled over first one side then the other. When the boat went one way the lines of the fishermen on that side went under the boat. When it went the other way the lines on that side went under the boat. A lot of them met in the middle causing lines to tangle and then lines were cut. Deckhands were kept busy unsnarling and cutting tangles, while bating hooks and putting ice on the fish. I felt something tug on my line and activated my electric reel. I felt decadent with my push button reel but before the day was over was thankful for it. I had on a smallish light colored fish. "That's a sand trout," said the deckhand. "They're food to eat though snappers are better. You can catch a lot of them in the Bay closer to shore or you can catch them right off the beach or a pier." I put my line back in the water. I began by catching a snapper the prettiest fish I've ever caught. About as much action as a blue gill but it was all new and exciting with the sky and water gorgeous. Someone hooked something big although we never saw it. It stayed deep and simply moved away in a steady drive and kept on going. Someone else hooked what the deckhand thought was a king fish and it was lost under the boat too. Someone else brought up a snapper bitten in half. "Shark," said the deckhand.

My neighbor to the left became sick and had to quit. A blonde girl replaced him with a figure like Daisy Mae Yoakum's with a vivid smile in a pretty sun darkened face. "This is fun," she said. "We don't have anything like this in Uvalde." I said that we didn't have anything like it in Kansas City either. She caught more fish in an hour than I did all morning. She put her line on the bottom and reeled it in to unhook two fish. She would put her line down and reel it in again to unhook two more fish and she did it all over again and again. Nobody seemed to be catching big fish. Mostly small snappers, a few small kings, and a small bonito were being caught. Most of the snappers were running three to five pounds. "Sometimes you'll get a big old sow snapper out here, said my friendly deckhand. They'll get up to sixty to seventy pounds, or you might catch a big grouper. You'll think you hooked the bottom if you hook a big grouper."

Daisy Mae squealed, "Oooh!" She had reeled in the biggest snapper I'd see yet, which was probably seven or eight pounds. "Wait till Daddy sees this!" The fish was a beautiful glistening creature, so was she. "Where's your daddy?" I asked. "He's on the other side and he'll never believe I caught one this big." "On the other side?" "You mean your daddy's dead?" I asked. "He's fishing on the other side of the boat. He doesn't like to fish with me because sometimes I catch more fish!" I could believe it. She certainly caught more fish than anyone else in sight, including myself. We struck up a conversation between reeling and unhooking and baiting. You could use the same piece of cut bait over and over as sometimes the fish hardly left a mark on it. She was 21 years old and she lived on a ranch near Uvlade with her daddy. She loved horses and did barrel racing at rodeos.

Clouds came suddenly as they do on the Gulf. It became dark and the rain started up. Everyone reeled in and crowded into the lounge. Thunder. Lightening. Rain. Storm at sea. This was great! The concessionaire was happy. All the fishermen were hungry and thirsty with a big run on the beer coolers. Limp ham and cheese sandwiches tasted like steak. All the dill pickles were gone because the sick people had eaten them in a vain effort to neutralize the surging currents in their stomachs. For the most part the sick people stayed sick. They would not feel good till they were on a steady unmoving surface. It amazed me that so many people were so ill and that I wasn't. In my ignorance I had never considered the subject as a part of going fishing. I sat beside Charles. He flinched away from the sight of my greasy sandwiches and adverted his eyes. I said, "Its about ten thirty Charles, many happy hours of fishing yet. I'm really enjoying this." I described my fish to him and told him about Daisy Mae. I'm going to ask her out." Charles was interested only in himself. At this point he was too sick to be embarrassed or to feel he was missing anything. He just wanted off the Thunder Ball.

The rain stopped abruptly. One moment it was raining and the next it wasn't. The sun shone. Clouds scattered and scudded widely in the turbulent air and there was a beautiful rainbow. The heaving dark blue water delighted me but it was rougher than ever and even more difficult to fish or even to stand without hanging on. We began to fish. Daisy Mae took over her old position to my right. She promptly began reeling in snappers. I asked how her daddy was doing? "He caught some fish but I don't think he's feeling too good. I hope he isn't getting sick." This was great news. Get old Dad out of the way and the possibilities were unlimited. She had said they were staying at the La Quinta Inn in Corpus Christi. I had the company car at my motel and could go there.

I brought up a fish. I surreptitiously rubbed my face with my sleeve hoping to remove all traces of ham, mayonnaise, and squid juice and fish scales. I faced her with the smoothest possible Kansas City suave and asked her out to dinner that night. "We'll tuck your old Daddy away in the motel and make sure he's clean and fed and wrapped up good. Then we'll go out and explore the city together. We can go just like two kids in the big town looking at the sights. Does that sound like fun?" She smiled ravishingly but her eyes were doubtful. "Sounds like fun, but I don't think Daddy would like it. He usually won't stay home while I go out." She pointed, "Here's Daddy now. You can ask him if you want to but I don't think I would he looks mean." I didn't ask him. It was instantly obvious that "Daddy" was not a term of filial description but rather a term of endearment or nickname for a young fellow about her age, 40. He was built appropriately somewhat like Lil Abner, although taller and heavier with a red angry face that had none of the friendliness of Lil Abner's. "He's mad cause he's getting seasick," she whispered. I put my attention back to the gorgeous creatures of the sea and put the siren of Uvalde almost out of my mind.

About 12:30 the rain came again with more wind and the seas rose. They seemed gigantic to me and it was impossible to stand on the deck and fish. The word passed around. "Reel in. Reel in. We're going in." Deckhands gathered up the equipment and the fish were lightly dusted with ice. We all went back into the cabin. I was the last one in, as I hated to leave the deck. The waves were so big that now I looked up at them. They reared angrily over the Thunder Ball that bobbed and slid like a duck on a rough lake. In the cabin I had beer and a liverwurst sandwich. I sat by Charles. "We're going home early," I said. "It's a little rough for fishing." He gave a pitiful flare of weak anger. "A little rough! It's a Hurricane. I'm never going on a boat again." I patted his shoulder with the hand holding the liverwurst sandwich. He looked at it with infinite disgust. "They say we'll be home in about three hours," I said. "It's going to be a little slow because we're going against the waves." In the ghastly ashy sheet of his features his eyes were dark tunnels and far back in the tunnels a light glowed briefly and then went out. "Oh God," Charles said. He kept shrinking away from me into the corner of the booth and I realized that the liverwurst and fish smell was aggravating his already deplorable condition. I went up to the wheelhouse and stayed there till we saw the jetties of Port Aransas late in the afternoon.

Captain Jimmy was undisturbed by the weather. "Too bad we can't fish," he said. "Jest a little too squally and it more than likely will be a little worse after a while. There'll be another day." I asked him how big the waves were? "About 12 feet." I had guessed they were closer to twenty but on consideration decided he was closer than I was. Since I'm not Joseph Conrad I won't go into detail on that violent passage to port. The waves were big, rough and it rained, thundered with lightning and I was thrilled to death. I stayed in the wheelhouse and listened to fishing stories and smoked a cigar. I enjoyed every minute of it. The chop inside the jetties that we had thought so rough that morning was even more pronounced now but seemed like no more than a ripple in the bathtub after the wild voyage home. I ran a stringer through my fish. I drank a last beer. I thanked the Captain and my friendly deckhand for their counsel and tolerance. They were pleased I'd had a good time as so many hadn't that day. Charles staggered on deck. He looked awful but his face brightened at the sight of the rain-splashed dock. He muttered "Land." He gave me the car keys. "You drive," he said and within minutes he was looking better. I drove through Port Aransas in the rain at about five o'clock. We waited in line for the ferry and Charles was coming to life. From the ferry we saw dolphins in mid channel sporting happily (I suppose) in the rain and whitecaps.

The siren of Uvalde smiled at me from the car window on my left. Her daddy was walking the deck of the ferry beside the car. He had his name on the back of his belt. "Damn Redneck," I said. Then I added, "She's too fine for something like him. He'll beat her after they're married." Charles peered at him. "Redneck? What did he say?" "He hasn't said anything all day, just scowls. But sometimes rednecks talk a lot." Charles replied, "He sure looks big and mean though." He was still too sickly to pay any attention to the girl.

At the motel on the causeway he washed his face in my room and his color was becoming pink again. He walked steadily. His spirits were improving rapidly. "I've got to work tomorrow," he said. "Otherwise I'd go fishing with you again," he lied. "It'll be quieter tomorrow and those poor people will have a better time." He drove off toward Corpus Christi in the falling rain and I went into my motel room and found the tricky guy had slipped the stringer of fish into my sink. That was not according to the plan. I looked in the mirror. I was stained and wrinkled and filthy. My face was red and puffy from the sun, wind and beer. I felt great. A real adventure! I drank a little scotch and took a long shower. When I finished the fish still laid in the sink. About a dozen of them, eyes glazed with their brilliant colors dulled. They were just dead fish waiting to be cleaned.

You must understand that ordinarily whatever I shot or caught I would clean, store and eventually eat. Today I had no facilities for any of that for all I had were the decomposing corpses of a dozen dead fish. I went to the front office. The desk clerk was a young Mexican with a wispy mustache and sad eyes. He looked at me mournfully but probably he was happy as hell, although he looked mournful. "How you do today?" I figured I'd let him have it right between the eyes and then browbeat him into submission if necessary. I thought of the drying and stiffened bodies in my sink. I looked straight at him. "Did fine. I'd like to give you twelve beautiful fresh red snapper." He followed me into my room and thoughtfully fingered the day's dead catch. It had been a good day for me. A hell of a fine day and my luck held. He smiled as he hefted the stringer of fish. He hesitated. "I'll clean em for you, fifty cents apiece to freeze and wrap them." I held firm. "I want you to have them." His lugubrious expression lightened as he'd made a gesture and I'd let him off. "Those snappers," he said. "They are awful good. Thank You."

I went up to the lounge. Through the windows the bay looked dark and ominous. Rain still fell. There were no fishing lights out there now. I sank gratefully into a padded seat. The girl came over.

"Beertininis," I said being tired now the seafarer home from the sea. "Heavy on the olives," I couldn't resist it. "In a dirty glass," I growled. She didn't get it this time either.

Jim O'Connor
10/22/87

BIRDING AND THE GREAT AUK

Forty-seven years ago two teenagers would meet resulting in them spending their entire lifetimes together. They were with their fathers who were attending a tradesmen convention at Goodland, Kansas. The convention was the Coming of Craftsmen Organization better known as the COCO convention. Back then the main speaker was Herman Sneezelweed who had earned the prestigious title and award as America's Sewer Worker of the Year. It was determined Herman was the best bucket driver in the sewer business. During that past year he had loaded and pushed more human waste than any other loading driver in the country. Quite an accomplishment by all standards when one thinks about it. As the main speaker Herman gave a speech concerning Modern Methods of Smelling Protection for individuals, communities and cities alike. In detail he explained how one could push sewer waste in a new proper system, which would decrease odor. His speech was riveting to all.

Well, almost all as the children Alexander Hurtsum and Kathy

Saltsman had no interest in such matters but rather took great interest in each other. At that time they lived in two small western Kansas towns only 35 miles apart. Alexander was lucky enough to have a 55 Chevy back then making their dating days easy and joyous ones. They would date through their high school days right into their 20's when wedding bells would ring for them. They would always recall their union was due to the COCO convention and Herman Sneezelweed's smelly speech which you might say they butted out of.

The forty-seven years of time had gone fast with their family of children and foster children now all grown up and on their own. During those years Alexander had earned a PhD in science and had become Professor Hurtsum while Kathy had been the perfect mother and homemaker. The Professor taught a variety of science courses at a small Kansas college although his goal was always to teach at a large university such as MIT. Three specific events by the brilliant yet eccentric Professor made it impossible for him to advance, as the acts were not acceptable at larger institutions. First there was the matter of the grading curve in education. There is the idea that if you gave 2 A's then you should give 2 F's and if you then gave 6 B's you should hand out 6 D's with finally the remainder of the class receiving C's. There is some leeway in the system but one term Alexander handed out 34 A's and 1 F. His superior, Dean Killjoy asked for an explanation on the matter? Professor Hurtsum answered, "Well 34 of my students did their very best and the one seldom came to class and was stoned all the time." The Dean did not care for the answer and wrote it up in Alexander's file. The next infraction was a much more serious one that would involve students. Professor Hurtsum taught an entire physics class for the semester on roller skates. He zipped around from student to student lecturing on the third law of motion. The students loved this and even took up wearing roller skates and skateboards in the hallways to travel from class to class. Many faculty members protested this practice and again Dean Killjoy wrote up Alexander's actions. The third infraction would guarantee that the Professor's lower college-level employment fate would be forever. He was in charge of a non-stop two-day chemistry workshop that included many intermissions in the two-day period. During the slow times approximately one half of the students took to drinking wine and other alcoholic drinks. By the second day this group was cold stone drunk! So much for chemistry, as the sober group complained to the Dean. Fortunately for Alexander no real proof came forth on the events which in turn protected his job. Dean Killjoy did write up the incident nonetheless. Once again the Professor's grading curve was lopsided with an abundance of F's which the Dean also took note of.

Alexander had wed the perfect wife for Kathy was the sweetest, kindest and most loving woman ever known to Kansas. Kathy's desires included being a good mother to her five children and many foster ones she helped through the years. Kathy was down to earth with practical Kansas living principles as her guide which she passed on to all the children. Her priorities in life where the children, Sunday school teaching, active PTA involvement and some local political activism. Being a lifelong loving wife to Alexander and sharing his dreams she excelled throughout their lives of supporting him in every way. Kathy was proud of all her children and foster children as well. Her youngest son took after his Father to become a science professor of note at Harvard. Then there was the foster child Oliver that became a Proctologist doctor practicing in Goodland, Kansas. In many ways this son made her think back to her teenage years, the COCO Convention and of course Herman Sneezelweed. Kathy's other sons and daughters gained success in all of their careers as well. Some were tradesmen, others in the medical fields and some happy homemakers as she herself always had been.

Alexander and Kathy were in their 60's with all the children gone from the nest. With Alexander retired from his teaching career they now could pursue their lifelong passion of bird watching. Back through the past thirty years they and the children had enjoyed birding at their country home. They had bird feeders located right outside of seven windows and two birdbaths in their yard. This afforded them the viewing of the local Kansas birds as well as migratory ones such as hummingbirds when they traveled North or South. On summer vacations they would travel to Canada, Mexico and most of the United States birding.

Now with retirement the loving couple was free to travel the world in search of a species he alone believed was yet alive, that being the Great Auk. This bird was a flightless bird that stood three feet high and history contends became extinct in the year 1844. Their habitat was the North Atlantic Islands ranging from Canada, Iceland, Greenland and Northern Europe. The large black and white birds were extremely awkward on land, hence their name, making them an easy food source for the early explorers. Then their feathers and down became popular commercial products in all of Europe. The Great Auks mated for life with only one egg per year to continue their species. Added up all of these factors contributed to their extinction. Only a few mounted birds exist in museums today for mankind's viewing.

Dr. Alexander Hurtsum could not and would not believe the Great Auk was extinct with plans he and his wife would set out worldwide if necessary to prove it. In earlier occasions he and his children had searched the Canadian East Coast to no avail. Now with retirement he would be able to search the seven seas if necessary although the North Atlantic would be the prime search area. He and Kathy would travel to Greenland for their initial search.

At the Kansas City Airport he said to his wife, "Well Kathy we are off to Greenland in search of the birds I know exist. Scientists for years have said there is no Bigfoot, there is no Loch Ness Monster and there are no Great Auks. Yet many people claim to have seen all three. Where we are going our Captain has said he has seen the birds, I'm very excited about this trip. By filming the Auk we will go down in history forever. Time to get on our plane." They were on the plane and seated as Kathy spoke, "I know we will enjoy this trip regardless of the outcome Alexander. This time is our time, how romantic, tell me again what happens when we get to Greenland?" Alexander seemingly went through the itinerary to his wife for the third or fourth time. "Dear we land in the Capital City of Nuuk, then take a flight up to the North East coastal town of Ittoqqortoormilt. I know dear I'm not pronouncing that right as only an Inuit Eskimo can, that is their part of the world for all times. Once we get to that town I've hired a Sea Captain and his boat for ten days. He is Danish and his name is Captain Blackout plus he is the man that told me he knows where the Auks are, how exciting." "Yes dear, I remember you telling me all about it, I just wanted to hear you say the Eskimo's town name again. I think you are getting better at it. Ten days huh? I packed a lot of warm clothes for us and brought three cameras and know you have the video equipment. Sure hope the Captain is right about the Auks. This is going to be one wonderful trip."

The flights to Nuuk and the Inuit town went well so next they went to the docks in order to round up Captain Blackout. The adventurous couple found the Captain all right. He was in the dockside saloon called Tie Down and he was as drunk as a skunk. "Say aren't you sea Captain Blackout with the boat named NEVER MOOR?" "Yes siree chap that's me," the Captain answered. "Well aren't you to take us tomorrow in search of the Great Auks?" "Yes siree chap that's me." The Professor wondered about his choice of this Captain and next asked, "Will you be in shape to sail at 9 AM as we have booked you for?" Once again the answer came, "Yes siree chap that's me." With that the tired pair left the saloon to find their lodging room that was three blocks away.

After their long day of travel they were pleased to find the room both warm and cheerful. Alexander said to his wife, "Well I'm not so sure at all about the Captain, in fact now I have grave concerns about him." Kathy replied, "Oh don't worry dear, you know what your mother always said, 'Things will look better in the morning.' For now I'm going to take a hot shower and go to bed. It's 9:30 back in Kansas so four hours later here and we'd better get up by 6:30 for breakfast in order to meet Captain Blackout by nine." With that said, she went to the shower and returned dressed for bed. A half-hour later Alexander did much the same and then both crawled into the bed together. Kathy spoke, "Boy that was a nice hot shower, how was yours?" He replied, "Yes the shower was fine but are we both sliding into the middle of this bed? I feel like we are in a taco in this thing." "Yes dear we sure are close, how romantic, so we could snuggle up just like when we were kids." He demanded, "Get up Kathy! I'm putting this mattress on the floor" and he did just that. He continued, "Boy my emotions are like an egg in the hot sun after little rest on the long flights with excitement to come here and now find a drunken sailor to lead our way. This will be one restless night sleeping on the floor, Dorothy was right, Toto I don't think we're in Kansas anymore." Kathy could only say, "Good night dear" as she kissed him good night.

Morning came with the two having a hearty breakfast at the lodge's restaurant followed by the walk to the docks. A delightful surprise came, as there was a young fellow on the NEVER MOOR cleaning the deck. He introduced himself, "Good morning I'm Lars the First Mate of this yacht and you must be Mr. and Mrs. Hurtsum, welcome aboard. Your cabin is the furthest in with the kitchen area also there. The head is down the hall to your right and towards this way is where the Captain and I take up quarters. Would you have any questions?" "Yes Lars we are the Hurtsums, so where is the Captain and by the way have you ever seen any Great Auks in this part of Greenland?" "The Captain is with the Dock Master checking on weather conditions present and the possible future. As far as Auks, no I have never seen one but many seamen have reported seeing many of them on an island north of us. Since it is August the ice breakups should allow us to travel up there with no problems. Captain Blackout will be along shortly." With that Alexander's excitement returned and the two made their way to their cabin with Lars helping to carry their gear. Now it was a matter of waiting for Blackout, yet they felt good and secure with Lars aboard.

Captain Blackout soon came to his boat to say, "Welcome aboard Mateys, all is good for our voyage, calm seas and to stay that way for at least the week. You have met First Mate, Lars and he will see to your needs as in fact he is the only Mate. For now let's cast off." The 28-foot boat with no sails did have two powerful diesel Cummings engines which started up to move the Captain and passengers away from the docks. They reached the open sea heading North with the Captain opening up the engines to a roar propelling the boat at a high speed. The Professor looked at his wife, "Look Kathy at the mainland where both seals and reindeer are on the rocky shore, I hope this Captain slows down now with all these ice hunks floating around. It looks like big icebergs ahead, we're not in Kansas anymore." Kathy responded, "With the telephoto I'm getting good pictures. Maybe you could ask the Captain to slow down as I've seen him drinking from his flask and you can bet it's not orange juice he's drinking." With that the boat hit some ice making a loud smack, which tilted the boat. Wisely the Captain did slow down and informed all aboard, "Well folks now it will be a slower ride making it a two-day trip to the Auk Island. May as well enjoy the ride and watch for whales in these waters. Hey Lars take the wheel I'm going to go get lunch up for these folks." The Americans felt much safer with Lars driving the small ship at a slower rate through the ice flows. Alexander asked, "Hey Lars does Captain Blackout drink all day at all times?" Lars could only say, "Pretty much, but don't worry I'll navigate 99% of this trip both ways. I definitely will keep us out of trouble at all times. When it is my sleep time I'll have the boat anchored by an island and with the Captain having his bottle in hand he'll snooze off then too. As you know now the sun never sets and with the light you can watch for icebergs coming our way and let me know even if I'm sleeping. The small ice chunks won't hurt us, don't worry, see that island ahead, it may have polar bears on it."

As they neared the island Kathy viewed it and turned to Alexander, "Dear all I see is some seagulls and rocks with ice and more ice. This indeed is the land of rocks, snow and ice with mostly ice. With the sun out all this clean white has it's own beauty and aside from the rocky shorelines it is pure white as far as the eye can see. If a bear didn't move how could you ever tell a white bear in all this whiteness?" Lars answered, "Easy just look for the bears black eyes." The Professor knew he was kidding but Kathy wasn't sure and hoped they never anchored close to any island. The boat slowly headed due North as they watched for icebergs and the three visited about Greenland's climate, people and history. Mostly on how the Canadian Inuit's first came centuries ago with next the Norwegians and Danish claiming the island but now the Danish owned Greenland. Kathy found it all interesting whereas the Professor felt it all small talk, as he knew it all from his past studies.

The Captain appeared, "All ready mess is on, come and get it Matey's." Lars put the engines in idle mode and the boat was free to drift with the current. All went to the kitchen table that was in the couple's large room. The room had two single beds, a stove, an icebox and the long table with eight chairs. The meal was a huge pot of clam chowder with crackers and hardtack bread as well. To drink was water or red wine only. It was hoped that the Americans would enjoy this meal, as it would be the exact same one served morning, noon and night for the next ten days. They learned this fact on the second day and intuitively knew they were in for eight more days of this exact meal. On the first lunch and evening meal it was delicious for the American couple, however on the second day the same meal served for breakfast gave them concerns regarding this diet. Alexander asked the Captain, "Is this the only meal we will have for the next eight days?" The Captain took a sip from his seemingly bottomless flask and answered, "Well matey you are on the sea and when on the sea we eat clams. You're welcome to cook them any way you wish, they are in the rear hole, a couple hundred of 'em. Oh yes, there is canned condensed milk too and all you want. I make the chowder up and it's easiest to just add to the pot. You might catch a fish or two if you really don't like just the clams, they make good bait if you want?" Kathy quickly responded, "Where's the poles?" With that said Lars put the engines in idle, the boat simply drifted in the current and the three began fishing. The Captain ate a few raw clams giving out some for bait as well.

Kathy yelled out, "I got something," as she reeled in to find no fish on her line. Lars advised, "You have to jerk hard when you feel a fish, that will set the hook in our next meal." With that the Professor had a bite and followed Lars directions to set the hook. He fought a fish for at least 5 minutes to reel up a good size Arctic Flounder and Lars used a gaff to bring the fish into the boat. Alexander beamed with his success, "Wow that guy fought a good fight, that was fun plus a real fresh seafood meal is ours." Then Kathy jerked her pole and yelled out, "I got one too, help me reel him in, oh please." Lars said, "Just reel him in girl unless you want clams the next eight days." Her husband added, "You can do it hon, just keep the line tight and reel him in slowly, no hurry, enjoy your Arctic vacation." Kathy was able to get her fish in with the help of Lars and the group stayed fishing until five were in hand. The Captain simply ate raw clams as he sipped on his flask as all the excitement was taking place.

With the fish cleaned by Lars he then took the controls and the boat headed back North once more. Floating ice bounced off the bow with little concern knowing Lars was the real Captain of this journey. The Professor asked Lars, "Say this is day two, is this the day we see the Great Auks as the Captain told us?" Lars answered,

"Travels have been slow so I expect we will get to the island he said most likely tomorrow." As they traveled more and more small islands made up the environment. One island was covered with puffins; a beautiful seagoing bird and the next island would be covered with seals. The North Atlantic Ocean was now the Arctic Ocean requiring more clothes to deal with temperatures ranging from 18°F to a high of 45° in the real day time. Greenland has over fifty birds that live on the mainland and islands giving the Americans plenty to photograph and record during their northern journey. They had plenty to see and enjoy besides all the vast white snow and ice. The Americans were happy with a meal of fish, seeing a large variety of wildlife and the anticipation of day three. With Lars at the wheel they would take to their cabin to enjoy a long sleep.

Since daylight occurred twenty-four hours a day in this Northland it was difficult to tell what day was what. Alexander had a wrist watch which would seemingly do every function known to high-tech modern man. It had GPS, a camera, connection hookups to the Internet and information regarding the year, month, day, date and time. With all this it was just next to impossible to tell what time of day it was unless you were high tech too. The mode of date did tell him it was day number three and hopefully the day of the Auk. The sea now was clear of the ice chunks with only icebergs the size of cruise ships floating South. They posed little danger as they could be seen for miles in advance to avoid them. Aside from the huge icebergs there were small islands on top of Islands in this part of the ocean that also broke up the landscape. Lars now ran the craft at full throttle most of this day except only at idle times when they all ate fish or chowder. Captain Blackout true to his name mostly sat quietly in his stupor except to sip from his pocket flask. Alexander and Lars would often wake him to ask if this was the right Island for the Auks? The Captain typically would say, "Yes siree matey, this is the one," only to discover more puffins or more seals but never an Auk.

Discouraged the professor and his wife now knew they were on their own with another day passing. The morning of day four found mother's saying of, "Things look better in the morning," would be true in many ways. To everyone's surprise the Captain came out of his cabin sober to announce, "Today is the day, I checked the longitude and latitude coordinates and we are a mere three islands away from the Auks, only about twelve km. Today's breakfast will be eggs and bacon I had set aside for this day of discovery. The last days of the ice flows had slowed us down greatly, but now with an open sea we will be there for lunch." Alexander and Kathy yelled out, "Hurray" while clapping their hands for both a new breakfast plus now their goal was close at hand. All went to the mess table and sure enough the Captain served up bacon and eggs with even orange juice being served. After the great breakfast all went deck side with anticipation of island number three. Day number four had the morning temperatures in the twenties as the twenty-six foot boat rapidly traveled Northward.

Around 11:30 island number three was in sight as Alexander checked his GPS location on the high dollar watch and then took notes of the information. Soon they would reach the hidden quest the Americans had come in search of. Captain Blackout using his spotting scope announced, "There they are, there's hundreds of them, there are your Auks." In a short time the birds were in eyesight view standing along the island's rocky shoreline. A discouraged Alexander looked at the Captain, "Blackout those are not Auks, they are puffins and penguins! You have put us on a wild goose chase!" The Captain responded, "They look like Auks to me." The American lectured, "Auks have large black bills, those birds have orange and black beaks, those are Emperor Penguins." All aboard knew the Professor was very angry over the present situation when all of a sudden he started jumping up and down to say, "EMPEROR PENGUINS!" Kathy seeing her husband's excitement asked, "What is it dear?" He now proudly announced, "Yes, three foot tall Emperor Penguins. This is a scientific discovery of historical significance. Penguins are only known to live in Antarctica and none have ever been seen in the Arctic, as the Southern Hemisphere is their habitat. The furthest North ones have ever been seen is at the Galapagos Islands and those were not emperors. Here we are in the Arctic to find a bird never thought to be here. Captain, I apologize for my rage, you did just fine. How about going around this whole island for further inspection." The Captain navigated and the Americans took countless pictures and videotapes of the birds on the island's shoreline as the small ship went around and around the

Island. Each full trip around the mostly flat island covered only by a whiff of snow took approximately one hour. It was learned that seals took up the West shore whereas the puffins and penguins called home to the other three sides.

The Professor asked the Captain to make land after many trips around the island and the Captain was happy to oblige by going into a deep cove. The Americans along with Lars went ashore to investigate while taking many close-up penguin photographs. Then the Professor asked the other two to help him arrange large sized rocks in order to spell out "HURTSUM ISLAND." With that done the three returned to the boat for a late lunch of what else but clam chowder. After lunch they made two more trips around the island taking even more pictures and videotapes. The Professor once again looked at his GPS readings and took notes of it, then said to the Captain, "Captain Blackout let's head for home port. I know this is only day four and we paid for ten, but I am most satisfied with this voyage. You surely may keep all the money we paid you and I'll even buy you a steak when we get to shore, even if it is reindeer in these parts."

With that said the passengers and crew headed Southward for the trip home. The Captain took out his flask and Lars took the wheel on the uneventful three-day voyage back to their homeport. During that time more clam chowder was added to the pot for all meals as Alexander's wishes to reach land overrode any idle time fishing. Once on shore all four went for steaks, type unknown?

The following day after sleeping the night on the floor all goodbyes were said and tips handed out with the most generous given to Lars. The Americans then took the earliest possible flight back to Greenland's capital city of Nuuk. In two days at Nuuk they visited the Ministry of Natural Resources as well as the Ministry of Tourism. At the offices the Professor had them make copies of the pictures and videotapes of the greatest natural find of the 21st century. They were happy to do so and it must be noted only the images with "HURTSUM ISLAND" were offered to ensure his own legacy.

Next they took a flight to Washington DC where they presented their findings to the National Geographic Societies Headquarters. Again only those with "HURTSUM ISLAND" were offered. Then a flight to Kansas and the drive back home. With the warm early autumn sun after the cold Arctic days the couple thought of days to come in retirement and how they could top their last journey? They looked up into the sky watching the endless flocks of Sandhill cranes making their Southward migration. The birds flew in their up and down erratic flight pattern while sounding their calls of hundreds of squeaky door hinges. He remarked, "Maybe the Auks are in Antarctica?" Kathy said, "Things always look better in the morning."

THE TWEETY BIRD

Everyone world wide knows of the famous writer Denny Hopkins that writes for the outdoor magazine "Happy Outdoors." Well maybe not everyone but many do know of his humorous outdoor articles. Okay, perhaps it is only a few that really knows of his writings. His is the only outdoor magazine that gets mixed up with gardening magazines on store shelves across the country. Store managers don't put "Sports Afield" in with the athletic section of their magazine racks; rather they place them correctly in the hunting and fishing section. Yet "Happy Outdoors" nine times out of ten ended up in the gardening section of the sales' racks, which accounts for very few outdoor readers knowing of the writer. One would think that the New York cigar chomping CEO of "Happy Outdoors" would recognize the problem and address it. He surely could change the magazine's name to label it as a hunting and fishing one. It could be called "Outdoor Sports," "Hunting and Fishing" or even "Hunting and Fishing Without Getting A Hook In Your Ear." The truth is anything would be an improvement in circulation however the cigar chomping CEO has a 21 year-old blonde wife that originally picked out the name "Happy Outdoors." Accordingly for the CEO to remain a happy man the name "Happy Outdoors" shall forever remain. Can you blame him?

Lucky for me I got to know Denny quite by accident. I had recently moved from Northern Illinois to Nebraska and I of the few faithful had read "Happy Outdoors" for several years. I had read the issues as loyal as a Lab is to his master. Once in Nebraska after the cultural shock of hearing and seeing, "GO BIG RED," one million times everywhere within the state I settled into living a slow life in the center of the State. Being retired I chose to live in the less populated area known as the Sandhills. Here the landscape is countless hills of cattle grass with ponds, lakes and rivers. Since I am an outdoor sportsman this was my idea of utopia. On one hot day in late August I was in a big city sports shop buying needed equipment as ammo, decoys and calls. As a kid in a candy store I piled up my boxes of goodies sky high knowing my fall hunting equipment would now be in place. As the expression goes, I was loaded for bear.

A young store helper and I were next loading my purchased equipment in my pick up truck. We were half loaded with many boxes to come when this fella walked up to us and asked, "You guys need a hand? This hot sun's beatin down like a flat tire in the desert. You guys need a break." He then held out his hand and introduced himself and accordingly the store clerk and I did the same. I did not connect him as the outdoor writer even though he was dressed from head to toe in camouflage attire. We sat down visiting on the tailgate of my pick up and asked the clerk to round us up some ice tea. The clerk was happy to go find us some and I gave him the money for it. In our conversation Denny told me he happened to live in this small village of Los Mindos. Oddly enough that also was exactly where I had put down my new roots making us neighbors. What a great coincidence I thought, as the clerk showed up with the tea. Our visiting continued and he said, "You got plenty number 8's?" Knowing he meant shotgun shells I wondered why such a low load. What in the world could a macho man use 8's for? Denny next advised, "Buy 8 boxes of number 8's and I'll take you shooting on September 1st and here's my phone number." I said I would love to go and gave him my number thinking this is the way people of the Sandhills say, "Let's do lunch."

Being a man of my word I did buy the eight boxes with thoughts of them as good as elephant hunting in the heartland. But if nothing else I could use them on the next Fourth of July to make some noise. Then after all the many shells and decoy boxes were loaded I was driving home on my ninety-mile trip when it hit me. I had in fact just met the humorous writer of articles I had read for years. Sure, he was Denny Hopkins, the writer in "Happy Outdoors." Plus he just happens to live in the same hamlet of Los Mindos that I also called home.

The day before September 1st the phone rang and sure enough it was Denny. He said, "Let's go dove hunting tomorrow, be ready by four and I'll pick you up." We visited some about the hot days and other small talk with the call being somewhat short. It never dawned on me which four he meant so sure enough at 4 AM the next day I was ready for my new adventure. Well 4 AM came with a no-show making me figure this was all a joke on me. Then 4 PM came and Denny showed up with four other local hunters. Denny said, "Let's go dove hunting." I didn't know if he was serious or not. I had never shot doves in my life although certainly was aware many people did. That was evident by all those articles in the sports magazines, which appears each late summer. So, surely many gunners did in fact find sport in tracking down the little bird. But Denny is macho and I'm damn near 70 so going to hunt a little Songbird for the first time was questionable. Denny is a deer hunter and bear hunter making it hard to imagine he was half serious about going to gun down tweety birds. After all he wears camouflage twelve months of the year, 100% camouflage including I bet camouflage underwear. I thought he was joking, he was not.

As a kid growing up I'll always recall how practically all the men folk gathered to shoot blackbirds flying during their fall migration. We'd all gather on the lakefront and await the flock after flock that offered us shooting practice most evenings. The idea was to sharpen up our shooting eye for the soon to open duck season. Shooting the blackbirds was simply shooting practice. It was a ritual and tradition practiced by most of the boys, men and a few women where I grew up. The object was to pick out one bird and not to flock shoot. What counted were accurate shots not number of birds downed. On a rare occasion some birds would be gathered and given to the older women who would make blackbird pies with them. Most generally the birds were left out for other creatures to feed on because the whole goal was in developing shooting skills not table fare. At best a lab would be trained to retrieve the birds once in a great while. I found myself a full-grown man even developing gray hairs and Denny was serious about shooting doves. Well they did things different here in Nebraska and with the absence of blackbirds the doves must be their way of practicing up for the "Real" fall hunting. That was the only logical explanation I had before we started out on this piece of cake adventure. My outdoor philosophy was if someone offered to take me hunting or fishing I'd go with an open mind. I'll do it their way, not mine, as I was the guest. This philosophy has been a good one. I have learned a great deal from other sportsmen and if all else fails I generally learned a new good spot to apply tested and proven methods later. With the case of Denny once I realized he was serious about hunting doves I also had to realize I knew nothing of this sport. Therefore, short of a flashlight and a gunnysack I had to do things his way. The gunnysack and the flashlight was a trick played on greenhorns and I was not a greenhorn so would not fall for that trick.

Dove hunting had its pluses and minuses from recalling that first day's experience. Primarily dove shooting is indeed a gentleman's sport as we left for our hunting at the crack of 4 o'clock in the afternoon. This was not in any remote manner linked to the insanity of duck hunting where you started the journey in the middle of the night. No, dove hunting is for the mild mannered gentleman that could easily shoot two rounds of golf prior to embarking upon the day's hunt. Here in Nebraska the season opener is Labor Day when temperatures yet may reach the 90 degree plus range. Weather would not be a discomfort factor and in fact sun tan lotion could easily be recommended. The leisure trip only offered one physical displeasure and that was mosquitos. It's hard to concentrate on being a great white hunter of the North when you have to fight off the annoying insect placed on earth for bird's food. The only other use for the pesky mosquitos that I have found is that they may be blamed for the missed shots you make. My shooting concentration is interrupted by the damn bugs is an excuse which works twice on every hunt. It is recommended that the excuse not be over used for credibility reasons.

Six of us left town in search of the morning dove. It was 4 o'clock in the afternoon, which made me instinctively wonder if we weren't a little late for hunting the bird with such a given name? I kept my thoughts to myself while I was sitting next to Denny as he drove the Ford pickup. The other four gunners followed in Denny's ford station wagon with two Labradors included. We rambled down rolling dirt roads and finally off the road to a cattle trail leading towards a canyon. Denny never walked any further than absolutely required in any hunting adventures. Accordingly the pickup and station wagon were put through the tests of bouncing along bumpity bump into the Sandhills. It was a good idea to hold onto something to avoid having your head bounce up into the roof. Denny never was going to outgrow his love for rodeo sports and a Ford bouncing along was no different than scoring a 68 on a bull. He talked about some other hunting or fishing memory as we approached the canyon. Riding shotgun I opened gates while the station wagon hunters closed them. No one was in a hurry on this late-summer day. Our vehicles finally stopped within sixty yards of where we would hunt. The area was overgrown pastures, numerous cedars and cottonwoods with a stock pond twenty feet over a ridge. We assembled our gear which had been scrambled in the 68 score ride and let the dogs run free. The dogs always have to run crazy for about five minutes it seems. Probably the ride and the fact they know this is their first hunt of the year had them super hyper. They were allowed to run crazy while we prepared. First we gathered the many, many shotgun shells. There were at least six hundred shells or one hundred per man, which indicated total positive action would occur. The shells ranged from new boxes of 8's and 6's, reloaded 6's, a bunch of miscellaneous old cells from fall hunting trips out of the ancient past and even a few old 2's. It's obvious this is a sport where you shoot up all the junk shells that had been collected in a coffee can over the years just like when we shot blackbirds. What is not answerable is why anyone would bring 2's to shoot a tweety bird. Next we gathered the life like dove decoys and put on camouflage. Denny slept in camouflage so it was only up to the rest of us to suit up while he calmed down the dogs. I wondered if birdcalls would be used, but was smart enough to not ask. I recognized these guys were serious about shooting doves. Decoys and 2's!

We climbed up the ridge and birds scattered but no one shot. Everyone was loaded down with decoys, shells, coffee thermoses and other assorted gear aside from their guns. There were many doves present, which made shooting not an urgent priority. The ridge turned out to be a dam holding a four acre waterhole to water cattle with the parameter being more cedars, cottonwoods and ridges. Decoys were set up in the most open trees including dead limbs. More were set in a line on top of the highest fence wires. We then spread out around the pond hiding ourselves comfortably within the trees and hemp plants that abounded. Denny held the dog as coffee or cold drinks were poured and only the damn mosquitos ruined a perfect set up. Everyone was in agreement to shoot only into the sky away from us all. No low shots allowed.

The doves came to the water hole in pairs and in small groups. They had not yet been attacked so demonstrated no fear or caution. We started shooting and shooting and shooting. Much later I would read Kansas statistics claim the average dove shooter brings down two birds for every ten shots. Based on those statistics I had to group myself in with the below average shooters. What I thought was going to be and easy piece of cake hunt turned into a nightmare. Shooting at and missing doves turned into laughs for all the gunners. The laughter saved our egos on that day as there were no heroes to be found amongst the six of us. All our explosions just sounded as if we were celebrating the Fourth of July a couple of months late. We had to get lucky and drop a few which gave the dogs some retrieving practice although not excessive practice. I can't account for where or when the foolish 2's were shot but they most likely fell into the next county. At evening minus approximately four hundred shells we considered going home with our 46 birds. I didn't compute the ratio because I figured someone lied about having "that" many unspent shells left.

The first day of the shooting was a day I shall remember fondly. All our shooting proved the dove is a difficult target at best. Myself an admitted poor shotgun shooter does not account for the other fellows. Some of them are excellent shooters and they did not obtain very good results either. The facts points out doves offer challenging shooting and relatively easy hunting. Other game birds would never decoy as easily and consistently in what must have sounded like a war zone. All of the facts made me contemplate the sport deeper. All right the birds fly in the most zigzag directions possible while seemingly dropping straight down in flight at will. Their flight pattern is as inconsistent and unpredictable as any bird ever hunted. There must be a reason? It occurred to me that here in Nebraska doves live in the wild hemp (marijuana) patches that abound. They literally live off of the seeds, which would logically account for their flight patterns. Nebraska doves are stoned all the time. Apparently the war zone explosions attracted them in the same manner the "drug generation" is attracted to what they call modern music. The sounds are most similar to music and the doves must have thought they were coming to a disco. It is no wonder they can fly crazy because they have eaten so much marijuana their flight is impaired. Based upon this most logical hypothesis it stands to reason that Kansas's doves would be easy shooting. In Kansas the doves eat legal milo and wheat while avoiding the few marijuana patches present there. The entire experience also unquestionably proves that in Kansas the success ratio statistics must have been conducted where the birds were not in possession of an illegal substance. Concluding these factual findings has eased my ego a great deal. Then eating the doves offered a gourmet experience equaled by none. They were delicious even if contaminated by THC. The birds were breasted out, hammered flat with a wooden block and breaded with flour. They were cooked with cracker crumbs and eggs so there can be no joke made about this delicious eating. The eating is reason enough to spend another one hundred shells on the next meal. With twenty-five shells in a box times eight dollars a box it comes to only $32 per meal!

Actually all the statistics, thoughts, ideas and bird eating came to me much later in life. I was still on the dove hunt that was coming to an end. We shot until dark and then rounded up the decoys and dogs. The heat of the day was letting up as I recall and all of us had sun burned faces that went along with dove hunting. Some of us had started the day with camo painted faces like a turkey hunter would use but now we all had blazing and glowing red ones. That ninety-degree heat all day in the sun did that to us. It only hurt when I touched my face. I did not swat any more mosquitos that landed on it as they now had, "a take my blood free zone." Finally all loaded up we made the journey back through the rough cattle trails towards home. The bumps and more bumps seemed worse than ever with me giving more of my blood to the mosquito's Red Cross for their use. I was tired and happy to be on our way home. I thanked Denny for the day and he said, "Yeah will have to do it again after you buy another eight boxes of ammo." It is funny how you needed one hundred rounds to get twenty or so tweety birds, as I call them. I thought to myself I would get better at it. I did get better at it as my average improved to 8.6 shots per bird.

Meeting Denny the writer living in the same village as myself made me very happy. It must have been destiny that I ended up living in Los Mindos. With my curiosity I did a detailed research to learn about the village that came about in the early 1800's. At that time there was a Spanish explorer, Senior José EL Bobalicon who was searching the area for a hidden gold mine. While searching, José did not find any gold or mine what so ever. The story goes on to say as a result of this failure he went mad and hung himself in a nearby cottonwood tree. The grim fact led the early settlers on deciding they would honor Senior Bobalicon in some way. The problem was they could not decide upon calling their settlement Lost Mine or Lost Mind? Consequently, Los Mindos ended up as the compromised name by the people. Once I learned the name's origin I definitely decided I would not dig in my yard or go near any cottonwood tree. I would be happy that I had met the writer, we were neighbors and leave it at that. Besides hunting tweety birds would forever be on my mindos.

THE HORSEMEN

During the month of September in1969 three good friends were discharged from their different units of the U.S. Army. They were all proud to have served in Vietnam and equally happy that they all would be reunited at their homes in Rehoboth, Delaware. Here they would adjust to civilian life as young men. First there was Joey that on his return friends nicknamed him G.I. Joe or simply G.I. for short. He was twenty-five years old but his war years had made him mature beyond those years. The suffering he had seen in Vietnam would leave emotional scars that lasted his lifetime. He and his brothers in arms had endured plenty suffering of their own during their war years. Watching his army buddies get shot with some killed gave Joey nightmares that lasted his life long years. He was an artist and had drawn many pictures while in Vietnam, but no one would ever see them and no one even talked about them. The drawings brought back to life the battles and for now he wished to leave Vietnam in the past. Joey was the happiest to be discharged and on home soil. To be reunited with his friends was his top present goal.

Bill Alexander was a red blooded fourth generation American. His great grandfather had fought with the Union soldiers during the Civil War and all the men in his family since had served our Country. He felt it mandatory that he should become a soldier too. He would have signed up for another tour of duty but a bullet in his arm prevented him from doing so. Despite that injury no one would challenge this six-foot twenty four year old to a fight. To do so would mean doom to any opponent with his reputation proving that fact. Bill never looked for a fight but never turned one down either if brought into one. In Vietnam he had become a Sergeant in rank giving him the name "Sarge" by his friends. Sarge and Joey shared an apartment in the low-rent waterfront district of Rehoboth, which was a good arrangement for both men. The last of the friends to be discharged was Louie. This six foot two hundred plus pound man was the jolly one of the three Vets. His joking around and seemingly inability to follow Army rules saw him peeling potatoes for two years while serving in Vietnam. He never was in battle although he saw plenty of the aftermaths from the war. Louie had lost three good friends during his duty and that he would never forget. He had great respect for the troops but never felt he was part of them. Louie had just peeled potatoes and all the other K-P duties assigned him. Once back in Rehoboth he would never talk about any serious actions that took place in Vietnam for in reality he never was part of any. His thoughts were he was happy his duty was over and that his two high school buddies had made it back home too. Upon his return Louie bought an eight-week-old Black Labrador puppy that he would love as his companion.

The three returning soldiers that had served in the war had three high school friends, which had not served. They were good friends all the same with no issues about the matter. These friends were Pete, Damon and Tommy. The three of them along with Louie and his puppy lived together in a house that Pete's father owned. They had the house rent free as the father owned many in Rehoboth and was a wealthy man. Pete helped maintain all the houses with the others at times doing their fair share that in a way was equal to any rent. Five of the six men had no full time jobs during this time so helping out was possible for them. The three Vets had ample money from their Army pay, as it wasn't possible to spend money while in a Vietnam foxhole.

Damon was the only one to have a regular full-time job. He worked on a fishing boat that braved the Atlantic Ocean and called Rehoboth Beach it's homeport. Most of the beach was for tourists to enjoy with only a small section remaining where commercial fishing boats had docks. When the ocean was too rough for fishing then Damon and the other mates would be on land repairing nets. Damon was a strong and intelligent young man that did try to join the Navy. He had flat feet and was rejected by the Navy. As the war went on his views on it changed and he became anti-war as many of his friends would do as well. Damon was happy to live in the house with his three friends even though he was the one home the least. Tommy was another friend to live in Pete's father's house. He was a happy go lucky young man that enjoyed humor and jokes as much as Louie did. Often the two would work together in order to pull off a prank on the other four. Tommy was a jack-of-all-trades working alone when his wallet told him to go to work. At other times it would be his play times that could last for weeks. When he did work sometimes he would haul away un-wanted items with his pick up truck and at other times he would be painting a house. On the doors of his pick up truck he painted, "Tommy's Enterprises, I'll Do Anything For A Buck, If Your Wife Needs Help I'll Dicker, Anything For A Buck." That was the sum total of his advertising efforts giving him spotty work which was okay with him. He was happy to work on Pete's father's homes that he knew resulted in his living rent-free. Tommy never considered joining the armed services although he had great respect for those who went to war. He thought the war would stop Communism and that was a good thing.

Pete was the rich one of the bunch that worked on his father's many houses when they called for repairs. There were eight houses in Rehoboth and Rehoboth Beach aside from the one that the four friends lived in. Pete's father had many other income sources as well making his family one of the town's wealthiest ones. Pete and his siblings enjoyed the wealth seemingly receiving anything they wished for while they were young children. The house he and his three friends lived in was near the Rehoboth Beach District. It was an older three-story affair with a nice fenced in backyard where Louie's puppy would live. Aside from helping his father he was never known to have any other employment. Pete was against the Vietnam War from its' onset but he was basically quiet about those views never bringing them up if his Army buddies were present. His wealthy father used his influence making sure Pete would never be drafted into the Army and this also was never talked about. Pete along with Louie, Damon and Tommy we're all grateful for the rent free house with all living in harmony. They would never say a bad word concerning Pete's wealthy father although plenty in town did.

The six young men often went to a local neighborhood bar called Charlie's with naturally Charlie being the owner. He was a big fellow in his seventy's that had a good laugh running his bar, which was a Rehoboth institution. Second-generation people that reached twenty-one started out their drinking days at Charlie's. He operated a place where swearing or fights we're not allowed as his was a family domain where his rules commanded his respect. In this pleasant atmosphere many called Charlie's their home away from home. On a weekly basis the six men would be at Charlie's and they became known as the six-pack by the locals. If together or not they all gave the seventy's year old man their respect and went by the rules. It was on a cold January night in 1970 that all of the six-pack was at Charlie's sitting at a rear table. They ordered up two pitchers of beer and three orders of the famous onion rings that could only be found there. The men were together to bond their relationships and visit about nothing specific. Their order came and Louie said, "You know what one potato chip said to another?" The friends all said they did not know. So Louie answered, "Are you free to lay." The six-pack had a good laugh as they ate, drank and talked about this and that. Eventually Tommy said, "You know guys none of us are really committed to anything and not much is going on for us six except for Damon right now. I know G.I. Joe and the Sarge will be going to college next fall on the G.I. Bill, but that's a long way off. So I got thinking." The other five men now made remarks such as, "Oh no, you thinking" or "You thinking, that is a first." They were kidding

Tommy as only friends can do. Tommy went on, "Well we should do something really different this year. Let's get some paper from Charlie and write down our ideas of something to do. We'll put the ideas in a hat and consider them one by one, but don't sign them and then we will talk about them. What do you say guys?" Louie loudly answered, "Geese laweeze, hey Charlie can we get some paper and six pencils from you?" Louie then went over to the bar and Charlie was happy to give him the supplies and while there Louie ordered up two more pitches of beer. He returned to the table, "Okay Tommy, here's your paper." Tommy used the side of the table to make six pieces of paper six by eight inches and handed them out. The six men each wrote down an idea as they drank their beer and this took about ten minutes for all the ideas to make it into the hat. Tommy then took the six idea papers and spread them out on the table with one of the papers getting wet from beer moisture off of the table. Without looking at anyone of them Louie said of the wet one, "That's the one for me, geese laweeze. If it can drink beer I'm for it." The others laughed and Tommy said, "OK Louie, let's look at each one of them and let's talk over all of them."

The first idea was to sail around the world. Everyone figured that this must have been Damon's idea as he was the ocean going one of the six-packs'. Nothing was said of whose idea it might have been however. The Sarge said, "That would be fun but it wouldn't work for G.I. and me as we are going to school next fall and that idea would take up too much time. Maybe when we finish school it might be okay." Tommy said, "You are right, that's a no go, what's next?" The second idea was to go to South America. Damon said, "That's a good idea but what do we do when we get there?" So the idea of going to South America was put aside to talk about later as the waitress Patty came to the table. "You guys need anything more?" Tommy answered, "Why yes, how about four nights with you sharing my bed? Maybe another order of the rings would be good too." Patty just said, "I'll get the rings." Tommy laughing then continued, "The next idea is start a company that the six of us can work at." The Sarge once again said, "With the two of us going to college that wouldn't work for us right now. Maybe we could do that in later years." Tommy put that slip with the all around the world one, which eliminated two ideas from the group's consideration. Tommy read another, "Ride horses to Mexico." Pete said, "We could do that given the time problems of the no go pile. Put that one with the go to South America one and we can talk about those later." Louie said, "Geese laweeze none of us know a darn thing about horses, geese laweeze." Damon butted in, "Hey that would be something totally different to all of us, put it with the possible pile." Then Patty arrived at their table with the hot order of onion rings. Tommy said to Patty, "Are you sure about the four nights, it's mighty cold out, could be a lot of fun?" Patty answered, "I'm sure, I'll just stay with my boyfriend, that will be two dollars and fifty cents." Joey paid the money as the others ate and drank their beer. Tommy said, "The next one is we all go look for gold in Alaska." Pete remarked, "That's a good idea and we all would have this summer to do it. Put that in the possible pile." Tommy did just that and said, "The last one is to go to Florida where it is warm." Four of the six all at once said, "Yes!" Tommy said, "Okay, this one goes into the possible pile too."

The four ideas of going to Florida, going to Alaska, going to and riding horses to Mexico and going to South America were laid out in a row on the table. None of the six were in any hurry to go out in the cold night that left lots of time to discuss the ideas. Tommy said, "Here are six more pieces of paper to write down one idea you like the least. The one getting the most votes we will eliminate which will leave three for our consideration." It ended up that going to South America was the one voted out. Probably because all of them knew that none of them spoke Spanish plus they felt it could be dangerous for gringos to be there. That left three ideas to talk over and Tommy told a joke with more beer ordered. The Sarge said, "Let's look at the idea of going to Alaska for gold, that is a good idea. We wouldn't get rich but it would be fun to be up there in all the beauty. Of the three left I like that one." Damon now talked, "Do you guys know anything about Alaska? I've talked about Alaska with two of my shipmates that have been there and they said they would never go back. We would face two problems, first the mosquitoes pick you up and carry you away and in the summer they are as ugly as the Sarge's girlfriends. The second problem is the big one. You have to own a claim to go for gold. You can't just start digging anywhere you want as a law up there is a claim owner can actually shoot you if you're on his claim. I've not been to Vietnam but I know I am not big on getting shot at. I think it's best we put this idea on the no go list and then someday we can go up there on our own individual basis. I wouldn't leave my job for Alaska." The Sergeant spoke, "Well someday I'm going up there and maybe then some of you will want to go with me?" The Alaska idea went into the no go pile with only two possible ideas left.

Tommy asked, "What about going to Florida?" In that it was January and they all knew there was plenty of winter to come this was a positive idea to the group. They discussed this idea for a long time. Damon finally said, "Only problem I know about Florida is rents and all else would be very expensive. We have both no rent and cheap rent here but that won't happen down there." Tommy took his turn, "Well ten million people live there so they must afford rent somehow. Sure we would have to get jobs but it sure would be nice to get out of winter." The Sarge looked at the other Vets, "You guys remember the heat and humidity back in Vietnam? Well when summer comes it will be like that and you three that weren't there let me tell you it was miserable. Florida is not for me, but will go if that is what the group decides." Louie said, "Geese laweeze Florida sounds good to me." Pete added his thoughts, "Well if we go to Florida we all would get jobs alright and I would stay down there and work longer than this winter." G.I. Joe said, "I am with Sarge, I've had enough heat and rain back in Vietnam to last me my lifetime. Count me out of Florida." Pete was the last to express the final Florida views, "I agree with Damon that rents in Florida will be sky high and here we have low and no rents, let's look at the final idea."

The going by horses to Mexico was the last to be considered and the one with the wet beer stain. Louie said, "Geese laweeze that's the one for me." He had no real idea what the slip would mean to his future but since it had the beer stain that was good enough for Louie. Then Tommy read the slip of going to Mexico by horses. Damon went first, "This sounds like a good idea to me. We would be camping out along the way meaning no rent. We could do this trip in the summer whereas Florida would have us being there a long time. We can buy horses in Maryland and sell them back out west somewhere. I agree this cold is a bummer but already three of us don't want to go to Florida because of the Vietnam heat and rain experience. I think it's on to Mexico unless we go back to the other ideas." Joey said, "Let's get more beer, it's only 9:30, we can call a cab if we overdo it. I'm going to brave a smoke outside, Charlie doesn't want any smoking in here anymore because of serving food. He even said he thinks some day there will be a law to stop smoking in all barrooms. I'll bet that will never happen. You want to come Louie?" "Geese laweeze, yeah I'll go. Can't have a smoke with a beer together anymore. Why don't they have bars with smoking and others with not I'll never know. Go fight in the jungle and get shot at but can't have a smoke cause it's bad for your health. A damn crazy country this is, let's go smoke Joey, you guys get the beer." Pete talked as the two left, "I had a pony as a kid and that was a lot of fun. We can't ride horses from Delaware to Mexico unless you guys figure on five years to do it. I like the horse idea but we'd better go to a shorter starting point than here." Tommy remarked, "Well Pete, I didn't know you rich kids had horses, I thought you all grew up with a Cadillac. Guess we will call you Tex. Going to Mexico is good by me as they have good pot and you can buy a lady of the night. Bet you can smoke anything in their barrooms too." With that said the Sarge went over to the bar, "Charlie we will have two more pitchers and it looks like we will need cabs later. We are making plans to do something different this summer and expect your till will go down a few thousand. Will you miss us?" The Sarge returned to the table with the beer, "Horses to Mexico, huh?" G.I. and Louie came back in from having their smoke. Louie said, "Geese laweeze it's cold out there." Joey then said, "The wind is strong from the Southwest meaning no one should hurry out in those elements." Then they took their places at the table and the talk continued. Sarge paid no attention to the returning two, "Might be fun to camp out in the old west and see the desert. That would be a switch from the jungle, don't you think so G.I?" Joey the roommate took his turn, "That could work as we'd be back here for fall classes. Only the horses would be the big costs and as Pete said we always could sell them back out west. Camping would cost a lot less than rooms in Florida. I've never been west of Ohio so it all would be fun for me. Between Florida and Mexico I vote horses." The Sarge said, "I think the six of us camping out would be fun and I agree that we would have to start at a reasonable starting distance with riding the horses. We could put together sensible plans this winter and head out in April. Okay, Louie what are you really thinking on this plan?" Louie took his turn, "Five of you for it, geese laweeze, why fight it? I'll go."

On that cold windy January night the idea of riding horses to Mexico was the one selected. The six-pack had no concept of what they were in for as they all had grown up by the Atlantic Ocean and thought going west would be like a John Wayne movie. To their credit they elected the Sarge as their leader and the one that would maintain order in the planning. The plan included what to take, how to get the horses and how far they actually would ride horses. Throughout the winter they would meet at Charlie's and talk about all the concerns of doing the trip. It was decided they would put a box cover camper on Tommy's truck to carry supplies. At any given time five would ride horses with the other one driving the truck. Each day they would switch the truck driver with one horseback rider so that all would get turns driving during the travels. This sounded like a fair and smart idea to all of them. Then they made a list of items they would need. The long list included; tents, blankets, cooking pans, plates, cups, silverware, binoculars, lighters, shovel, rope, packs, guns, axes, compass, soap, playing cards, trash bags, note books and any other personal important items such as whiskey and Lucky Strike cigarettes. Then there was the matter of horses and the saddles. Damon suggested that they go to a riding stable in Maryland to learn something about horses and the gear needed to ride them. All agreed with those ideas and decided that on a warm February day they would go to a stable where they could rent horses.

A nice late February day came when three of them rode up front in Tommy's truck and the other three rode in the back. They were going to Maryland and a riding stable they had learned about. Tommy had built a nice big box cover for his truck that even included a cook stove and a bed. On the way to the riding stable one would rest on the bed while the other two sat on cushions watching out the three windows of the box. They even turned on the small propane cook stove, which made their ride a warm and cozy one. In Maryland they finally arrived at the Buck-A-Rue riding stables. They met the owner, Slim Jim right away who actually looked like a runaway convict to the six-pack and they wondered if that was his real name. Slim Jim was fat unlike his name but very helpful and explained all that was necessary to the amateur green horns. They learned about tack with the Sarge taking notes and then soon they would all ride away on a trail. Slim Jim picked out the horses they would ride based upon each rider's request. Pete said, "Man this is easy, it reminds me of my pony days." Tommy responded, "Okay Tex, for you it is easy but I feel every jump this guy takes is going to give me hemorrhoids." Louie added, "Geese laweeze, are you sure you guys want to really do this?" The Sarge said, "All hold on it will get better we're not going that fast. Kick them in the sides, let's speed up some." With that they all did and they all went faster with Damon and G.I. remaining silent. After two hours of riding at the Buck-A-Rue all but Louie had felt foolishly they had mastered riding horses. The Sarge bought some books on horses and equipment in the Buck-A-Rue Book Store that also sold tack of many descriptions. The Sarge said to the others, "Let's not buy any equipment yet but let's talk to Slim Jim about maybe buying some horses." They all agreed those were good ideas and felt for now it was too early to actually buy or own any horses. They thought to talk about it and get an idea about the prices would be a good plan for now. Sergeant Bill approached Slim Jim and the two talked about buying the horses and the prices of them. Slim Jim said he could outfit the group with six horses in April as they wished. The prices varied from three to six hundred dollars and he would give them all needed tack except for the saddles. This meant; bits, halters, reins and blankets would be part of the deal. The Sarge told Slim Jim that seemed very fair and they would return in the first week of April to purchase six horses. He also said they would like to return in March to the Buck-A-Rue to ride for more experience and look at the horses they could buy. Slim Jim told the Sarge that was a smart plan and he looked forward to seeing them in March. That concluded the six-pack's successful day at the Buck-A-Rue and then they headed back to Delaware.

It was late in the evening when they arrived back home making Charlie's their first stop. At Charlie's Louie said to him, "Hey Charlie you would never guess where we were today? I'll tell you, we all were cowboys today and we're as thirsty as the dust on your floor. How about two pitchers of beer?" Charlie poured the pitchers and remarked "Were you out on the Atlantic smoking that funny stuff again? You guys don't look like any cowboys I've ever seen." Louie answered, "Really Charlie we went to the Buck-A-Screw or Buck-A-Do or maybe it was the Buck-A-Sue stable out in Maryland and this summer we are going to ride horses to Mexico, believe me." Charlie handed out the pitchers and took the money due him but made no further remarks. He almost believed the six-pack was going to try a feat unheard of in Delaware. From this point forward he would call them the 'six-pack gang.' As the men drank their beer most complained of being stiff and sore from they're riding. The Sergeant advised them that the discomforts were temporary and when on the big ride all would be fine. Charlie could see that they were walking like ducks waddle and in time the Sarge went up to the bar for refills. Charlie asked the Sarge, "Were you guys really riding horses today and do you plan on going to Mexico on horses?" The Sergeant answered, "Yes we were and yes we are. This will be an adventure so different for all of us we just have to do it." He returned to the table to announce a plan, "Hey guys I've gotten state maps looking into our trip. The road map from Nebraska says, 'Where the West Begins' so that should be our starting point. There is a place about half way through the State called Grand Island and I figure we can start there. We should get U-Haul trailers here or in Maryland and haul the horses out there to that point and from there off to Mexico. That's the way I see it. We can load Tommy's truck with all our supplies and the only thing lacking now are the saddles. Slim Jim said the horses will cost between three to six hundred dollars so the fair way is to total up the final cost and divide it six ways. That way we all pay the same price and when we sell the horses we will do the same. I'm sure we'll think of other things for the adventure as it is plenty early now to do so." Louie remarked, "Geese laweeze you have thought of everything." With that the six-pack gang drank their two pitchers of beer and headed for home.

During the month of March the group made another trip out to the Buck-A-Rue where they rode horses for two hours. Slim Jim showed them a lot of different horses they could buy and they took some of them on rides. The Sarge rode a spirited thoroughbred with the name of Table Legs. The Sarge asked the price of this black horse and Slim Jim answered, "I would sell him to you for three hundred dollars, but I must warn you another fellow is also interested in buying him. You rode him okay today but sometimes he acts up and will take you into the trees. Because he sometimes will do that he doesn't fit here, as I can't have customers on the ground. I let you ride him today because you said you wanted a fast horse and that he is. You did a good job of riding him today I'll say that." The Sarge talked it over with the gang for he really wanted Table Legs. The group decided to buy the horse but none other on this trip. Slim Jim agreed to board the horse for another month at an additional fifty dollars. Table Legs would belong to the group although all knew he really would be the Sarge's horse. Slim Jim also showed them many saddles and some would cost more than Table Legs. They purchased no saddles on that trip thinking they could find some which would cost less. As usual they made the trip back home with their first stop being Charlie's. At Charlie's the Sarge proudly told the bar owner he had bought a horse with only five more to go. Charlie said, "You goofy guys are really going to do it aren't you? Brought up at the ocean and you guys are going to go be cowboys. Let's see Delaware cowboys, a gang of sorts, what can we call you guys now? Maybe the Della-boys gang that won the West." With that Charlie laughed and gave him two pitchers of beer free of charge. After the long day they ordered hamburgers and onion rings while talking about how much fun Table Legs would be.

During the remainder of March they obtained supplies and began loading up Tommy's truck. They bought canned goods and powdered food only requiring water along with countless cans of Spam. They bought six guns and two rifles with ammunition for the trip. Then they bought hats of various styles according to their individual choices, so they had everything they needed but the saddles and five more horses. They checked with the local U-Haul outlet to learn they did not rent any horse trailers. They decided to solve that problem they would rent one trailer for Tommy's truck to pull and one cargo truck. They would put three horses in each one and drive them out to Grand Island, Nebraska along with taking hay for the horses on top of the trucks. Now it seemed to them everything was in order with all anticipating their adventure. Damon talked to his boss about his plans and how he would like to return to his job in the fall. The boss laughed at it all and said he could come back to work if a rattlesnake didn't kill him out west. In late March the six-pack gang all went to Charlie's once more to celebrate their trip. The Sarge went up to the bar while the others went to a table and the Sarge told Charlie, "Well this is it, won't see us all this summer as we will be in the west. Better give us two pitchers, three orders of onion rings and six of your biggest hamburgers to start. I think for sure we will be here till your closing time so we will need two cabs when that time comes. None of us will be in any shape to drive the way we are drinking. Happy night to you Charlie." The Sarge brought the beer to the table and in a short time Patty gave them the food. G.I. asked Louie what he was going to do with his dog Sparky? Louie said, "Geese laweeze of course he's going with us. I got a bag he can ride in with me when he's tired of walking. He won't be any problem and in fact may warn us about lions and wolves coming into our camp. What's a cowboy without his dog?" The six-pack gang kept drinking, eating and talking about the trip to come. Damon told the others, "My boss said it's okay to come back next fall and I sure feel good about that. My last day is April 1st, Fools Day so I hope I'm not one. What day are we going out to Slim Jim's to get the horses and then what?" Sarge the leader said, "Let's go out to Slim Jim's on the 5th and pick out the other horses. Then ride them with Table Legs for a day or so at the Buck-A-Rue to make sure we have sound horses and ones we like. After that load them up and head out, no sense in coming back here. That means when we leave here everybody needs to have everything they want. It will be westward Ho!" Now that the date had been set the six-pack continued drinking until Charlie told them the cabs were there and it was time to leave the saloonkeeper. They all staggered out of the bar like a bunch of drunken elephants walking through a bed of hot glue. That would be the last night at Charlie's for a long time to come.

April 5th of 1970 came and the six-pack gang along with the five-month-old puppy made up their caravan. They had a U-Haul trailer being pulled by Tommy's truck and a U-Haul self- driving moving van. They left early in the day leaving Rehoboth and the ocean heading to the Buck-A-Rue ranch. They had five thousand dollars amongst them with plenty of six guns to protect that money. The plan was to travel ten hours a day until they reached Nebraska where they would unload and return the U-Hauls. When possible they would take the newer Eisenhower Interstate Road and camp out nights along small rural roads. They would go from Maryland into

West Virginia and then through Ohio to Indiana. Next was Illinois, Missouri, Kansas and finally into Nebraska where the west begins. According to the Sarge's calculations they would arrive in Grand Island on a Monday to unload the horses and begin the real journey to Mexico. But on this day the matter of buying horses and saddles was on everyone's mind. They traveled along at 55 mph, which they determined would be a safe speed with their loads as well as maximizing their gas mileage. Around mid- day they arrived at the Buck-A-Rue to greet Slim Jim and look at horses. He showed them ten horses they could ride to pick from and of course ride them free of charge. Also they were welcome to camp on the grounds as long as they wished. Slim Jim thought it was odd that they had no real horse trailers but said nothing as his interest was in selling them horses. He figured they all would find a way to load the horses when the time came.

The six-pack gang went to look at the horses in detail. Slim Jim was honest in telling them the age and characteristics of each horse. It was decided each man would choose a horse to ride a few hours today and tomorrow to make their decision on which horse they wanted. In that the Sarge had already picked out Table Legs it was a matter of choosing five more horses out of the ten. They saw this as their top priority and decided to set up their camp later after riding various horses. Since they had rented the U-Hauls back in Delaware and not in Maryland they would have more time in selecting horses for each member of the six-pack gang. Louie said to Slim Jim, "Geese laweeze, I need a slow horse nothing like Table Legs." Slim Jim pointed out several older horses that would fit the bill and told Louie, "Here's Snickerdoodle, a nice older mare quarter horse that would be perfect." Louie replied, "Geese laweeze I want a whole horse, I don't want one fourth of one. What good is a quarter of a horse to anybody?" Slim Jim then explained that a quarter horse was a breed and the one real cowboys use. Louie calmed down once assured that Snickerdoodle was whole and thought to himself that he was a real cowboy at that. Damon picked next and he went for a four-year-old gelded thoroughbred named Thinkaboutit. Slim Jim told Damon that this horse was the fastest of the ten and had even raced as a three-year-old. Damon said he was used to rocking on the ocean and they put a saddle on him. At that point only three horses were remaining to be picked out. Tommy went to his truck and return with a deck of cards. He said, "Okay, there's three of us left so let's draw cards. High card picks first and low card goes last." They agreed that was fair and G.I. went first as he had an Ace. Tommy won second and Pete would pick last. G.I. Joe decided he would like to try the horse named Annabel, as that was his grandmother's name. The horse was a gentle six-year-old mare of mixed breeds and Slim Jim said that would have been his choice for she was mindful at all times. Tommy asked Slim Jim to name again all the horses remaining. He picked out Snaggelpuss because of the name while paying no attention to any of the facts the horseman was attempting to tell him. Pete had the last pick and he could not decide between two horses. One was Lame Duck and the other was Last Chance. He finally decided to try out Lame Duck. Slim Jim told Pete that the horse was a very fast thoroughbred and he had better be prepared for a fast ride. With the choices made the six-pack gang went out for a ride on a long path and then to a meadow.

The earth was waking up from the winter now growing green grass with beautiful wildflowers of every shape and color. It was a field of splendor where the horses could run free and fast. Thinkaboutit and Table legs took off like jet rockets while the others went into a peaceful pace except for Lame Duck. That horse was apparently named correctly. He would be for kids and no wonder he was for sale. How wrong Slim Jim was as this horse could hardly walk and never would make it to Mexico. Pete was very disappointed and knew tomorrow he would try Last Chance. The two fast horses gave their riders fast ones with both men holding on for dear life. The three other horses went along very well and Louie liked Snagglepuss a great deal while wondering how Sparky would do on a horse? He decided he would try that out on the next day. Only Lame Duck walked along slowly way behind the other five. Pete became so disgusted he headed back to the barn leaving the others to ride. Once there he said to Slim Jim, "I thought you said this horse could run? Well, that's not true, I had a Shetland pony that could out run her. What's the deal? A turtle could out run this old nag." Slim Jim looked Lame Duck over to find she had thrown a shoe. He explained the situation and said he'd have it fixed by morning. Pete finally understood and helped take the tack off of Lame Duck and learned how to use a halter. Pete's was the last one of the six-packs' to have a horse so he decided to try Last Chance and thought it probably was destiny. Then he took the opportunity to learn all he could about horses from Slim Jim. He learned horses at times laid down to rest but are the only animal that can sleep standing up by locking their knees. Pete learned a lot more about horses that could be valuable later. Finally the other five returned to the barn all happy with their horses. As night came Tommy and Louie slept in Tommy's truck's camper while the other four put down straw in the U-Haul truck's back for their bed. They found no need to set up their tent and Louie untangled Sparky's rope and took him to bed with him.

The next day Slim Jim had all the men put on the saddles and bridals by themselves. Pete would take Last Chance on this day and found the eight-year old quarter horse a nice horse for him. When they were getting ready to ride Louie's horse bucked up and kicked and kicked. Louie said, "Geese laweeze what happened to this horse? Did she find the other three fourths of herself? Or did she eat that funny green stuff like Tommy smokes?" Slim Jim explained that Louie should always mount a horse on the left side. Louie made no sense of it and his puppy didn't care for it either. Finally Louie and his puppy in a bag with his head sticking out were on the horse. The other riders awaited Louie and once all were on the horses they took the path leading to where the pretty meadow was. Once there Table Legs and Thinkaboutit took off again racing each other all over the field. It became apparent Thinkaboutit was the fastest of the two. The Sarge asked Pete how he was doing with Last Chance and Pete said, "Fine this is the horse for me." The Sarge said, "Good Tex, now let's all go back and have lunch and so they did. Five of them after lunch went back to riding whereas the Sarge stayed back to pay for the horses. Since Table Legs had already been paid for they had to pay for the five horses and six saddles. The bill came to $3,330 that Slim Jim explained in detail. The Sarge was surprised to see the big bill and checked the figures to find them correct. That meant their travel account was down to $1,670 and a concern for the Sarge. He hoped some of the gang had extra money as he had. Once they got to Mexico they would sell the horses and he hoped that money would get them back to Delaware somehow. He thought the biggest expense would be the gas to Nebraska where the west began according to the roadmap he had. With the business concluded he rode out to the meadow to join the others. Around 5 o'clock they called it a day, returned to the barn and asked Slim Jim where a good restaurant was in town? They took the rental truck into town with three up front and three in the back. On arrival the three from the back said something had to be done in providing air into the back and before returning they wired cardboard to jam the doors slightly open. They had their meal, purchased some six packs and headed to sleep as they had done the night before. The next morning Tommy made coffee on the camp propane stove and they had some donuts to call it their breakfast. Then they loaded three horses into the U-Haul truck and three into the U-Haul trailer. They went into the trailer easily but the truck was another matter because it was so high off of the ground. To solve the problem they backed the truck up to a small hill and led the horses in. They wired boards to the doors, which held them slightly open for plenty of air to enter both rigs. They said goodbye to Slim Jim and went off to West Virginia where a hot meal would be their next stop.

Tommy drove his truck with Louie and the Sarge with him to direct the caravan. Pete drove the U-Haul van with Damon and G.I. being his passengers. Tommy led at a moderate speed and soon it began to rain. They finally were on Highway 45 leading to Martinsburg, West Virginia where they would stop. The Sarge said they had to get their food at a fast food place and eat it while continuing to travel and not stop to eat. He knew daylight was soon to end and twenty miles out of the town he stopped the caravan to set up camp. The April rain had turned into two inches of snow making it difficult to set up their camp. Louie and G.I. Joe were given the jobs of feeding and watering the horses along with cleaning out their spaces. The others would set up the camp and build a fire. Despite the snow and cold they sat around the fire drinking beer while talking about their slow travel day in the mountains. Tommy said he felt sorry for people that didn't drink because when they got up in the morning that was the best they were going to feel through the whole day. The rest of the gang had a good laugh and soon all went to bed on a cold night. Tommy, Louie and Sparky slept in the camper as the other four slept in their bedrolls in the tent. Morning came with a campfire and coffee to warm everyone up. They decided that in this part of the trip Louie and G.I. would tend to the horses, the Sarge and Pete would take care of the camp needs and Tommy and Damon would be the cooks. When all doing their jobs Louie yelled out, "Hey guys there's a bunch of brown golf balls where the horses are. Who brought them?" The Sarge went and looked, "You idiot, those are the horse droppings and your job is to clean them out." Louie and G.I. Joe reluctantly cleaned them out using a shovel and their hands. Louie said, "This is like an Easter egg hunt finding them hiding in the straw, kina fun." G.I. told Louie he really didn't need to go west but should go check himself into a nut house. Tommy and Damon made a great breakfast on the campfire while the other two broke down the camp. The puppy ran around in the snow stealing the men's bacon whenever he could.

After all was packed up they made their way up and down the mountains until lunchtime. They had cold Spam sandwiches with beer as they kept driving for the Sarge said they had to keep going. He told them because of the slow pace in the mountains there was no time for stopping and he alone was the navigator. Tommy did not like the Sarge's tone or plan. Tommy then said, "You know Sarge, you are like the skeleton that didn't go to the party because he had nobody." Everyone was quiet for some time after that. Driving hours and miles on top of miles zigzagging through the mountains they arrived at Highway 64, which led to Huntington. Once there the Sarge decided on Ohio over Kentucky as the route they would take. They traveled twenty miles into Ohio and finally stopped to camp, which everyone was more than ready for. The gang did their chores as Tommy and Damon made juicy hamburgers with fried potatoes that were so good everyone ordered up seconds with of course beer being their drink of choice. The hot meal seemed to be a treat after so much Spam and hurry up meals. After the meal they sat around the campfire and marveled at the thousands of stars above. They never viewed so many while in the city lights back in Delaware. Around the fire they told stories and jokes while drinking their beer and Louie offered up a bottle of whiskey. Tommy passed around a joint to those who cared to smoke some. Tommy asked, "Hey Sarge, what are you going to study in college to become?" The Sarge said that someday he would be an attorney. With that Tommy said, "Well listen to this. One of my buddies was cleaning out an old lady's basement for her and found a bottle with something in it. He opened it and out popped a Genie. The Genie said to him that she would grant him three wishes but whatever they were every lawyer in America would also receive two of them. So my buddy said he'd like to have a BMW car and presto he had one and every lawyer in America automatically got two of them. He next asked for a million dollars and presto he had the million. Then every lawyer in America received two million. The Genie said he had now but one wish. My buddy thought about it a long time and said, 'You know Genie, you have been very good to me and with one million dollars I can buy anything that I want. With all your kindness I should help and give back. I wish to donate a kidney to someone in need in America.' What do you think about that Sarge?" Louie said, "That's a good one Tommy, but I wish I could laugh more but the pain in my knees are killing me. I walked so much in the Army all three of my knees are a wreck. After this trip I'm going to have them replaced." G.I. said, "Three? You don't have three knees." Louie said," Oh yes I do. I got my left knee, my right knee and my weenee." They all had a good laugh, passed the bottle around and then they all went to bed.

After another good breakfast they packed up and continued on the Ohio road. Sarge told them they had to hook up on Route 35, which would go to the new Interstate 70. Then the Interstate would take them straight to Kansas in a day or two. That sounded good but they needed ice as none of the other five wanted to drink any more warm beer. The good news was Ohio turned into flat land with many small farm towns along the route. They stopped at one for ice, beer, gas and groceries. The Sarge told them to have more cold Spam sandwiches and keep driving on. Once on I-70 they only went a few miles to exit onto a small county road. They made camp along the road and this time had two hours of daylight to tend to their chores and relax. The cooks made a splendid meal of pork chops, potatoes and hot green beans. After the meal they all did their assigned duties with Louie cleaning up the brown golf balls as he always did. They built another big campfire and talked about their successful trip so far. All were happy to have the mountains and snow behind them and were looking foreword to the real trip of riding the horses to Mexico. Sarge told them, "Once we are at Grand Island we will turn in the U-Haul's and then ride on the original Oregon Trail with the horses. Highway 30 runs parallel so the truck will always be close by but for now many hundreds of miles on I-70 are yet to be traveled." On the fifth day since leaving Rehoboth they had a good breakfast and wasted no time getting back on I- 70 heading west. After three hours they passed through the big city of Columbus and kept on going into flat black land the farmers were preparing for the crops to come. Finally they stopped in a small town for gas, ice and of course more beer. It was another day of Spam for lunch and even the dog was getting real tired of it. The Sarge kept saying, "Push on." To this point the puppy was no problem as he was in the camper and took long naps with his master Louie. He did pee on the floor once or twice and Louie cleaned it up saying it was no big deal since he had to clean up golf balls every day. The caravan kept traveling west on I-70 with plenty of daylight remaining. They exited on a lonely county road, which had become their practice. With luck along the road they found a grove of trees among the flat barren land. They started setting up the tent and tending to the horses when the County Sheriff showed up. He asked, "What are you boys up to?" The Sarge was the spokesman and told him their trip details and that three of them were Vets. He asked the Sheriff if they could stay for the night? The Sheriff said okay but if they wanted to stay longer they had better go to the State Park that was ten miles away. With that he left and the six-pack finished their chores, built a fire and made their supper. Around the fire that night Louie brought up the fact it was lucky the Sheriff didn't search the camper to find their pot. The Sarge thought that since three of them were Vets he gave them the slack. The next morning they cleaned up the area as if no one had ever been there and G.I. Joe even buried the golf balls. They had coffee and rolls as a simple breakfast and went back on I-70 once more. Indiana was a narrow state so in five hours they reached Illinois. A few miles into that state they stopped at a small farm town for gas and supplies. The Sarge said today they would go to the local restaurant for a hot lunch since they had no real breakfast. A bunch of hoorays could be heard on this news with even Sparky barking in the excitement.

They had a hot home cooked meal just like grandma would have made in the town restaurant. Then they went back on I-70 and Tommy talked the Sarge into driving. He went into the back camper with Louie and the puppy and after an hour down the road a huge bang could be heard. The Sarge thought he had blown out a tire so pulled off the road. The following U-Haul pulled off behind the Sarge while he was walking around inspecting but finding no problems. He asked Tommy and Louie if they had heard the bang and they said they had indeed. Tommy would drive again and give the Sarge a rest. Of course Tommy nor Louie never said a word about the big firecracker they had thrown out of the back. In a few hours they went through St. Louis, Missouri on I-70 and drove twenty miles into the state and stopped to camp once more. There were plenty of hills so they let the three horses out of the U-Haul truck by backing up to one. These horses had been in the truck the past three days so there were plenty of golf balls to pick up. Plus the horses from Tommy's trailer were let out with more golf balls exposed. All the horses were fed and watered while Sparky ran around them wanting to play. Setting up the camp, taking care of the animals and making supper left no time for riding the horses so the puppy would have to be content retrieving a ball. Not a golf ball either. It seemed the Sarge kept the caravan only traveling with no time for play every day so far. It was the night's campfires with the whiskey bottle being passed around that allowed for any real relaxation. It would be the same event on this night after another day of long travels. Then to bed with a solid sleep, that stopped their bodies from the motion of traveling.

Waking up the next morning afforded a very cool one making all of the six-pack gang having coffee around a nice campfire. No one was in a hurry to leave it except the Sarge who said that familiar, "Let's push on." With no breakfast they did and once more were on I-70 going west. After four hours they were in a small town again for gas, ice and needed supplies. On this stop the Sarge decided a restaurant lunch would be allowed since again they had no real breakfast. The men loved the hot food and the fact they had a break from moving down the road eating Spam as they had for too many days. The Sarge not saying anything but realizing their funds we're going fast wondered what the future would bring. Back on the Interstate their goal now was Kansas City and then the state of Kansas. Tommy and Louie were again in the back camper with the dog. Louie said, "Geese laweeze I'm getting tired of this nonstop road traveling. I thought we'd ride the horses some on this trip but

Sarge keeps us going and going. It's almost like being back in the Army the way he keeps pushing." Tommy lit a joint and replied, "Louie calm down. This road trip has turned out to take much longer than anyone expected it would so he's pushing in order we can get on the horses. It will be maybe two more days and this part will be over, here take a toak." The two men mellowed and then took a nice nap with the puppy. When they woke up Louie said, "Geese laweeze I dreamt I was back in Vietnam pealing potatoes. I was picking up brown golf balls too. I wonder what pealing the golf balls would be like?" Tommy said, "You know Louie you are completely nuts and you should try that tonight."

The caravan drove through Kansas City to keep on going one-half way to Salina. On a state highway they found a Kansas wayside and set up their camp. They had the area to themselves and Tommy and Damon had plenty time to make a nice meal of hot ham with boiled potatoes and corn on the side. At the campfire that night the Sarge announced, "Tomorrow we go to Salina and then off the Interstate to Highway 81 North to York, Nebraska. Then only an hour or so to Grand Island where the west begins." The gang clapped to hear this news. The long ride from Delaware was almost over and soon they would be on their horses riding down the Oregon Trail. It was on a Sunday when the six-pack gang arrived in Grand Island to set up their camp south of town in a nice park where a small lake, trees and the Platte River was located. The horses where unloaded for the last time and a nice camp was set up. With the lake water and a broom the U-Haul trailer and truck were cleaned out to leave no horse evidence and the saddles and one remaining bale of hay was taken down from the camper's roof. Tomorrow the U-Hauls would be returned to have some needed cash deposit money back and then to find some hay was on the agenda. When night came on this day everyone was amazed that how in April it was daylight until 8 o'clock at night. The evening did get cool as the sun went down so a campfire with beer and whiskey gave them a celebration meeting. They talked about their future rides and how they wanted a slow one to Mexico and not a non-stop one. They were thankful for the safe trip with no breakdowns except for the one loud bang. They basically congratulated themselves for making it to where the west begins. Louie didn't understand why he didn't see any mountains. How could it be just flat black soil where farmers were out in their fields? There were no cowboys to be seen and only the trees along the Platte broke up the flat horizon. This was not the west that all the movies portrayed by a long shot. Henry Fonda was born in this town so how did he ever learn to be a cowboy since none were here? Louie and many others pondered all of this as they went to bed.

Morning came and after a hot breakfast Tommy, Damon and the Sarge went to return the U-Hauls. That went well and next they went to a local coffee shop. In the shop they spotted two men with cowboy hats and asked them if they knew where they might buy some horse hay? The men directed them to Fonner Park where there was horse racing going on and they thought for sure they could either buy some there or find out where to get some. The three drove to the park where the gate security man allowed them to walk in where the horses and horsemen were. They talked to a horse trainer by the name of Mr. Anderson and he was helpful in selling them eight bales of hay, which was the maximum they could put on top of the camper. They next talked about horses and Damon told him about Thinkaboutit and how he had raced on an eastern track. Mr. Anderson showed an interest in the horse and suggested that he could possibly run in a race on Friday but he would have to work out and do some gate training during the week. He also advised them if all went well the horse could be in a five thousand dollar purse race and make some money if he finished in the top four spots. That sparked Sarge's interest, as he knew they were running low on funds. Mr. Anderson said he would need the horse's papers on past race results, which the Sarge replied by saying that information could be sent via Western Union from Slim Jim with no problems. They agreed they would bring Thinkaboutit to Mr. Anderson later in the day and then he could work with the horse during the week. At Fonner Park there were races on Thursday's as well the men learned while they loaded the hay. They went back to camp and as promised Damon rode Thinkaboutit back to the track as two others drove Tommy's truck there. Mr. Anderson liked the looks of the horse and already had received all the needed paperwork from Slim Jim. Then a $300 entry fee was needed which the Sarge paid. Now all was in order if only the horse could make the grade? The six-pack gang we're all excited about Thinkaboutit's prospects of being in a race and possibly earning some needed money. They were also happy that they were taking a break from traveling after the non-stop road trip and especially since they had such a nice camp along the Platte.

During the week they rode their horses along the river during the days and enjoyed their campfires during the nights. When Thursday came five of the six went to Fonner Park to watch the races while G.I. Joe remained back at camp to watch over it. At the races they pooled $42 for betting and twenty dollars for beer. Hot dog costs would have to come from each man's private money as some of them had only one and others like Tommy had five during the day. They enjoyed watching and betting on the nine races during the crisp April day and in the end they were eighteen dollars and twenty cents ahead for the day. When the races were over they went to talk with Mr. Anderson to see how Thinkaboutit was doing and if he indeed would race on the next day. Mr. Anderson gave them the good news, "Well men your horse has worked out this week in very fast times and is doing fine in getting out of the gate. J. R. Heywood is the jockey that will ride him in the fifth race tomorrow and he is a top jock. Other trainers have asked me where your horse has come from as no one has seen him before. I just told them I fished him out of the ocean with six owners that are a bunch of rough cowboys. Anyways all is in order and you should put some dollars on him because he will finish in the money, I'm sure." This news really excited the five men as they returned to camp after buying a bottle of whiskey and some treats for Sparky. Back in camp they shared the news with G.I. and cooked steaks and potatoes for their meal. The beef was a special treat and was delicious which convinced them they really were in the west as back east there were no steaks as juicy. After the meal they continued the campfire tradition with a big party late into the night. It was decided Damon and G.I. would go to Friday's races and the other four would draw cards to determine which one of them would stay behind as the camp tender. Pete drew the low card so he would have to stay with the camp and take care of the horses while the others would go watch Thinkaboutit run in the fifth race. That night few of them slept well as they did mind racing on how their horse was going to do and how much money they should bet on him.

The following morning's big day came with Tommy and Damon serving up a breakfast with lots of coffee for the hung over gang. Apparently they had over done it with the whiskey. During the meal the Sarge declared, "Guys our funds are lower than I like but I also have great faith in a winning horse today. I think we should bet one hundred to win, one hundred dollars to place and two hundred dollars to show on you know who? If Mr. Anderson is right we will have some tickets to cash. As far as other races you are on your own." The morning dragged on with a lunch not made, as the gang knew hot dogs awaited them at the track. Pete had a Spam sandwich with beer and gave Tommy five dollars to bet on the number seven in the seventh race and at noon the men dressed in their best new Western wear. They had on snap button western shirts, Levi pants and cowboy boots. The Sarge wore a white cowboy hat and Pete a black one even though he'd be at the camp all day. The other four had on ten-gallon hats they had bought back in Delaware. They were all white as they thought for sure they were good guys and all good guys wore white. The hats were so tall a bird could have made a nest atop of any one of them. These hats might have been worn in Texas but not in these parts making them look like clowns. They piled into Tommy's truck and went to the track around 1 o'clock. Once at the track they went directly to Mr. Anderson's private box to join him. The trainer told them, "Your horse is going to do well today and if he does win after the race you all need to go down to the winner's circle to have your picture taken with your horse. For your information, I think the number four horse in the third race today is going to run good so you might want to put a few dollars on him. He is a horse that I own that's done real good at this track, he's a Kentucky bred." The men thanked him for the tip and individually placed bets on the first and second races with Tommy and G. I. coming out ahead but the other three just bought hay for their losing horses.

With the third race next they put their money together and followed Mr. Anderson's advice. They bet twenty dollars to win and twenty dollars to show as they figured they had to hold back some money for hot dogs and beer plus their big money was going to go on Thinkaboutit in the fifth race. The third race went off and the number four got out of the gate first to lead the pack all around the track by over two lengths. The men were jumping up and down yelling, "Come on number four" and the horse kept leading down the first stretch as they kept yelling, "Go number four." The horse was a cinch to win the race and all could see it. Then three feet before the finish line the horse stumbled and threw the jockey forward off of him before the finish line. The horse still finished first way ahead of the others. The men were giving each other high fives and were as happy as larks. Then Mr. Anderson said, "No good boys, the jockey has to be on the horse to win. That's racing." The gang could not believe it and thought this was a goofy sport. The fourth race they did not bet and elected for more beer with hot dogs. The Sarge went and made the bets on their horse, which would be running next as the gangs excitement built. Thinkaboutit came onto the track with his head held high and was groomed to perfection never looking better on this his big day. J. R. Heywood the jockey had on white pants with a blazing orange top that could be seen for miles. Damon was proud and thought they would be able to watch their horse through the entire race with the jockey's bright colors. The group of horses all entered the starting gate and they were off. Thinkaboutit started in fourth position as the five men in the box stood up to watch and never sat down during the entire race. The horses thundered down the Grand Stands for the first time going into the first turn. Their horse ran wide into it and another horse passed theirs, but coming out of the turn they entered the backstretch where positions changed once more. The men were now jumping up and down yelling, "Go number five, go!" The horse that had passed Thinkaboutit now was first with Thinkaboutit running with him in second place. The two horses ran several lengths ahead of the pack making it now a two horse race. The guys now were uncontrollably yelling for their horse while jumping in the air seemingly as high as a bird could fly. With their ten-gallon hats they stood out like sore thumbs in the crowd. The two horses came to the finish line neck to neck and hit the wire together. The men were yelling loudly as the entire crowd was and now it was up to the photo finish picture to decide the outcome. The gang was convinced they were the winners giving each other high fives and hugging each other. It seemed forever but the results were posted as 5- 3 -8. They had won and now the men in the box really went into a celebration mode. Mr. Anderson told them to go down to the winner's circle with the horse already there. Once there and the picture taken with the ten-gallon hats along with huge smiles had many laughing in the crowd. Thinkaboutit paid $8.20, $5 and $3.80 as apparently the low payouts were due to the jockey's wives having inside knowledge that the horse was a good one. The Sarge calculated their returns as $460, $250, and $380 with a total of $1,090 from their $400 bets. Then they would receive over two thousand dollars coming from the purse money. The Sarge was elated with this boost in the gang's pool of money. He thought how could things get any better?

Then the track announcer over the PA system said, "Number five, Thinkaboutit has been claimed by trainer Bill Mallery." What? Mr. Anderson then explained that the race was a claiming one and the horse was no longer theirs. They would get to keep the winning purse money and they would also be paid the claiming price of $3,500. The men went from joy to sorrow in a split second. Damon was about to punch Mr. Anderson in the face but the gang held him back. The trainer took Tommy aside to tell him something and then he left to not be seen for the day's remainder. The Sarge went and cashed the tickets and they left Fonner Park to never return as a group ever again. They left just as like leaving a funeral for in a way it was one. Few words were spoken and Tommy drove straight back to the river camp breaking all speed laws. No evening meal was made as the six-pack wanted none but rather snacked on comfort food if there were any in the present situation. What did ease the pain was the night campfire with lots of beer, plenty of whiskey and some pot as well. They talked over the highs and lows of the day and considered trying to buy the horse back, but the Sarge talked a long time about his thoughts. He said, "Okay guys we only paid $300 to get him and he has returned over $6,000 to us which we never would get close to when selling him in Mexico. All the horses belong to all of us now. One guy will be driving the truck and five will ride the horses meaning nobody has to lead an extra horse. That is a good thing and we will switch horses every day so every one of us will get to ride every horse. This is the fair way, what did Mr. Anderson tell you Tommy?" Tommy replied, "I am real sorry Damon on how things ended up and Pete here's your five bucks as we left long before the seventh. Well he told me we could pick up our check and photo tomorrow after 3 o'clock. He was sorry for what happened and did not expect it. Send me the whiskey bottle." They drank and smoked late into the early morning before retiring after a stressful day.

The following day after breakfast and lunch the Sarge and Tommy went back to Fonner in order to receive their check and the photo with the big smiles only matched by their hats. The Sarge took the photo and basically hid it and knew now they would have to remain in camp until Monday in order to cash the check. Saturday came and they again ate and drank a lot while preparing for the ride to Mexico. They knew when Monday came as soon as the bank opened they would be on the Oregon Trail along the Platte River going wherever the west begins. Damon hid his grief and the others their sorrow. Monday finally came and the Sarge went to the bank while the five others rode horses down the river trail. Damon was on Table Legs and now was attempting to accept the loss as he was enjoying the river's nature. There were thousands of big geese on the river and in the fields of stubble, which had not been planted. After they passed the town of Lexington the trail and Highway 30 met close enough that the Sarge with the truck met them. They had a lunch of Spam and beer as they watched the birds in flight. They devised a plan where G.I. and Sarge would take their two rifles and shoot some geese for a fine meal. The men had on their western clothes ten-gallon hats and a six-gun strapped to their side. They were real cowboys now so no laws would apply to them and a couple of geese would be nothing in the thousands that were there. The rifles would be the guns of choice to get a couple hurting nothing in nature. They would meet up again near dark to find out each man's results on having a goose or two to eat. It would be a far cry from all the Spam feasts on this trip. Around 5 o'clock G.I. got off his horse and took steady aim to fire at the geese. The cracks of the rifle took down two birds, which he retrieved from the river's edge. A half hour later the sounds of two shots where heard which meant maybe the Sarge had some birds too? By 7 o'clock the horseman met up with the Sarge to learn he also had two birds. With the truck near the river they made camp, cleaned the birds and were surprised that the daylight continued for another hour. Louie said, "Geese laweeze these geese have long necks and long feet too. Let's cook them up and try them out." They did that and found them to be great eating although on the skinny side as far as geese went. They went through the nightly party routine and the dog chewed on the bones to make things better on this night.

The next day Tommy drove the truck while the other five rode with their six-guns on their sides. Tommy stopped for gas and got talking to a fellow about all the geese. The man told Tommy, "Those were not geese and they are Sandhill cranes. The birds have stopped in this valley for centuries on their north migration and they are our state bird and totally protected." Tommy thought to himself, Yikes! The Oregon Trail met outside of North Platte where they all met at two o'clock in the afternoon. They cooked hot dogs on a fire Tommy had going before their arrival. He told them what he had learned about the cranes, which wisely meant no more would end up as their dinner. The gang knew being a cowboy was one thing but going to jail for shooting a long necked bird was not in their plans. They decided to make camp at that location to just relax and have the horses rest up. Louie said, "Geese laweeze there are no mountains here and where is the west? I see lots of hills to the north but no mountains. The Sarge advised him that the Rocky Mountains where in Colorado which was their next state. Sparky in the meantime was acting up and getting into the men's food. Pete asked Louie, "Hey are you going to take care of this dog? He is kind of useless on this trip." Louie did not like hearing this so defended Sparky, "Geese laweeze what are you talking about? My dog does every command that I ask; yet sometimes I have to wait a day or two but he does it. Sparky is a wonder dog; you have to wonder where he is and what he is going to do? He knows everything even your smelly socks. He brings back the ball every time. What more could you ask for? He will bark when the lions are near. Wait and see." With that the two men calmed down as the dog chewed on Pete's pant leg.

The next day the men rode to Big Springs, Nebraska where the Oregon Trail headed off into Wyoming. This meant they left the trail to go to Colorado in the south with the horses now following the truck along the highway. It was not as nice as the river trail had been but it was the route to Mexico. Towards evening they came to the Colorado state line and made their camp. Tommy said, "We are in Colorado, where are the mountains? Did somebody steal them?" The Sarge had to explain they were in the High Plaines and the mountains were half the way across the state. For now they would ride south in the plains and meet up with the mountains at Raton, New Mexico. It made no sense to Tommy or Louie that there were no mountains and things looked like a desert to them. This was not the west that Hollywood movies portrayed with John Wayne shooting up the bad guys. All Louie and Tommy saw was a black top highway with brown weeds in all directions. It was in the early month of May as the horses followed the truck to Brush, Colorado. In that town they loaded up with needed supplies and felt better as the men there wore cowboy hats. They spent the night camped by Brush and went into town later to enjoy a local saloon and the friendly people. The next day they started out on their long ride to Trinidad, which was over two hundred miles to their south. The ride was in the High Plains with no mountains to be seen but the stars at night were spectacular. They watched shooting stars and even what looked like a UFO. Louie said, "Do you guys think the little green men will come down here and take us away?" Tommy answered him, "They might but your safe, the green men wouldn't want to take a lunatic like you. Now let's go to sleep."

Along the long route there was the town of Ordway to stock up on gas, beer and ice once more but traveling next to the highways was not what the six-pack had thought the west would be like. They made the best of it with their late night parties burning tumbleweeds as trees were not to be seen in the sea of grass. Finally after many days they reached Trinidad to spend some of Thinkaboutit's money at the local watering holes. The next day on to Raton Pass, New Mexico where the mountains were higher than any of them had imagined. They were beautiful after so many days of flat travel and now they knew they were in the west. After three days of riding again along highways with the mountains to their right they reached the town of Las Vegas, New Mexico. They went into the town seeking saloons and gambling casinos. They found a nice small saloon that had tables just like Charlie's. They took their seats at one of them and the waitress came to take their order. Louie asked, "Geese laweeze where are the slot machines and card tables? I want to play them." The waitress answered that they were two states away from them in Nevada. They were in the right town but the wrong state. With that solved they spent the night drinking and eating the local hot spicy food. They drank a lot of beer to cool their throats, as this type of food was new to them. Later when they returned to their camp all had a great need to use lots of toilet paper and this went on during the entire night. In fact it continued through all of the next day making it impossible for any travels. The men were all saying that there would be no more hot food for them. They grunted and groaned all day and Tommy made the point that they no longer where the Delaware gang but now the diarrhea gang. They ate and drank nothing but water all that day. Next to their camp Louie discovered a nest of rattlesnakes in a pile of rocks. As someone yelled out, "No! No!" Louie drew his gun and BAM! BAM! Six shots went off. The snakes jumped like lizards on a hot frying pan in all directions. The diarrhea gang ran into the weeds with more toilet paper and that event put some excitement in the day of hot food recovery. On the next day they were once again on their horses headed to Mexico. It took two days to arrive at a big town and on arrival they found a McDonald's to dine on safe food. They camped outside of town but all of them avoided drinking anything outside of vanilla malts as none had fully recovered from the native food. The good news was now the horses could follow the Rio Grande River down to Mexico while the truck would be on a paved parallel road. Traveling along the river with mountains everywhere convinced them they indeed were in the real west. This route however did take many days leading to El Paso, Texas and Mexico their final goal. The days were hot and the nights were cold. They built large campfires to furnish them heat through the seemingly long nights to temper the cold. The river trail led into heavy forests where many dead trees were available to them. They recalled their travels through the High Plains where no trees lived making this part of the journey a much easier one. They could have great campfires with all of the abundant wood so easy to just pick up. The trees and the beautiful blue skies were a western utopia to them. Soon they would be in Mexico and all of them privately thought on how proud of themselves they were in accomplishing this journey with only the spicy food as a snag in it.

Their journey continued and one day while in the mountains the Sarge was on Table Legs forgetting what Slim Jim had told him about the horse and trees. After being so good for the past weeks the horse took off into the trees at a gallop leaving the Sarge hanging on a branch. Everyone in the six-pack gang saw the event and broke out in laughter except of course the Sarge. They helped him down from the tree and made certain that he was not hurt and then they continued their laughter once they knew he was okay. Louie said, "Geese laweeze, Sarge I didn't know you could fly up trees? You had better take a parachute if you're going to fly around like that." The Sarge didn't find any humor in Louie's remarks and it took two days to find Table Legs in the mountains. Then it took another five days to reach El Paso after finding Table Legs. It was slow traveling along the Rio Grande however an enjoyable beautiful one. If there was a tree nearby then the rider on Table Legs got off and walked him, as they believed Slim Jim now. Once just outside of El Paso the six-pack set up their camp to decide on their Mexico plans. They liked Texas as the men here wore cowboy hats with some even being ten-gallons ones just like theirs. However they knew they had to go into Mexico to make the journey complete. Around the campfire it was decided five men would ride horses into Mexico and one would walk in leaving the truck in El Paso. That way they all could say they made it to Mexico. The next day they followed their plans and rode into Juarez and learned it was a huge city and no place for a horse. Then when they tried to come back into America the horses were not allowed back in without inspection papers. Of course they had none resulting in two days in Mexico to find a horse buyer.

They found a hotel that allowed the horses tied up in the rear where space allowed for it. During the two days they enjoyed Mexico and drank the nights away. Tommy and some others even spend a night with the señoritas. Eventually they sold all the horses at a fair price and sadly said goodbye to them all. The tack and saddles were also sold and the grieving men walked back to their truck in El Paso. With three upfront and three in the back they traveled to their El Paso Campground where Sparky was awaiting them hungry and thirsty. That night the big decisions of returning to Delaware had to be made with the calendar saying it was late June. They had thought the trip would have gone into July but they had made record time. Around the campfire they drank their beer along with whiskey and smoked some Mexican pot. This would be the six-pack's final party and they all knew it. The Sarge, Pete and Damon decided they would fly back home while Louie and G.I. elected to travel back with Tommy and Sparky in the truck. This three along with the puppy new more adventures awaited them in the west. Tommy even said they needed another night with the señoritas. Louie said, "Geese laweeze let's go for it."

THE FISHERMAN OF MALAX

It is mid-June in northern Minnesota where the town of Malax and the actual Lake of Malax is located. This day marks two important events. The first is it is the opening day where all species of fish are legal to take by state laws. More importantly it is Malax's annual celebration of the fish. For the past two days cars, campers, and trucks with hundreds of people have come to celebrate and enter the Malax's annual fishing contest. Most are camped out here and there as the town's two motels are filled to capacity on this weekend. Malax is a typical mid-western town of about 2,000 souls with three churches, two grocery stores, a hardware store, a car wash, two motels and most importantly one bait shop. Then of course two saloons, a restaurant, a bank, a travel agency and one mechanic's shop. For other services like a barber shop or hairdresser the people would travel to other close towns. This weekend the Malax's businesses would all be busy with most of the conversation just about the fishing event. The annual celebration long ago started with the winner of the fishing contest given prizes and the covenant title known as "Hooker Of The Year."

The people and town board members take this event with great pride, so much so they have erected signs along Route 61 entering their town that read, "WELCOME TO MALAX, THE HOOKER CAPITAL OF MINNESOTA." Needless to say the billboards raised some eyebrows, especially from the town's Lutherans, but the signs remain to this day. Traveling salesman and quite a few drinkers from out of town that have drank too much often ask to the whereabouts of the hookers? Local pranksters send them on long journeys into the woods where only mosquitoes live.

The goal of today is for the fishing contestants to catch the big one, as well as many other fish to be fried up tonight on Main Street where the party will be. The huge celebration includes the free fish fry along with drinking, dancing to the polka band, and carnival rides for the kids. Most importantly the awarding of the title, "Hooker of the Year" for the largest fish caught. Other prizes include deer jerky, bear stew, a Zebco rod and reel, many lures, two dozen worms, and best of all Mrs. Butts one gallon of super hot chili for the cold nights to come. Mrs. Butts Chili is nothing to sneeze about. Most of all the chili is saved to be used in later cold months that always come. In the winter it will be consumed giving off hot tongues, hotter lips and great memories of the honored "Hooker of the Year" award. You might say it will provide many hot hookers many a nights. This year there are four hundred and seventy two fishermen and fisherwomen registered in the fishing contest. In one boat are the trio of Karl Humpstead, Ole Nottestad and Axel Gustoson. These men have fished together for many years resulting in great friendships on and off the water. Karl is the owner of the sixteen foot used Lund boat with the equally used fifty horse powered Johnson motor. The men are signed in so it's now just a matter of getting out on the lake. Karl backs the boat and trailer down the ramp into the water and Axel yells out, "Hey we forgot to put the plug in the boat, it's filling up with water, drive er back up!" Karl replies, "You idiots, you stupid idiots" as he pulls up and the water now drains from the boat. Axel says, "Oh well, boat floor needed a little cleaning and we did a good job of it, saved money from the car wash too, now let's go fishing for the big hooker." He then finally puts the plug in. Once again Karl backs the boat in with Axel at the controls. Kazoom! The trusty Johnson takes off and after parking their vehicle and trailer the other two men board their "yacht" and off they go to their favorite spot on the lake which is on the North side far away from the ramp and piers. Even though of course most fish are in fact caught where they launched. Nonetheless they arrive at their North side spot to commence fishing. The trio are rigging up their poles when Ole in his broken English advises, "Hey, okey-dokey then, we gotta sing our good luck song first." Ole couldn't carry a note if it was mailed to him, Axel always sounds like a rusty drain pipe but Karl can sing some as he is in the Malax's Lutheran choir. As tradition would have it the men sing their song:

> Oh I wish I was ah fishin'
> what a beautiful day
> ta be on the way
> where the water is calm
> and we might catch some
> oh, I wish I was ah fishin'
> where the big ones swimin'
> and no tiny ones livin'
>
> May the pole bend as ah willow
> mine not the other fellows
> oh, I wish I was ah fishin'
> oh, I wish I was ah fishin'
>
> The big hooker could be mine
> ah, wouldn't it be so fine
> now some brandy
> ta make it all so dandy
>
> oh Lord, I wish I was ah fishin'

With their tune over, their laughs done, the lines in the water and now coffee with bandy poured for all as they drift about. Axel who drinks too much guzzles brandy straight from the bottle and Ole, the joker says, "Okey-dokey then, Axel if yous a keeps drinkin like tat we could've made a bathrooms pee song fer ya. We could call it, your-a-nation, by golly." The men's chuckle as Axel adds, "I don't drink so much anymore, used to fall down loaded and had to crawl across the street, nowadays I fall down at the curb and swim across the street." Karl says, "Got one!" He reels in a nice four pound walleye and put it in the live well. He says , "One for the fry and you both owe me a dollar for the first fish of the day, now to catch a lunker to get that hooker award." Ole replies, "I talks with my Sky Pilot las Sunday bout Jesus gettin all those fish ta feeds da hungries, he says. "Jes Jesus dit its as miracles." I says, "I needs a miracles ta catch ta lunker of ta year, okey-dokey then. Does I prays fer it da happen?" Ta preacher says, "Prays and fish." Axel advises, "You need more than a miracle to catch the lunker cause I'm going to catch him. I going to put my secret bait on my hook." "What's that," Karl asked? Axel replies with caution, "Well since we're out here and you guys can't make any here I'm going to tell you my secret. First, I take hunks of carp and let them rot in the sun, in a jar of course. Then the real secret is I take a sock I wore every day for two weeks and put the rotten carp in the sock. Next I hang it in the sun, boy it smells so much by then it attracts skunks and òther critters from miles around. I take a long cane pole, tie the sock at the end and make the skunk spray on it. Next I put it in this gallon jar I hid from you guys. This is my killer bait indeed." As Axel opens the jar the stench fills the air as Ole gags, coughs and spits. He now says, "By gosh, my golly, uff da that stuff stinks ta high heavens. Yous goin ta stink ups ta whole lake and kills everythin in tit. If ta fishes don't die ans they eats tat stuff yous coulds never cooks em in ta house or tits wood smells ups ta place so bads you'd have to move outs. Fer now we's gotta smell tat stuff alls day in tis little boat, Axel yous a cruel man, okey-dokey then." Karl added, "That is the smelliest concoction I've ever smelt in my whole life. Do you really think it will catch fish or just have the smell kill them and us? So rotten carp, ripe socks and skunk spray is your idea of bait? Do us a favor, keep that jar closed and keep your hook in the water at all times, will you?" Axel takes a big swig of brandy straight from the bottle and replies, "Wait to you see the big one I catch."

Malax is a mid-sized Minnesota Lake not to be confused with the much larger Lake Millie Lac. The lake does offer all the summer fun for all ages. Water skiing abounds in the warmer afternoons which fishermen dislike. On this day one skier is coming close to boats and giving the occupants water spray from the skis to verify the dislike. The trio will soon be victims it seems. A boat roars by with a young girl skier coming within eight feet of the Lund creating a large splash with spray hitting our fishermen where they are not hurting a flea. As it is happening Axel digs into his tackle box to pull out a 22-caliber revolver and then fires off three shots at that young skier. Kaboom, kaboom, kaboom the 22 cracks out! Karl yells out, "You crazy imbecile idiot! Are you insane or what?" Ole adds, "By golly uff da yous could ave kills tat girl, wat's wrongs wits yous? She's gots on a pinks bikini and nots much of tat ons er, she's addin my days lots mores tan yous stinkin bait okey-dokey then." Axel replies, "Ah, quit wagon your tongues like a dogs tail. It's only a blank gun and surely will keep those terrorists away, works every time." Karl not happy adds, "What if they come back with a 12-guage to blow us out of the water? They don't know your shooting blanks."

Eventually all of the men settled back down to seeking out the lake's lunker. Axel was correct in that no more skiers would harass them on this day. He continued to drink the brandy as if it was water with a second bottle showing up. As the day goes on for the trio each caching a few walleyes and some bass but the smelly bait is catching nothing. Seems the fish don't think much of the skunk spray anymore than humankind ever has. They drift along in a light breeze with a small water chop of waves offering perfect conditions on this beautiful Minnesota day. Now if only one could catch the lunker that might make him the biggest hooker. As luck would have it, Axel's smelly bait pole jerks and bends like a bow to say a monster fish is on hand. Perhaps the Loch Ness monster? Axel grabs his pole and yells out, "Wow, something big is on here, I feel his strong pull and weight, I can hardly reel him in, yippee." Ole in his joking way says, "Okey-dokey then, you wants me ta cut yous line, I gotts a sharp knife and yous woodn't have ta works so hard?" Then the big fish breaks the water to fly out ten feet in the air. Karl advises, "Keep em coming, I'll get the net ready, he is a dandy." The big fish offers up a good fight taking and giving up line in a fifteen minute period. Once at the boat he runs off with two more spectacular leaps from the water he calls home.

Finally Axel reels in the giant fish with Karl managing the net to perfection. The great fish his battle lost is in the boat. Karl grabs his tape measure from his tackle box while Axel places the big fish on a flat seat holding him firmly. The two men measure the lunker as Axel proudly states, "A muskie, a giant of the sea, did he fight or what? Ah, the tape reads forty-seven inches, bet that if I step on him he'd be four feet long, oh what a fish, see my smelly bait is the trick." Ole just jokingly adds to the big fish talk, "Okey-dokey then, yous steps on him and it's be like a lawyer tat never talks. Ain't never happins and yous ain't goin gets ta one inch eithers." Axel takes a huge swig from the brandy bottle and offers, "Well men this calls for a drink. A muskie that surely will win the hooker award and Mrs. Butts chili to boot." Karl answers, "No booze for me, let's move on to catch his grandpa, the day is getting shorter."

After the big fish and skier events the day continued with more walleyes and even some more bass being caught, but no more fish go for the skunk bait. With the sun drifting down and the clock reading 5:30 the trio needed to call it a day. They headed back to the piers, boat ramp and where the official check in station is located. Once there they add their walleyes and bass to others, which will be fried up later tonight.

Axel is full of brandy yet staggered over to the officials with his prize muskie. "Here you go, this guy will surely win Hooker of the Year or my name ain't Jimity Cricket!. Cause it ain't." The official looked on and in a friendly Minnesota way told Axel, "Uff da, yep, sure is a dandy. We will weigh and measure him up for you. You need to fill out this form, it'll only take a minute or so." Axel slurring his words told the official, "Okay, I'll dos that, but you takes care of my prize fish, will yous?"

It is early evening now with Main Street alive and blocked off as the Hooker of the Year Festival already is in full swing. Free food is as abundant as Minnesota mosquitoes and the beer tent has the populace getting their fill too. Dancing on the street to oopta oopta has all ages having fun. This indeed is an early summer mid-western festival all are enjoying. There are carnival rides for the kids while the older folks sit in their fold up chairs watching the events. They visit and talk about the good old days and those no longer on this good earth. Just the same laughter and joy abounds on Malax's Main Street as it does every year during this festival. Naturally the fishermen and fisherwomen talk of the ones that got away as they also exaggerate about the size of the fish they did bring in. According to tradition this is not lying but rather telling a fib or two as fishermen have this luxury created throughout the centuries. Grandpa did it so I can do it is the code. It's as if they are all used car salesman and good at it. Better yet they all could be lawyers!

The fish fry, dancing and drinking continues until eight o'clock when the MC takes the stage to start the process of the Main event, "The Hooker of the Year Award." First of course town dignitaries go through their lineup of introducing each other to maintain their egos while patting each other on their backs. It seems this is necessary in all small and large festivals. However, the next day the general public seems to have forgotten who any of them are. Finally the Mayor is introduced, as he is the one to hand out the awards. The MC announces, "Ladies and gentlemen please give a big hand to your Mayor, Mr. Bigbottom." The Mayor takes the mike and starts out, "Say folks, haven't we here at Malax had a wonderful day with lots of great competitors? Let's give them all a big hand." So, clapping and hooting from the crowd goes on for quite a while. "Now let's get on with the awards and find out who will be the biggest Hooker of the Year?" The crowd now really hoots, yells and hollers which is proving indeed a good time is being had.

Mr. Bigbottom now announces, "Our third-place winner is Mrs. Dryland of Duluth catching a huge twenty-six inch walleye. She will receive a Zebco rod and reel with two-dozen words, I mean worms, contributed by, 'U HOOK EM BAIT SHOP' of Malax. Let's hear it for Mrs. Dryland." The crowd yells, claps and hollers. "Our second place runner up is Axel Gustoson of Lost Lake, Minnesota and he receives an all expense paid weekend of ice fishing here at Malax provided by 'ACE HOLE OUTFITTERS' of Malax. He entered a forty-seven inch muskie, a great fish, let's hear it for Axel?" The crowd once more gives their approval sounds. "And now folks, the

Hooker of the Year goes to Bill Boober of River Falls, Minnesota. Bill landed a forty-eight inch muskie that wins him an all expense paid vacation trip for two to Hawaii provided by, 'CRASH TRAVEL AGENCY' of right here in Malax. This is a two-week dream vacation folks, let's hear it for the Hooker Of The Year!" The crowd erupted in applause. Oddly enough, Mrs. Butt's chili was not given out this year. Not a word about it would be heard and some concluded that either the dignitaries or the Mayor himself kept the hot, hot Chili. These are the same men that at election time talk about honesty and righteousness. They must be politicians.

The applause continued and the polka band started back up to its oopta oopta. Axel took a big swig from his third bottle and made comments that small ears should not hear. Karl looked at Axel and said, "You did a good job, I'm happy for you. Maybe I can go ice fishing with you? Besides Hawaii's too hot in the winter and there's no hookers there, uff da." Ole said, "By golly there's always tis next year, okey-dokey then."

THE REST OF THE STORY FROM A WOMAN'S PERSPECTIVE

I had lived out west most of my life, however climbing the "ladder of success" had taken me to a position working in the Chicago suburbs. As time went on I met the girl of my dreams as she was very pretty and had the perfect figure. Any red-blooded American boy would say, "Wow, wow" to this gal. Her personality was with great fun and for a city girl she had an open mind towards events outside of going to the mall on Saturdays. She was willing to try new travels beyond the city. My experience had been that you go out with a woman and after the third date she would say, "when are we getting married?" Well, to my surprise this never happened with Mary Ellen as she was most happy within herself and not looking for a man, or so I thought.

After the normal city dating routine of movie shows and out to dinners it occurred to me to really test Mary Ellen. I would ask her if she wanted to go fishing? To my delighted surprise she answered a most positive, "sure." As time went on I would learn she was always positive and a Pollyanna of sorts. It seems she was willing to try new things way beyond the city lifestyle. Boy, this was the girl for me as I had experienced the opposite earlier that had ended in a divorce. That wife's idea of life was a fancy new car with going out to a fancy restaurant on Saturday nights with work in between. Now I'm a pickup truck, bring on the outdoors and have a smelly old dog kind of guy. Needless to say that wife was not a match and it seemed possible Mary Ellen was the type that could fit into my lifestyle despite being a city gal.

Due to my schedule it would be at least three months before we could go fishing and that was all right as I asked her in the month of March the first time. In June that year I called to ask about going fishing again and the answer once more was a positive "yes". During those in between three months we had dated on and off. It seemed we always ended up eating at Greek restaurants and I had no idea that she had any ability of cooking a meal. To be honest I did not care as a hot-blooded young fellow I had other interests on my mind anyway. The day did come when Mary Ellen cooked a delicious meal at my apartment. I thought to myself, wow, she can cook, she's beautiful and then there's that "playboy" type of body. This girl is the one for me I thought. Wow, she can cook!

Later on I would learn city girls don't cook wild game but that's her story. I had learned about the good fishing at Lake Mendota up at Madison, Wisconsin from a friend. That would be a three-hour drive on Highway 12, which I thought ideal for a fishing outing. This would give us plenty of time to visit outside of the hectic city life we were in. The drive through the countryside might tell me if we would be compatible on a long-range relationship. The ride went very well and it became time to go fishing and for Mary Ellen to tell her story on all things considered.

"THE REST OF THE STORY"

The rest of the story or a woman's view of the man's world. This city-raised girl would like to enlighten the women readers as to just what she is getting into when she decides to hook up with the "Outdoorsman." It was a hot June day when the phone rang and it was that interesting fellow John I had met a while back. His voice sent a cold chill down my spine. "How would you like to go fishing?" The next thing I knew we were in a small fiberglass boat on this beautiful lake right in the middle of Madison Wisconsin. Yes, this most beautiful lake was located right in the middle of this large city. Since I had grown up in the suburbs of Chicago I was not too hip on what fishing entailed and so it was a wonderful outing for me. He rigged the tackle and bait and handed me the pole and then after it was in the water all I did was hold on until something at the other end started pulling. As he was the captain of this expedition he regulated the motor and accordingly killed the engine while I fought to get the fish to the boat where he netted them for me. Why there was nothing to this fishing and I got a real charge out of it and with such a handsome skipper to boot!

While fishing that day he looked me straight in the eye and said, "If you are looking for a forever relationship, forget it". I thought he was pretty big on himself (I hadn't even thought of him as marriage material yet) and with that in mind I said, "Okay, can we just fish?" It was my first fishing trip of my life and I was really excited about fishing, especially when the first fish I caught was a fairly large Northern. By the end of the day we had caught four very large sized Northerns and we both had our pictures taken with the fish. I still have my copy in my photo album and the smile on my face shows my enthusiasm. August brought several more fishing trips and many different kinds of species. This was truly the most exciting fellow I had dated for sure.

After many months of dating and not dating I heard how he and a fellow outdoorsman had traveled all the way to Nebraska to go duck hunting which turned out to be a picnic with dinner cooked on a Coleman stove in a nice warm motel room. I was beginning to feel this city girl should be in the country. Carefully I set out my plan of attack and after some time and a year later I let him catch me and it was off to Nebraska for "The Good Life!" He was gonna be a keeper.

Our first month in the slow-paced community we had chosen to live in was the month of August. We fished but mostly we enjoyed our new country living and became better acquainted with Mother Nature. City people just don't know what they are missing but that's okay, Nebraska is not for everyone. September came and I occasionally became annoyed with the amount of preparation time he spent for the opening of the "Big Hunt" but I was still enjoying all the differences between city and country living. I also was aware of my big let down in September because the fishing season was all but over in our area and I was saddened when all the fishing gear was put away as well as the boat. So hunting was here and I truly wanted to learn all about my outdoorsman and learn I did. Hunting doesn't seem to be a sport that women folk in this area were or even wanted to be a part of. I did enjoy trying the different game that he brought home but it was quite lonely while it was being hunted. Seems that before dawn and after sundown was an incredibly long time for him to come home with the small amount of game that was procured on that day. It takes 27 turtledoves for one meal and that required sometimes two long days to secure. They were good but I mostly enjoyed eating the grouse and pheasants. If I thought this was intense hunting I sure was in for a shock when duck season arrived. Being that this was my first go around with John, my outdoorsman, I maintained my good humor just seeing the pleasure on his face when he would come home with the considerable number of meals that he did.

October 6 was the opening day for ducks and I had already been a part of the preparation of the duck blind including painting it in all camouflage colors that was not exactly brilliant colors. Then the placing of the blind that had to be hand walked with three of us inside to the exact spot from where we would shoot all the unsuspecting ducks. Next of course the camouflaging of the duck blind with reeds and such vegetation that was in the immediate location, as you don't want to get weeds that were not already familiar to the ducks. This took most of the weekend before the season even started. Then the big day arrived, since it was my birthday and the first day of the duck-hunting season it was all intertwined by an invitation to go duck hunting for my birthday. So with another couple off we went at the early hour of 4 AM. We were heading toward the concealed duck blind we had previously placed at our exclusive duck hole. The drive was at least an hour and good strong coffee helped me awaken and get all hyped up for this new experience. I was dressed with all the proper clothing that was just like the paint we had put on the duck blind, not any to feminine either. I might add the other lady came out in a shocking pink coat. Along with the promise of a new experience the breakfast was cooked for the ladies on this trip. This was quite a treat to be taken out of our natural roles and be waited on. So with all this anticipation I smiled to myself when thinking of all those city folks that were about to face a new day fighting traffic and time schedules. I commuted to the downtown "Chicago Loop" (it's called) every day by train and when arriving at the train station I felt like going "MOOO." I always thought there was a better way to do this thing called life and I was right!

Yes, this is going to be a day I would not forget, not even if I wanted to. We transferred all our supplies from truck to blind with many trips for the four of us. We were in the blind with the dog and the sweet smell of bacon, which was a good way to start the day. With breakfast over and the sun just about to come up the excitement mounted. I was given my first lesson of shooting a gun while on a turtledove hunt so I just needed a little refresher course. Then the time came and our outdoorsmen started with their duck calls, I was amazed how real they sounded. Of course not knowing which was real and which was not I had to wait for the signal from the men as to when to shoot "NOW!!!!" By the time I got up in position shots had already been fired and ducks dropped before I knew what had happened. Then the sun was really up but the ducks for some reason were coming right towards us and they would split to completely bypass our blind, what could be the problem I wondered? Then the men looking right at me said almost in unison "Keep your big white face down." This must be why all the men in our area had started growing bushy beards come late August. They never mentioned the other ladies bright pink coat was a problem. With this new development I found myself hunched over in the blind while the duck callers began their new barrage of calls. Again the ducks came and again the familiar "NOW!!!!" sounded and again it was all over before I even got a shot fired. Besides not even having shot my gun there were thousands of little frogs that were inside the duck blind and while hunched over keeping my "big white face down", I was beginning to see this was not as exciting as fishing had been. Then they devised a way for me to tell not only when the ducks were ready to be shot at but also when to shoot. They started to explain that they would say, "12 o'clock, nine o'clock, or three o'clock" and it was then that I remembered I had not even brought a watch. What they meant was that if the ducks were coming from straight ahead that would be 12 o'clock and so on. Was this city girl ready for this much of the outdoors? Well, it was time again the "NOW"!!!!! Came and I was just about to fire when the patience of the other fellow had run out and he got two of MY ducks. I tried again and again and out of the whole day had only gotten one duck in the air. It was right in the water amongst our decoys and upon my rustling around got up and he tried to escape but I nailed him about 2 feet in the air. Shoot at least 3 feet in front of them they told me but I was not sure of my distance like they were. About late afternoon I decided the only way I was going to get any ducks of my own was to bushwhack them in the water and that is exactly what I did. The excitement of duck hunting was not what I had hoped it would be and I'm sure it was because of my "big white face."

Well the very next day I was going out with my outdoorsmen alone to try for some more ducks. This time we again got off long before the sun came up only upon "my big white face" I had smeared brown Halloween makeup. Now I could be a part of the watch and not have to dodge those frogs again. I recently found out what a good laugh was had at my expense for attempting to be in full camouflage without shaving my face to get a good beard going. Much to my surprise it did not improve my shooting except for the ones I bushwhacked in the water nor did I really want to get up before the crack of dawn and come in after the setting of the sun to cook a big meal. So next time I begged off and then the long lonely hours began again. From October 6, until sometime in January we spent only five days alone as the rest were taken up with endless people that came to hunt OUR duck blind. Those days alone were then taken up with the next phase that was coming. It was trapping, dying of traps, waxing of same, getting stakes ready and the like. Mostly beaver trapping that first season and I saw for the first time that these outdoorsmen's were all candidates for 'ONE FLEW OVER THE CUCKOO'S NEST.' The amount of money and time spent was beyond my comprehension but I went along with it because it all started when I was to get a beaver pelt made into a vest to combat the cold winters we had or at least the one we were having that particular winter. I have yet to get that vest much less the beaver pelt. I don't know the count for that particular trapping season but it did pay the phone bill once in a while and provided gas money for vehicles back and forth to the drop-off and pick-up places. When asked by my new acquaintances "where's John?" I would laughingly tell them, "I just threw him in the river," not letting them know that is exactly what I would have liked to do.

So the winter was a long lonely one and I amused myself with two little stray kittens that someone had dumped off by our place. It took me 2 1/2 months to get them to come and eat and get a peaceful nap without looking over their shoulders. The rest of the time I spent finding out how to prepare all this wild game that was being hunted or trapped and much to our delight we enjoyed beaver and made some delicious beaver burgers. We even contemplated opening a beaver burger chain but quickly abandoned that idea when realizing the FDA would never approve our methods of preparation. One of our friend duck hunters brought a gift of two very large deer steaks, "Oh good," I said "I never had eaten deer meat." While the men were out cleaning their ducks and geese I put the steaks in the frying pan. I started to prepare potatoes and corn when I smelled a very foul pungent odor. It was the deer meat. I was close to vomiting so opened all the windows in the small trailer we were living in and promptly took the meat still in the frying pan out to the garbage can and tossed them in. I got some hamburger meat out and in a different frying pan started cooking them. When the men came in with their dressed birds they asked where the deer steaks were? I said, "I threw them out as they were rotten and stunk up the whole place". "Threw them out?" They said, "That's the way they are supposed to smell." I told them I could never eat anything that smelled so nasty. Then someone else presented us with more deer steaks and said to soak them in vinegar over night which I did. They didn't say to dilute the vinegar so another trip to the garbage can. To this day if offered deer anything I politely refuse.

As time went on I thought we surely would have some time to rekindle the spark that started way back when. And sure enough the boat had to be repainted and all gear cleaned up and while on that first fishing trip in May, Memorial Day, to be exact we caught over 100 perch and I was back in the swing of things when from out of nowhere he says, "Well, only three more months till hunting season!" This story started on a beautiful lake in Madison when learning he did not want a "forever" relationship. That was 34 years ago and I say I caught the biggest fish ever and he's a keeper.

AND THAT IS THE REST OF THE STORY

THE RESORT DAYS

In 1906 a Swedish immigrant came to America and specifically to Chicago where he would start his new life. His name was Axel Jorgenson and he came to America with wealth, for in Sweden his family had several large businesses. Once in Chicago, Axel purchased a saloon in the Swedish section of that city. The building included upstairs living quarters giving him a business and a home. In that era Chicago was a city of neighborhoods with the Swedish one located on the near North Side that Axel enjoyed a great deal. He was equally liked by the people living there making his saloon business a very successful one. In that day and age the saloonkeeper was many things to many people. Axel would be a banker, the helper of the poor, a marriage counselor along with being the general psychologist to his patrons. He was well respected throughout the Swedish neighborhood, as he was the helper to many people living within it.

Gustaf Swanson was one customer that required Axel's assistance in many ways. The main problem was he did not provide adequate funds for his family although he had a good job working for the railroad. Gustaf's wife would often come to Axel in need of food, clothing for the children and heat in the winter. Axel always would assist her with money but Mrs. Swanson wished he would talk with Gustaf hoping for a long-term solution. She knew if anyone could set Gustaf on the right path it would be the saloonkeeper. Axel assured her he would make every attempt to assist her with Gustaf.

The day came when Gustaf came into Axel's saloon very intoxicated. He staggered up to the bar to say, "By jimity I'm tey richest guy in this place, buy everybody's in this joint a drinks. I can affords ta even buy out this whole place, give everyone's two drinks." Axel did serve everyone one drink and Gustaf a black coffee with a pinch of brandy. He collected the money taking some extra which he would give to Gustaf's wife later. With that Gustaf was broke once more and no one offered to buy him a drink seeing his drunken condition. Axel did pour him more coffee saying, "Gustaf you need to consider your family, you cannot keep being the fool you have been. They need your paycheck over you spending it all at saloons." Gustaf replied, "Fool huh, I shows you what a fool tis." With that he went back to the barrooms rear and out the door to the outhouse in the back. He returned totally naked and jumped up on the bar to do a jig of sorts. Axel angrily commanded, "I'm as frustrated as a toad in a rainstorm with you! Get your clothes back on and get out of here! You should never come back here again, never!"

Sure enough Gustaf went and put his clothes back on. That is exactly what he did to the barroom's customers surprise for all his clothes where on backwards. To see his shirt and pants reversed from normal was a site no one had ever seen. He staggered out in his clown like dress and said just before going out the door, "Vie umpity lizards I's never spends a dime ins here veers again." True to his word he never did return to spend a dime but three years later he did return to Axel's saloon. He ordered up a black coffee and was as sober as a judge. Well maybe not as a Chicago judge but as one somewhere. He was with out drink. Axel came over to him seeing he was a new man with clear eyes. Axel questioned, "How are you doing?" Gustaf said, "Axel, I wants to tank you for throwing me out three years ago. Tat opens ups myself and i's changed accounts of its. No more drinking since, I's a changed man, tanks you." Axel was very happy for Gustaf and his family and they parted friends.

During those same three years Axel met and married an immigrant Swedish girl named Ida. The two continued to operate the near North Side saloon but both had thoughts of leaving Chicago for a new adventure in the country. They read ads in the newspapers for possible options and one day this one appeared:

FOR SALE:

Once in a lifetime paradise can be yours! An
Operating country resort on beautiful Grass
Lake. Includes barroom, sleeping rooms,
Dining room, several out buildings along with
Rental boats.
A Fishing and Hunting utopia. This property must
be seen to be appreciated.
  - Contact Joe Conman at 427

It was in the springtime of 1914 when Axel made the phone call to Joe Conman that would change his and Ida's lives for many years to come. "Hello, my name is Axel Jorgenson and I'm calling regarding the resort you have listed." "Ah yes, I'm Joe Conman and I can help you on the matter. You need to take the North Western train north to Wilmont, Wisconsin and I'll pick you up there. The train runs on Wednesday, Friday and Sunday. Tell me what day works for you and I'll meet you at the Wilmont Depot." Axel told Joe, "Next Wednesday would be best for my wife and myself." Joe said, "That will be fine, I'll see you then."

That next Wednesday came with great excitement for the big city couple as they boarded the train. Axel told his wife, "Dear this is a dream come true as ever since leaving Sweden I have yearned to be in the country with nature. Our years of running the city saloon have been good training towards having a resort to operate. How I hope it all works out." The train traveled along leaving the city civilization for the small farms and where few people lived. Ida had her doubts about leaving city conveniences yet on the plus side she was happy about possibly leaving the saloon business. In America she was ready for a new start and trusted Axels' judgment on all matters small and large. She enjoyed the ride into the spring countryside away from the big city. The open spaces and many wildflowers provided great beauty to her eyes.

Two hours after boarding the train it finally arrived at the Wilmont Depot. The Swedish couple along with four other resort customers departed this first leg of their journey. Next, Joe Conman greeted them all. "Hello folks, I'm Joe and we all are headed for the Klondike as our resort is known. Just follow our motor man Zak down to the river and we will head out to paradise." Accordingly all walked a short distance from the depot to the river where an excursion boat awaited them. The boat was loaded with supplies leaving just enough room for the passengers. Then the canvas topped boat traveled down the Fox River for two and one half miles. Water wildlife was seen everywhere, turtles and frogs appeared in the water while shorebirds and songbirds filled the river's reeds. Hundreds of many duck species flew in the air on this pleasant springtime day. It was a drastic change from their city life where only pigeons and hundreds of mice made their home. The river then met the lake and offered a view of what Heaven itself must be like. Only path like roadways broke up the miles of beautiful green vegetation that was covered with white lotus flowers. Thousands of ducks filled the air and even large fish broke water to jump into the sky. This indeed was the utopia that nature lovers sought out through the ages.

The beautiful scenery and unlimited wildlife had Ida and Axel sold on buying the resort long before they would ever see it. To leave the congested city for this environment had them convinced to make a business deal indeed. They both had these same thoughts as the boat continued through the lotus flower paths to the Klondike. Zak skillfully docked the boat at one of the many piers and then all passengers walked up to the sandy beach. They looked up on a small hill to see one hundred yards away the three-story resort. A flower bordered pathway led to the building and once there they were introduced to Matilda who said, "I am the cook, room keeper and chief bottle washer." She next took the four guests up to the second floor and their rooms. The Swedish couple remained on the first floor with Joe who showed them the barroom and dining area. Both these rooms were large in comparison to their Chicago business and Joe then showed them a room adjoining the barroom. In this room were stacks of filled beer boxes, large ceramic crocks producing beer, a workbench to cap the beer and best of all an artesian well. This was the crystal pure water used to make the beer.

Then the three took the steps up to the second floor where there were ten sleeping rooms. One of the largest was Zak and Matilda's own private quarters with the others set up for customers. Finally they climbed up to the third floor, which was divided into two huge rooms with large windows looking out at the grounds. Joe explained, "One room will be your quarters and the other can be used as an office area. Now let's go down to the beach after I show you one more room down on the second floor." They went back down to a room that had a large padlock on the door. Joe opened it to view a room filled with a still making corn whiskey. Joe explained, "You can buy corn from the farmer that is your neighbor or grow your own. With the artesian water you can make the best whiskey money can buy." Then they left the building and went back to the beach.

Joe said, "There are four piers for boat tie ups and over there are ten boats stacked up yet from winter storage. That building is a workshop and oh yes I forgot, behind the resort are his and her out houses, any questions?" Axel asked, "Joe where is the roadway?" Joe, as any smart salesman answered, "Well Axel there is no road which is the beauty of this property. You pick up your customers by boat from either Wilmont or the town of Fox Lake where the trains stop. Customers love this feature as it adds a great deal of romance to the Klondike." Joe next pointed to land across the water one hundred yards away, "Over there is your horse Nelly and a wagon she hooks up to. You can take Nelly to Fox Lake by a dirt road on that side for supplies if you wish but it is faster to just go by boat. There is plenty pasture and hay growing for Nelly year around there giving you no extra work. You have seen how beautiful the lake is and I would think someday it would be a National Park with you now on the ground floor. Any other questions, Joe asked?" Then Ida asked him, "Do you think Zak and Matilda would stay on with us and what about close neighbors?" Joe answered, "I am sure they will stay on with you as they have been here over ten years, of course you will need to ask them. Well neighbors, behind the building is a large piece of land that you could plant a big garden in and from it is a path leading to the Zinger's farm. They are about four hundred yards away down the path and are great friendly people. Matilda goes there to buy milk and vegetables from them in season. Also from their farm there is a dirt road that leads to roads going most everywhere. Someday the road may come here and then they also might build a bridge over the water to where Nelly is."

The trio next walked around the property as Joe explained how many flowers could be planted here and there which would beautify the Klondike. On inspection it seemed that only a coat of paint was needed on the main building and Axel and Ida by now were ready to buy the Klondike. Ida then asked Joe why he was selling the resort? Joe responded, "Well Ida it is my wife. She is in poor health needing doctors all the time so we have to be close to them in the city. It breaks my heart to have to sell and give up this utopia for a life in Chicago." The Swedish couple both said that they were sorry for Joe's wife's health and hoped she would improve. Then the three went into the Klondike to the barroom. The bar itself was made out of oak with expert craftsmanship equaling all ever made. Behind the bar was a large mirror, which helped light up the area, as the building had no electricity. All of the Klondike had kerosene lamps and candles for lighting purposes as a result. The four paying customers were at the bar enjoying the homemade beer and some Canadian whiskey. They talked about the fishing they were to do on the next day and fishing they had done in past years. Zak was tending bar as all seven of them sat enjoying a drink when someone brought up the women's actions in Kansas. Joe said, "Yes, have you heard there are women taking axes to saloons and booze stores now out in Kansas? Those crazy women are prohibitionist as they call themselves. They want to take all our alcohol drinks away from the workingman. With our crazy government and the crazy women someday they might get that done. If they ever do they will never affect the Klondike as nobody would ever give them a boat ride out here." With that Matilda entered the bar room to announce supper was ready and all should take to the dining room.

Matilda with Zak helping served a fine three-course meal. A potato soup was followed up with a ham and then beef steaks cooked to perfection. A strawberry cake with coffee topped off the delicious meal. Ida asked Matilda, "You certainly have served us a meal fit for a king, and may I see your kitchen?" The two ladies went to the kitchen area, which was simple yet complete. There was a large black cook stove that operated by a wood fire. Ida especially liked it as it brought back fond memories of one back in Sweden that her mother used. Then there was a table in the corner with a wall telephone above it. Ida asked, "Matilda I see that there is a telephone, does it work?" Matilda answered, "Oh yes it does, behind the building along that path to the Zinger farm are the poles with the wires. We share the line with the Zingers along with three others and our incoming calls are four rings. I use the telephone to talk with the Zingers about what milk and produce is available but you could call Chicago if you wanted to." This was wonderful news to Ida as it meant they would not be isolated from the outside world. This was another factor that convinced Ida that they should buy the Klondike. Ida then asked, "Matilda would you stay on with us and Zak too if we increased your wages some?" Matilda answered, "Oh yes, we will be happy to stay on and work for you as we wondered about that? We have no other place we would care to go, you can count on us staying." This was music to Ida's ears.

Then the two women returned to the dining room. The four customers along with Joe and the Swedish couple finished their meals and next went to the bar for a nightcap drink. Then up the stairs to their rooms for a good night's sleep. Ida and Axel were given the large third story room and before sleeping they talked over their day, which had started with a two-hour train ride. Axle started, "What a day, this area and lake is absolutely beautiful. I believe we should move here but the only thing I don't like is no electricity." Ida added her news, "I know no electricity is bad but someday perhaps we can get that. The really good news is in the kitchen there is a telephone and it does work. I am real happy about that. I agree with you that we should leave the city and start a country life here at the Klondike. Tomorrow we need to talk with Joe about a price and terms to see if we can really afford this resort." Axle then said, "I think that will work out as my family will help out plus we have two different guys that want to buy our Chicago saloon as Wrigley Field is to be built by it you know? Plus his poor wife has to stay in the city and he has never brought up others are interested in buying the Klondike. I'm sure we can make a good deal. Today seems like a dream, I wonder if Zak and Matilda will stay on with us? They both know so much on running the place." "Well Axel I talked with Matilda about that back in the kitchen. She assured me they would be happy to continue with us." Axel happily replied, "That is great news, in fact the best news. Now let's hit the hay, it has been a long wonderful day." With that the two took to sleep.

The next morning was Thursday and a beautiful sunny day it was. The four fishermen had an early breakfast and went out fishing. Matilda told them that she would fry up their catch for them as an evening meal. Joe Conman and the couple had their breakfast followed by coffee with Brandy. They talked over business proposals and to all's delight the agreement of $12,500 with thirty days to make payment was agreed upon. This was a huge sum of money in 1914 but Axel felt assured he could raise that amount. He knew his family back in Sweden would back him along with the money from the Chicago saloon sale would make the deal possible. In thirty days they would meet at Joe's attorney's office to complete the Klondike sale. After their business completed Axel and Ida took a boat out to the lake. Ida said, "This sure is so different than the city and I love it. We will have a big job bringing all our belongings out here by boat." "I know Ida, I've thought about that too. We will have to account for that when we sell our Chicago place. Today let's enjoy this beauty as tomorrow we will be taking the train back and then work on getting all the money together." The two enjoyed the sunny April day on the water and on the resort's land. Axle once again looked over both the beer making room and the whiskey room on the second floor. He thought about the beer he could make for pennies and sell for a nickel a glass. The whiskey costs would only be corn and could be sold for twenty-five cents a shot. He knew on the long run this new home would be a perfect business if only someday he could have electricity. Ida spent most of her day with Matilda learning all she could from her. She asked her, "When we return what could I bring you and Zak from the city?" Matilda said, "I'd really love to have one of those big black hats with pretty feathers and I know Zak would enjoy a cigar or two." Ida said she would be happy to bring them on her next trip. With the day ending the fishermen came in with enough fish for all to enjoy a meal of them. Following the meal all had a few drinks and then off to bed.

The next day, Friday the two would make their journey back to the city while the four fishermen stayed at the Klondike. Joe and Matilda stayed as well with Zak giving Axel and Ida a ride to the Fox Lake train station. This boat ride was not as beautiful as the Wilmont ride had been, however it was a much faster one. The town of Fox Lake was a good-sized one and Axel saw he could buy any future needs there he would want. They said goodbye to Zak and boarded the train back to Chicago. In route Axle and Ida talked over plans of their new venture as both beamed with pride. It had been an eventful three days, which would change their lives forever. The train ride through the farmlands to the city seemed much faster than the ride to Wilmont and back in the city they made their way to their city home. They both thought the busy city was a different world than the Klondike and soon that would be their home.

Within three weeks the necessary funds came from Axel's Swedish father along with a buyer for the city saloon. Axle telephoned Joe at 427 and the next day they met at Joe's attorney's office. The deal was completed with the deed drawn up giving Axel and Ida the Klondike once all the money was paid. Three days later the business deal selling the Chicago property was concluded and the Klondike was paid for in full. The Swedish couple next had sixty days to have their belongings moved from the upstairs apartment. This would give them the time to transfer their belongings to the Klondike while the new owner could still operate the business. The couple boxed up their belongings and arranged for them to be sent as freight at the end of May. On their first trip back to the Klondike they would travel with their necessities and a few boxes of other items. Axel bought a box of Cuban cigars for Zak and Ida purchased a fancy big hat for Matilda. She remarked to Axle, "I wonder what Matilda will do with this fancy big hat out at the Klondike? She is a big woman but why out in the country is beyond me? Maybe the bullfrogs will croak her a tune she can dance to under the stars. I can see her doing a jig with the feather bouncing around to the frog's and cricket's music."

It was on Friday, May 18, 1914 when Axel and Ida arrived back at the Fox Lake depot as the owners of the Klondike. Two paying customers were also with them to their delight. Zak was there to pick all of them up for their boat ride to the resort. Upon arrival the gifts were at once handed out. Zak greatly appreciated the cigars and Matilda immediately put on her feathered hat and danced around the beach. Next, she escorted the two customers up to their rooms with her new huge hat on at all times. It was a comical sight indeed. The customers took the remainder of the day walking around the grounds and spending time in the barroom. They were in no hurry to do any evening fishing although they talked at length about it with Zak. They were indeed two gentlemen with professional backgrounds enjoying a get away from the big city. Axle and Ida took their own belongings up to their third-floor room. They arranged it as they wished while Zak tended to the barroom and the guests. Matilda with her soiled apron and big new hat worked away in the kitchen. Dinner was served at six followed by more barroom drinks and polite visiting. By nine o'clock all would retire to their rooms after a long day into this peaceful world. Things are not always what they seem, Axle and Ida would learn. On their first night in their new venture a thunderstorm came about. Drip, drip, and drip the rain came into the resort seemingly everywhere. Matilda was running around placing one-gallon empty lard cans to catch the water as it poured down from the heavens. "My God is there any dry place in this building?" Ida screamed out. Matilda answer yet placing the tins out, "Oh it's nothing, this always happens when the rain comes. Didn't Conman tell you the roof needed repairs?" All through the night the water kept coming through the leaky roof, first into the third floor and then into the second floor sleeping rooms. Then somehow it worked its way down to the barroom. Zak was placing cans there to catch the rain when Axel came down the steps to see the fiasco happening in his barroom. In disgust he said, "Zak how come no one told us about the leaky roof? I sure would have brought supplies to repair it and would have deducted it off the buying price. This is a disaster!" All Zak could do is continue placing more lard cans where the water dripped and he said nothing.

The second-floor sleeping rooms were taking the worst of the situation. The guest's room was soaking wet making it not fit for use. Ida and Matilda learned that only the room where the whiskey still was had suffered the least. They rounded up two mostly dry mattresses and placed them on the stills floor. Next they found dry bedding in a closet to make up the two beds. It was the best they could do given the situation. Axel escorted the guests to this room hoping they would understand. They did not. The taller of the two went into a rage. He yelled out, "This is the worst place we've ever been. Do you expect us to sleep on sponges and become sponges ourselves? We demand a full refund and want out of here as soon as possible! Get us back to Fox Lake and sanity the first thing in day light, we want out of here!" Axel replied, "Look, we are very sorry about this which we did not know about. I apologize and you will get a full refund and we will fix our roof. If you would like we will give you three days free stay in the future and Zak will take you to the depot in the morning. That's the best we can do and again I apologize." The two men grumbled and shut the door to their new room. When morning came few words were spoken and Zak took them to Fox Lake. Axel told Zak when there to buy roofing supplies, lots of them.

A half hour after the boat had left Ida, Matilda and Axel settled down to a breakfast. "Ida said, "Our first night and our first guests, what a disaster. Why no one told us about the leaky roof I'll never know. Joe sure pulled a fast one on us. I can see why he didn't want his sick wife here." Matilda said, "Wife, what wife? Joe is not married he has no wife." Axel in amazement, "Well he lied to us about that and said nothing about the roof. Yeah, his name is Conman which really is con man, I wonder what else he failed to tell us?" They slowly continued eating their breakfast when KABOOM! Another crisis, the still on the second floor had exploded setting off a fire. The three ran up to the fire yet confined to the one room. Matilda grabbed the rainwater filled lard cans to throw on the fire. The other two followed to do the same and eventually the fire was out. Axel talked, "It looks like the fire is out but we had better keep an eye on this room. Seems like the only damage is the walls are blackened and the mattresses are ruined. We had better throw them outside for safety's sake. Those guests must have left a cigar burning in here to cause the fire and it was lucky we had the rainwater to put it out. For our first day as owners like Ida said, "Maybe we aren't so lucky." Having a leaky roof, then a fire and our first guests gone forever. Wonder what could be next?"

As the springtime and summer progressed there was plenty that came next. The stack of rental boats all needed major repairs in order that they could float. Zak and Axel solved that problem as well as giving them a bright orange color of paint. This would enable them to see their boats anywhere on the lake. Of course the roof and whiskey still both had to be repaired which took time to get it right. Next the two out houses had reached their capacities. That meant dig new deep holes and then move the buildings over the holes. And lastly the kitchen received needed upgrades, which made Matilda very happy. By the end of the first summer the Klondike was operating in top condition. Then the lake froze with open water only where springs sent up warm water. Now the problem would be how to have anyone come or go from the Klondike. Axle went across the yet open water where Nelly lived. He thought this would solve the problem by having Nelly and the wagon bring the customers from Fox Lake until he saw Nelly for the first time. Nelly was old. Nelly, in fact was very old. She was as sway back if there ever was one not fit to pull any wagon. Her back hung so low it almost touched the ground. Axel realized this option of bringing customers would never be. That winter there would be no customers so Axel and Zak took to trapping raccoons and muskrats with the traps found in the workshop. By trial and error they learned to be good at it and collected many furs that winter. They built a fur shed to work up the furs and when spring arrived they sent them to Sears and Roebuck. That company at that time bought furs as well as sold trapping supplies. The two finding trapping a good way and profitable one to use the winter bought more traps, which they would use in the future winters.

Summer came and went and soon it was 1920 and the Kansas women won. National prohibition was the law making all alcoholic beverages against the law. Axel had become good friends with his neighbors the Zingers. He bought a Model T Ford car that held six passengers, which he could leave on the Zinger farm. Now he could drive his winter guests from Fox Lake to their farm and have the guests walk the path to the Klondike. At the other times of the year when the lakes were ice-free all guests would still come by boat. Klondike was now operating on a twelve-month basis plus the men continued trapping during the winter. Old Nelly wandered off never to be seen again with all believing she peacefully went to pony heaven.

The roaring 20's was a boom to the Klondike bringing in the largest profits ever known to the resort. Having beer making and whiskey at will had tourist and business people coming to this sanctuary in droves. Axel convinced the electric company to run power on the telephone poles to make the resort modern. A city electrician came to run wires everywhere in the resort to make it light up like a Christmas tree. Now music would come by a radio and eventually a machine was bought that played records. Jazz music and booze flowed through the Klondike, a place the feds would never come. They knew nothing about the road and they would never come by boat. This was a free for zone where all had fun in the 1920's.

Zak and Matilda stayed on through the years and received good raises and bonuses for their loyalty. They even would take the train to Chicago during slow times that were few. Zak did not much care for the big city but Matilda did and always came back with another big fancy hat. She bought fancy clothes too that she wore in the kitchen so she was the best-dressed cook to be found anywhere. When the fall season would come many duck hunters came to the Klondike and Matilda would always cook their ducks to perfection. She was excellent at preparing all types of wild game and always received compliments from the hunters on her cooking.

Once during the duck hunting season a group of sports writers came to the Klondike. Matilda asked them to shoot a bunch of mud hens for her and the writers fulfilled her request but wondered why as no one ate that bird. After their first hunting day they returned with both a few ducks and mud hens. Matilda told them she needed a lot more mud hens, in fact at least twenty. The hunters wondered why the cook wanted so many of the undesirable birds but that night gave her two dozen of the birds and many ducks as well. They had great fun hunting and guessed she wanted the feathers to put on the big fancy hats that she wore. The writers thought that it was unheard of that anyone would eat mud hens.

That night Matilda served up a meal with both a large ham and meat in a gravy sauce along with other foods to complete another one of her outstanding meals. One writer asked, "The meat in the sauce is wonderful, what is it?" Matilda answered, "Why it is the birds you brought me, it is the mud hens." All the writers were amazed and finished off the dish not having any of the ham. One said, "Mud hens, huh, is there anymore?" Another asked, "Can we have some more?" Matilda said, "I'm sure of it, you have a drink while I fix you up some more for you hungry men." Matilda returned to the kitchen to learn Ida had served all the mud hens to other hunters. Matilda told Axel about the situation and he said he had a solution. He went to the fur shed and returned with muskrats he had cut up to look like mud hen parts. Matilda cooked them in her gravy sauce and served that meal to the writers. They ate the entire dish and even remarked that they were even better than the first bunch. One writer asked her how she made such a wonderful meal? Matilda said it was a secret and Axel and Ida said not a word.

THE PROFESSOR ON NATURE

It was nearly one in the afternoon as the students at the University of Moose Jaw were taking their seats. They also were visiting with each other awaiting their highly anticipated lecture. Professor Kadiddlehopper, the renowned Geopsycophysicist scientist on this day would be the guest lecturer on the subject yet unknown by the students. This was an exciting event for Dr. Kadiddlehopper was known throughout Canada as a leading scientist in the field of Earth's properties. The student's regular Professor, Dr. Mudson also was a Geopsycophysicist and with the assistance of many government grants for years was studying why rainwater produces mud. Many in academic circles considered his research to be ground breaking. Although most of his students secretly thought the huge and many grant funds he received for such a foolish study proved how government money simply goes down the drain. They also secretly called the Professor Mr. Mudwater behind his presence. Dr. Mudson would take a front row seat and also waited for the visiting lecturer to take over his class.

"Good afternoon students, I am Dr. Kadiddlehopper and it is a pleasure to present a very significant topic on this day, `eh. During my presentation today if you have any questions or wish to add your experiences please feel free to do so, `eh. If you raise your hand I will be more than happy to address you. With that said I will begin, `eh." The noted professor then took off his suit coat and loosened his bow tie to begin his lecture on nature.

"Muck, Muck, Muck is not to be confused with duck, duck, duck. If humans could fly as ducks can there would be no need to even deal with the dreaded muck, `eh. Since we are unable to fly, yet have the love and call of the great outdoors we place ourselves into the necessity of learning about muck , `eh. It does not show up at boat shows or at the early spring sport shows. For that matter it does not appear at Safari Conventions that the wealthy attend either, `eh. It seems muck has no place at those events as they are designed only as money making venues, `eh. That leaves us with the highly educated students, which you are, wondering just what is muck? How does muck apply in the great outdoors and perhaps is muck just made up you ask yourself `eh? Nope, muck is real, `eh. In fact I expect some day in the distant future NASA scientists may add it to the chemistry and element tables for all the high school students of future generations to marvel about. You the student are now putting yourself light years ahead of your time as a result of this present study. You will be "in the know" of muck, quite an achievement `eh?"

The visiting Professor next went over to a desk that was cluttered with objects. There he poured himself a glass of water or perhaps clear vodka and drank it. He began once more, "Muck is as old as the dinosaurs and Noah's Sea and that is to say it has been around for a long time. Muck as we know it is seen as the pile of the fine silt which forms on the shorelines of rivers and lakes. This fine silt forming muck may go as deep as your mother in-law is tall an even deeper `eh." With that the students laughed but were yet on the edge of their seats listening to the Professor. "Muck is not mud and should not be in any manner confused with it `eh. Now Dr. Mudson has intense important research on mud as we know." With that he addressed Dr. Mudson, "Say Doctor, I know you have been studying the effects on rainwater when it hits dirt for the past eight years, `eh. My question to you is how many years will it be prior to you learning and sharing the findings of your studies?" Dr. Mudson answered, "Well if all goes well and the grants continue we anticipate final results in approximately 12 more years. I have been approved grant money for the next four years so I pray at night the government powers that be will continue the study, `eh." Professor Kadiddlehopper then went back to the cluttered table and picked up some props. He poured some water into a large clear jar and added some dirt. "See mud is plain old dirt and water which you can make in your back yard or living room for that matter, `eh. Although, I am sure your parents would prefer you to do this difficult experiment in your backyard, `eh. Now your Professor is studying the effects of rainwater making it a much different study by all means."

"Muck is not mud as I have just made. Our good old muck takes thousands of years to form and generally is in depths that seemingly can go to China, `eh. You can say in the beginning there was muck and more muck as others say there was Adam and Eve, `eh. This known fact accounts for why someday NASA will indeed classify muck. To describe muck we must consider color, texture and smell, `eh. The color of muck ranges from a rich dark brown to an absolute coal black. The texture is just like used coffee grounds, `eh. Once any object as you included goes into it and emerges the outgoing surface will be covered with small clumps of the muck. You would be polka dotted with the gooey stuff on your skin and clothing, `eh. Not a pretty site by any means. Once again think of yourself as if you had just emerged from a bathtub of coffee grounds, `eh. Now for the smell which truly distinguishes muck from plain old mud. It can be best described as if you had just fallen into a septic tank, `eh. Therefore, once you are free of the muck you would appear as a polka dotted clown that smelled in such a way no one would care to be near you, `eh. One might find this useful to keep bill collectors away." The students chuckled at the joke and a beautiful young woman came on the stage. The professor went to the table and gathered some objects from it. "Now students my assistant Miss Peabody will aide in a demon-stration which will offer you a clearer idea regarding texture as well as odor, `eh." With this said he poured a mixture of old coffee grounds slowly down her hair and back. "As you see students how clumps form just as muck does." Next he mixed up a concoction in a 3-gallon pan with no lid on it. Soon the mixture produced an awful stench similar to sewer gas, which filled the room. "And there students we have the odor of muck, `eh." Now the odor unfortunately would fill the room for the next hour as the Professor continued on. Many of the students were very displeased with this present situation and they made comments to each other calling the noted lecturer a mad scientist or sewer man and even worse names. The young lady with the coffee grounds left the stage but the foul odor pan continued producing its vapors.

"Another feature of muck is it is much like quicksand making it very dangerous to be in. As with quicksand the more you struggle the deeper you descend, `eh. I must tell you of my experience while walking in a swamp one day when I walked right into a muck hole. It was very fortunate that only my left foot and leg was in the muck, `eh. With only one foot in and the other out I was able to free myself, `eh. My lesson was one foot in the muck okay, both feet in means it is over and I would have been terminated." At this point the stinking odor was continuing from the pan with several students leaving the lecture hall due to illness from the odor. One student finally raised his hand. "Yes, young man do you have a question?" "Yes Professor, is there any way you can neutralize this room full of stench? Several students had to leave due to getting sick from it." The Professor answered, "Oh my, I can cover the pan that will help. Why don't you all open any doors and windows to let fresh air in, `eh?" The students did just that however now the odor went through the entire building creating more problems. An English class down the hall had to evacuate due to the odor. However, at the gym the ones working out were so accustomed to BO odor they just took the new odor in stride. It did not affect them in the least.

The Professor's lecture hall did improve as he continued, "I hope that is better for you, `eh? Now back to our most important subject. As I was saying muck has the properties of quicksand, `eh." Now another student raised his hand. This lad was truly into the lecture as he was called upon. "Doctor, I sure can tell my story about muck as quicksand if I may?" The Professor advised, "Go ahead please tell us, `eh." "In the spring time as children my friends and I would go along lake shore edges spearing Carp. We would often sink up to our waists in muck as we toiled away. Wisely we always had a boat along so we could pull ourselves free into the boat and we always wore Levis and gym shoes and never boots. When we were done spearing we would go for a swim to rid us of the clumps you talked about but the smell lingered on. The next day in school the teacher always sent us home for a bath. Of course we took no bath but returned to spearing. However, on the next day of school we did wear new pants. So that is my story of nature and muck." The Professor pleased said, "Very good, does anyone else have a muck story?" Now two students raised their hands and the professor said, "Well great we have students willing to share their nature experiences, this is wonderful, `eh. Well this fellow up close to me why don't you go first?" "Thank you sir, well my experience was we would build duck blinds in bogs that included both mud and muck. We would pound wooden posts down into it and then place a platform on top of the posts. One day one of my friends fell off the platform and went ker-plunk right into the dreaded muck. He sank right past his waistline and at first we were at a loss as how to save him. One quick thinking friend had the sinking friend tie a rope around his midsection and then he took the other end and tied it to our boat. Next he reved up the outboard and at full speed ahead he yanked him out of the muck. He came out with quite a holler and stunk to high heavens. The lake water was very cold so he did not go swimming and we had to endure his smell until we reached our home shore. From that day on none of us ever saw him again as he did not go to our school. We understood he did go into the sewer business in later life. So Professor the quicksand effect and smell you have demonstrated is one that I experienced is absolutely true. I learned that in nature you want to avoid muck at all costs, it is very dangerous to be around. That's what I know." The Professor responded, "That is a very good story that I do hope all listened to, `eh. Now the fellow in the back please speak up so we will all hear you." The student in the rear now took his turn, "Well

Professor you know our national sport is of course hockey, `eh. Well as kids we had no iPhones or iPods but we had hockey. What did happen to us is a true story. One time a light snow covered thin ice where we were playing and the ice broke through. Our friend Ian went through it and down into the muck. Naturally with our hockey sticks we were able to pull Ian back onto thick ice away from the muck, 'eh. Once on the solid ice he faced the problems of the clumps on him plus the smell. It being winter there was no open lake water to rinse off with so he went home. Now the funny part, his mother would not let him into their house in such a disgusting manner, eh.' Thus he stripped down to his drawers outside and sprayed himself with the house's outside hose. Local girls happened to watch him clean his goose bumped body and they got some good laughs from the scene. Later the girls nicknamed Ian as the gooey foot and the goose bumped bunkin,'eh. His dating days were numbered." The professor now took over, "That is a funny story except for poor Ian and I'll bet he does not find it so to this day. Well students you now can understand muck is dangerous and may appear in nature were you least expect it, `eh."

"At this point why don't we take a ten minute break, eh?" With that all the students left the lecture hall to exit outside and to fresh air. The building yet had that terrible odor and only the athletes continued inside as if nothing had taken place. Aside from them and the two professors the building was void of human life. After the ten minute rest time was over only two students returned to the classroom. All the rest felt they had learned all they ever needed to know about muck for their lifetimes. That meant only two students along with the two professors remained in the lecture hall. Professor Kadiddlehopper nonetheless continued on with his muck lecture for another hour. He concluded by saying, "I sure do hope this has been a very interesting and educational talk today, `eh."

THE MUD HEN PUSHER

Each year in late September of the 1950's and '60's a unique event occurred on Grass Lake, Illinois. In fact this event only took place there in the entire United States. To begin the event there would be many local camouflaged colored boats with ten horse-powered outboards pulling eight to ten 14-foot boats behind them. This process took place for several days with the lines coming from adjoining lakes and their resorts. They appeared to be long snakes slowly swimming all headed for different and many of the Grass Lake resorts. The boats being pulled were all colors of the rainbow as bright orange, neon yellow, red, blue and all of the other colors ever made. Over one hundred of the different colored boats would be brought into the resorts once this first part of the event was completed. The logical thought was that a major fishing event was about to take place. Perhaps big fish would be attracted to neon yellow boats?

Grass Lake in size is one mile wide by two miles long and generally only eight feet in depth. The shorelines being much shallower abounded with water plants of countless types with lotus flowers providing beauty. For many decades the lake had provided food for all species of southbound migratory ducks, geese and all the other water birds. Thousands of birds on any autumn day would be seen on this lake, which had always made it a prime hunting lake. The North end of the lake had thirty duck blinds that were allocated out by state officials each August. This was a major and serious event by all the local duck hunters. The Hailing clan led by Charlie brought huge numbers of people to sign up for the drawing, which the official's conducted. Little did they know that Charlie even signed up his relatives that were permanently resided in the local cemetery. Needless to say his group always walked away with the most duck blind locations and then it was up to the location winners to build their own floating blinds at each number they had won.

The floating blinds could be very basic as just a floating box with a wooden seat. Then there were the luxury blinds designed like a Holiday Inn built by the wise old serious duck hunters. These guys were old and their blinds were their homes during October through December, so maybe their wives kicked them out of their real homes? It seemed they did live in the blinds that had heating stoves, cooking stoves, couches for naps, radios to hear the World Series and buckets to poop in. With all that they sometimes hunted ducks too. But mostly they just sat in their cozy warm chairs and played poker. If you had all that why would you go home? Then every blind had a camouflaged garage to park the hunters boat in. The rich guys even included a doghouse for Fido too.

The duck blind drawing and fishing however had nothing to do with the hundred and more of the colored boats. The opening day of the duck season would find all the boats anchored throughout the lake filled with what loosely could be called hunters. Normally hunters did everything in the world to camouflage themselves and not sit in a brightly colored boat in the middle of a lake. It was obvious that Grass Lake was unique to the hunting world with the hundreds of hunters in colored boats expecting to down a duck. The local folks had their homes filled with long lost relatives showing up to be in a colored boat as well. This was a big event having every soul in the community focused on the duck season's opener. The big event was so big that even the rural elementary school joined in. All the boys were given the school day off in order that they might go

153

shoot a duck too.

On the North side of the lake there was and yet is a saloon only reachable by watercraft. It is Blarney Island where the state officials would announce the beginning of the waterfowl season. Picture the lake dotted with hundreds of colored boats, thirty duck blinds as well as countless shoreline gunners all awaiting the signal. The Wardens would send it off all right, it was an aerial bomb that would reach the high heavens and be heard for miles around. The explosion indeed was a monstrous ear piercing ka-boom! That in turn set off hundreds of shotguns that fired for fifteen minutes nonstop at every bird in sight. The mallards and all other intelligent ducks during the first three minutes took flight a mile high and headed to nearby Lake Michigan seeking refuge. That left the poor low-flying mud hens as the targets of the multi-colored boats, duck blind hunters and shoreline shooters. There were thousands of mud hens that would endure this unbelievable flurry. After the first 15 minutes of non-stop roar the hunter's guns would still be heard shooting at the mud hens for over an hour, as it seemed the birds had no refuge. As odd as this all sounds it did in fact take place each and every year like clockwork. There were limits on the number of birds you were allowed but that was a mute point as only a very few shooters would collect any birds. Hundreds of the dead mud hens simply floated throughout the lake.

The city hunters that came and rented the orange or yellow boats came simply to shoot with no intentions of ever retrieving a bird. The same was true of the hundreds in the other colored boats as well. Perhaps in earlier years they took some mud hens home to learn all they received was a smelly kitchen with an angry wife. With such results there was no need to ever pick up a bird again and they didn't. They came for the comradeship of their buddies, shooting of their guns and to enjoy the pleasures of the many resorts. To them the countless dead mud hens could just float away. After the first opening day barrage three-fourths of the shooters simply stayed at the resorts, for the lake's big event was over. On this weekend the remaining living birds had found refuge or had left the lake for another.

The local hunters and people had a secret and that was they knew how to turn mud hens into delicious table fare. That meant my brother Lad, our friends Johnny Burke and Jerry Heywood with myself at young ages could have as many mud hens as we wished without firing a shot, but of course we did. We would give the birds to our friends and families that were excellent cooks of the birds. On opening day after our own shooting we would take our boats and motors to pick up limits on top of limits and run them home. Other locals of course did the same with the Game Wardens of that day actually approving of this practice. With hundreds of dead birds floating they felt it was better to see the birds go to honest use rather than to no use at all. On the second day we could continue running in even more birds. The wind and waves had piled up the dead birds on a shoreline with the cold water making them as fresh as the previous day. By the third day the unique one-of-a-kind event was over for one more year. The resort customers with their booming guns were gone and the long snake-like multicolored boats would be returned to the different lakes where they belonged. Worst of all the boys had to go back to school.

A week after the big 'mud hen shoot' the lake would return to its normal state. Cooler October days would have the North end blinds being used by the serious duck hunters. There would be three or four in a blind only concerned with shooting ducks and having no interest in the mud hens. They were thought of as the old hunters that sat in their heated blinds cooking and eating as if they were at a picnic. If a poor duck flew over twenty shots went off from adjoining blinds with the duck flying away. Then they would yell at each other that the others had shot out of range making it impossible for anyone to down the bird. This yelling match could be heard each and every day. About four of the floating luxury blinds bordered the State Refuge where the entrance was illegal and it seemed the ducks knew this. There they would swim in large flocks taunting the hunters. In a vain attempt to make the ducks fly several illegal attempts were made to do so. First, Fourth of July rockets and explosions would be sent to the ducks. Secondly, dumb-dumbs were made and shot at the safe ducks one hundred yards away. A dumb-dumb was when a shotgun shell was cut with a knife at the point where the lead B-Bs and the gunpowder met. When fired the front slug would travel out the gun's barrel to the ducks. Neither method seldom caused the ducks to fly more than ten yards safely yet in their refuge. But both methods were tried and tried by the old hunters who often ended up with gun barrels blown apart by the dumb-dumbs. It seemed the old hunters in their heated blinds would do anything for a duck.

Then there was the last desperate method to scare up the refuge ducks. Towards the end of the season with few or none of the Game Wardens around a hunter would pose as a fisherman to motor around the refuge and thereby put the ducks into flight. This was illegal but if stopped with only fishing poles in the boat he could say, 'I'm only a dumb fisherman.' The Game Wardens would warn him and chase him out which scared up more ducks. With the mission accomplished he would go from 'fishermen' to be known as a 'Grass Lake Outlaw.' It seemed everyone in the thirty blinds was one or would become one during the season. There never was a lack of volunteer "fishermen." Now I know about all of these "hooligans" that went on, as I am a Grass Lake Mud Hen Pusher through and through. Of course I never did anything illegal, well maybe a little but I never was a real Grass Lake Outlaw. I think I was too young in acquiring such a treasured title. I sure viewed all the other hunters blowing their barrels up, shooting Fourth of July rockets and then posing as fishermen in a war zone. They would go to any lengths for a green-headed Drake Mallard! But mud hens had lost the interest of their gunpowder.

With each week passing more and more newer northern mud hens would come to the lake. They would swim in large groups throughout the main lake and since no one ever saw the flocks arrive it was assumed they arrived during the nights. This situation created a new type of hunter, that being the 'Grass Lake Mud Hen Pusher.' To be one was a badge of honor and you would be one of a very few for life. The pusher was young and healthy as the old hunters could only sit in their heated blinds. Being a pusher was way too much work for them as the pusher was in an oar-powered boat that would chase the swimming birds around the lake. The mud hens wanted to swim and stay in the safety of the lakes center out of guns range but the pusher had different ideas and plans for the birds. He had to corral a flock and make them swim into a shoreline in order to force them into flight. Once flying at their low levels shooting would bring some down. This process of shoreline pushing could go on throughout the entire day making the boat rowing only for the young and determined. Often the low swimming ruddy ducks would be with the mud hen flocks. This turned the pusher's attention solely on the duck that had the ability to dive and swim great distances away. Even if in range nine of ten shots simply did no good in obtaining the duck. Somehow his low profile protected him making it great efforts to down him. With his unbelievable diving abilities it was next to impossible to make him fly but the skilled pusher once in a while did force him into a shoreline and flight. To down a duck was a great prize for the pusher that then returned to the mud hen pushing.

To be a mud hen pusher had its dangers and my older brother, Arlad and I tested them all. Our duck boat was a Mississippi River one that was only eight foot long, forty inches wide with a depth of only twelve inches. In this small low profile craft was even a smaller cockpit. The hunter would sit on the floor in an open area of only three feet by four feet. Needless to say the design was for one hunter only which meant somehow both my brother and I would dangerously cram ourselves into the tiny cockpit. Since he was the oldest he always took the forward position to be the shooter and I always had the work of rowing him around the lake. Throughout life in any and all activities this exact scenario took place with me doing the work. Obviously that explains why he became an attorney. Yes, his real name is Arlad, which our parents came up with in 1943 by thinking 'our boy' equals Arlad. Well just think if he had been born a girl? Would it have been Arlady or Argail? Then they give me the common name of John. Sure glad I wasn't Arjon. Anyways, we had no business of having two in the boat made for one. This resulted in ice-cold water coming over the sides proving our dedications as true pushers. Even alone in the boat danger could lurk when the wind and waves were at seemingly gale forces. In November when the temperatures were below freezing being out in large waves was not a good idea but never deterred me, the 'real' mud hen pusher. The waves would splash on the boat's deck to freeze and create an ice coating, which added weight to the boat. That in turn made the low-profile boat even lower in the water. More than once this scenario sunk the boat in the icy waters. The solution was to swim to shore and await the boat, ever so slowly coming into the shore with the waves pushing it in. Then some how knock the sheet of ice off and bail the water out as you were shivering near death. All of this for a few mud hens! Of course you did it all again and again. One time I was alone in four feet surf like waves that resulted in flipping the boat over which in turn resulted in swimming to shore once more. How we survived the dangers must have been our lucky stars or an angel must have been with us while we were doing these stupid acts. We called this thrilling. To be a mud hen pusher did develop certain qualities that would guide us through life giving us courage to accomplish any and all of our life's goals it must be said.

While in high school during one opening day we enlisted three friends to help skin over one hundred mud hens we had gathered up. We were skinning the birds until very late into the night when the friends quit leaving Lad and I to finish the job. We then stretched them and put borax on them which preserved the birds. My brother traded the original Herters of Waseca, Minnesota the skins for their best mallard decoys. They would sell the skins to fishermen for flies they would tie and we would go hunt ducks. We also learned the art of taxidermy while in high school to mount every bird and animal available to us. The Racine, Wisconsin zoo gave us a deceased monkey, which we mounted in a hanging position and then gave it to Charlie Hailing for his barroom. We would always be pushers but I must admit the day did come when we too would join Charlie and the wise old men that sat in their cozy warm blinds.

As life went on I was living in Northern California and hunted pintails in a friend's blind. In his rice field blind we sat and waited for the ducks, which I found boring at best. Next I lived in central Minnesota and had one of the 10,000 lakes as my very own to hunt. My wife and I ate mallards, sweet corn and wild rice as often as we wished. In that I had no hunting competition there were no challenges involved compared to the Grass Lake days. I got thinking, which is dangerous by itself. When I was young I often heard the old-timers talking about their live caller ducks. Sure enough, I purchased a pair of English Callers to try the present day illegal method out. Mind you I was only testing history out as an experiment and certainly meant no wrong. On the other hand I wouldn't mention any of this experiment to the local Game Wardens. They might have foolishly mistaken me as a Grass Lake Outlaw. In my "history" lesson I anchored the callers just beyond my decoy spread and awaited their quacks. Once the wild mallards filled the sky my tame ducks made no quacks, not even one. After an hour or so no quacks, which made me think the ducks must be in a conspiracy or the old-timers stories had no truths. There I was breaking the law solely to test history and I must have purchased the stupidest ducks on the planet. Then the wind kicked up and the tame ducks began flapping their wings that did attract the wild ducks. By pure chance I happen to have my Browning along so more mallards we would eat. It seemed testing history with a modern-day 12 gauge worked out pretty good. That was a one-day event and I next gave the caller flapper ducks away.

To prove I was not always an outlaw in later life my father and I were hunting ducks on Sterling Reservoir in Colorado. A storm came up bringing forty mile per hour winds and my father wisely advised we head for home and call it a day. I took him to shore and then saw my golden opportunity to be a pusher once more in life. I went back out in the surf where a flock of Canadian geese were bobbing up and down in the large waves. It ended up that they let me within ten yards of them and they kept swimming rather than taking flight. I never fired a shot to return back on shore where my father was watching the event. He questioned me of course and I explained that it was just too easy and I felt sorry for the geese. He in turn felt sorry for me thinking I had my lights on with nobody home. However, in following years we did shoot many geese together in Colorado.

Once a pusher always a pusher. During the 1980's I had a beautiful Sandhill's, Nebraska lake leased for hunting and needed to push the governmental system to take full advantage of the situation. The first year of the lake's lease I was eligible for unemployment benefits and decided to dedicate my life exclusively to duck hunting. The government naturally required that I applied for employment opportunities in compliance with receiving my unemployment checks. I did so by applying to the required number of applications per week in one of the finest styles possible. Each week on Sunday I would hap hazard tear off three used pieces of brown grocery bag, preferably with a few grease stains. Then I would write my plain requests for a job clearly legible in red crayon and stuff my correspondence into their respective envelopes to be mailed on Monday. During my previous employment I had been a College Instructor, which meant I sent off the somewhat unprofessional requests to Yale, Harvard and MIT. I figured they must be uppity up as I never obtained a job or a response but did accomplish my true goal of hunting ducks. I would highly recommend that everyone owes it to himself to take a fall and do much the same.

My wife kept track of the statistics that fall, as I was covered in feathers. The season opened on October 6th and ended on December 18th that year. She presented me with the fact that during that time I had only missed five days of hunting and that was due to traveling to the North Platte airport to pick up or leave off guest hunters. Another statistic to her disdain was we had only been without hunting guests ten days of that total time resulting in an abundance of extra cooking and cleaning on her part. Finally, she presented the fact we had eaten 350 ducks that season. I concluded it was indeed a very good year!

Our favorite guest that autumn was my then 80-year-old father. He joined me to hunt in our luxury blind made for old men just like the ones back at Grass Lake. It seems age and wisdom was catching up with me, as blinds were no longer boring. The spectacular number of ducks in our area brought my father to remark that it was just like hunting back in the 1920's and '30's. One particular windy day a large flock of mud hens formed a reef in the lake's center. I positioned my father in the front seat and rowed out towards the birds. Once more I was doing the work and then it dawned on me that my brother must have learned that I should always do the rowing directly from our father. All kidding aside my father did the shooting once the mud hens took flight until he had downed enough for one of his most favorite meals. That was my father's last hunt and on that day we proved once a Grass Lake Mud Hen Pusher one was just that forever.

Finally regardless of where I hunt on any opening day of the duck season in my mind I always hear that gigantic Ka-boom of my youth!

THE VOTE ON NATURE

Our magazine "Happy Outdoors," is dedicated to bringing our readers current vital information, which will affect nature's future. In our recent issues we have brought forth both the Democrat and Republican views that seem to be identical regarding nature's future. In this issue we have interviewed Mr. Harry Lonesum, the third-party Freedom Party candidate, with platform ideas unlike any others. All three candidates are seeking the office of the Presidency, which will have a huge impact on America's outdoors presently and into the future. Happy Outdoors' Chief Editor, Edgar Penwright conducted the following interview with Mr. Lonesum three weeks ago at the neutral site of the Lazy Tie Me Down Motel in Albany, New York.

Mr. Lonesum's ideas and positions have been labeled as far, far left wing being radical and extreme. Both politicians and the press along with especially his opponents are delighted to see such a label given to him. The media also questioned Mr. Lonesum's qualifications to be President in that he has been an animal control officer throughout his life. The fact his family owns Raw Meat Dog Food Incorporated does give him unlimited funds to operate his campaign. With his family's immense fortune backing him it is refreshing to see a campaign putting up a candidate that is not always politically correct. Like it or not, Mr. Lonesum was straightforward in answering our questions. We wish to advise the reader even though many of Mr. Lonesum's positions may seem distasteful to some of our readers, we highly recommend you read the entire interview.

Please note: This publication in no manner supports or endorses any candidate for any office. The following views do not reflect any of "Happy Outdoors" policies and are only offered for the reader's consideration.

Editor: Mr. Lonesum, you are running for the office of the President in the Freedom Party. Automatically, the questions arise as to why you are running and what does the Freedom Party stand for?

Lonesum: First, I am running for the office to give Americans a real choice. The other two parties are really one. They offer the same solutions to all the problems facing America today. The Freedom Party is the only one that will give Americans the truth in all matters, no more lies. In the past I have voted for both parties based upon what they said they would do and once elected they did just the opposite. Their moral actions were disgraceful once they had secured the office. Nixon with Watergate, Reagan on the Contras, both Bushes on wars and on the other side Kennedy with women, Johnson on Vietnam, Clinton who had no sex but unloaded his Willy Wacker in a girl's mouth and Obama both on wars and taking our personal information. You can see both parties do not have a very good record.

Editor: Has there been any honest Presidents?

Lonesum: Yes, both Ford and Carter. Since they were honest they only served one term. They were good Presidents however the American public could not deal with the truth so did not re-elect them.

Editor: We are an outdoor magazine and it is known you have strong views on the outdoors. What would you like our readers to know on them?

Lonesum: I am a big ASS.

Editor: That sure is an odd answer. Will your bumper stickers read, "Vote for a Big ASS," or, "Put a BIG ASS in the White House?"

Lonesum: I'm a proud Big ASS. That stands for Association to Save the Sparrows. I belong to as many animal rights organizations that I can. I have many friends in all those organizations and support Green Peace, PETA, and the Friends of Animals, just to name a few. My favorite is ASS.

Editor: What about Ducks Unlimited and Pheasants Forever?

Lonesum: No, they are only manufacturing birds so they have more to murder. I support only associations that help species live in freedom, hence our party's name.

Editor: Okay, what is your position on guns?

Lonesum: I believe every American over the age of eighteen should have all the guns they want. The only exceptions would be the mentally ill and felons. Others should have whatever they want with no paperwork. When the militias went against the British all had guns of equal power and that is the way it should be today. The common man took up arms back then, as then there were no Armed Forces or government armies. They formed militias to over throw the British with basic weapons of that day. Today the homeowner should be allowed to have every weapon made including tanks and jets with nuclear bombs. With that position how can anyone be called a radical? Look, the Forefathers wrote the Second Amendment for the common man to own weapons of his choice. Again, back then in history all guns were equal. Today the government has the military and all of its firepower on its side. If the American public ever had a rebellion what good would it do? None. That is because the common guy cannot go up against the military with just his deer rifle. To make all things equal the common man should have nukes too.

Editor: Most people would be afraid if their neighbors had nuclear weapons. You said age eighteen, what about the little boy that gets a BB gun for his birthday?

Lonesum: No more BB guns period.

Editor: You're saying no BB guns but it is okay to have nukes?

Lonesum: Yes, that is right. You could not own a bomb until you're 18 or older. At age 18 you are responsible based upon the fact that you can have a drivers license and drive a car. Look at the number of people that die in cars, now that is a real weapon. No BB guns as they are given to kids and what do they do with them? They go out and kill songbirds and sparrows with no regard for life.

Editor: You seem to have a high regard for birds.

Lonesum: Yes, and the public over all has very little. Look at the common phrases used today? People say, "He doesn't have his ducks in a row," When they should be saying there is something mentally wrong with that fellow. Or they say, "He's a dead duck," which means he has been eliminated from something. Another is they say the guy is, "cuckoo" which again means a mental problem. Then there is the "lame duck" President. Why don't they speak the truth and say he's without power? The public made extinct both the Passenger Pigeon and the Great Auk to name just two of many. They could easily do the same to the Sparrow and other birds. That is why at ASS we have to stand up for Sparrows and all birds.

Editor: Are you saying all birds ?

Lonesum: Yes, because hunting is not fair. The hunter has a gun, which kills and the birds have no guns. That is not equal.

Editor: Now we understand your position on birds. What about animals?

Lonesum: Same thing, no more killing of any animals until they are taught to shoot guns back at the hunters. Of course that will not happen. People can shoot at targets or better yet make it legal that they can shoot at each other. That is the ones that find it necessary to go out and kill animals.

Editor: That seems like a radical idea.

Lonesum: I think not, in fact it seems logical to me. If hunters were allowed to hunt and shoot each other it would be a fair situation. It seems mankind has always liked wars.

Editor: What about animal over population and all the deer hit on the roads each year? Wouldn't you be afraid of the animals gaining numbers in turn causing more accidents?

Lonesum: Good question. Nature always has and always will have a balance. It is called, "the balance of nature" as a matter of fact. We as humans do not need to murder our birds and animals. The caveman did to continue living, but today that is not the case.

Editor: Well then what about farm production animals and birds such as the Thanksgiving turkey so many enjoy?

Lonesum: That is fine as those animals and birds are raised with a specific goal in mind. They were never free. I eat McDonald's hamburgers from a cow that never knew freedom.

Editor: What about fish?

Lonesum: If we farm fish I have no problem with it. The natural fish we should just leave alone. How would you like it if someone threw hooks into your mouth and dragged you up on a beach or into a boat? China and Asia are raising most of the fish in the grocery stores so we need to build more fish farms. Sport fishing and commercial netting will be illegal once I am the President.

Editor: The fact is billions of dollars, are spent each year by outdoors people. That must mean millions of people are hunting and fishing.

Your positions will eliminate all hunting and fishing so why would any sportsman vote for you?

Lonesum: Most won't, but to equal that out I'll get the vegetarian vote as well as the sensitive peoples' vote. Perhaps, just perhaps, I might not win this election but I sure am going to get the public to think.

Editor: I know that your family owns a huge corporation where you could have held an office position but your career was that of a dog catcher. Why is that? Can you explain how does being a dog catcher prepare you towards holding the highest office in our land?

Lonesum: I highly object to your portrayal. I am an animal control officer not a dog catcher. My career has centered on saving both domestic and wildlife animals, and this fact must be emphasized. Sure, I could've had a cushy desk job in my family's corporation but all the world's money is not equal to saving one brown Sparrow. I made that decision early in my life and stand by it to this day. Think about it? Money is only paper whereas I went out and saved beating hearts. Money is nothing more than filthy paper held by thousands of dirty hands with different numbers printed on it. The American public will certainly see the merits of my ASS efforts, I am convinced. I have held the office of Executive Director of ASS and at times belonged to my local PTA. Those experiences dwarf the Presidency that will translate into votes for me by all fair-minded people.

Editor: Are you saying being on the PTA is equal to the highest office in our land?

Lonesum: Certainly. In the PTA you agree and disagree with your neighbors to reach compromises in order to have your local school function. As the President you have the power of executive orders and need not answer or compromise with anyone. Since World War ll our Presidents have started wars on their whims or better yet as paybacks to the oil industry's demands. The PTA does not work like that and everyone knows it. In my case I do not need any outside money as my family's fortunes are supporting me. Therefore no one or no corporation can buy me off. Running this country is a piece of cake.

Editor: I am finding many of your solutions simple in a complex world. Do you think this is true?

Lonesum: Those that hold the power makes the rules. The Freedom Party lays out the rules pure and simple. The American people will respect and vote for our world rules and views.

Editor: You have made your hunting and fishing positions clear. Now what about the nature lover that enjoys hiking in the wilds hurting nothing?

Lonesum: Are you kidding, hurting nothing? Do you realize how much damage that is done to rocks and trees by this group? They totally change the organization of nature. Their big flat feet crush all they step on which in turn changes insect life. Bugs that live on the ground are in fact food for birds. How would you like it if some giant took your food away? Then hikers seemingly always have to take a tree's branch for unknown reasons. In doing so they potentially take away the exact spot that a bird was going to make a nest at. Anyone can see these reasons alone should stop all hiking.

Editor: Your position is clear. It seems then we should close all State and National Parks.

Lonesum: Oh no, I don't want people to lose their jobs there. The existing roads there may stay just not the hiking trails. People can hike on the dirt and paved roads. Birdwatchers can view them with binoculars from the road locations. Animals as well can be seen from the roads. Most Americans never get out of their cars in the parks anyways. So any logical and rational person can see why the hiking trails have to go.

Editor: Well back to the fishermen and hunters. Since they will not be doing their sports anymore what will they do with their time as you see it?

Lonesum: It seems the answer is that we need to start more wars so they have some entertainment amongst themselves. They could have fun killing each other I would think. As for the fisherman I don't know. Maybe they all could take up stamp collecting?

Editor: If we all have nukes wouldn't you be afraid they would get into the wrong hands? The entire world could be in a disastrous situation it seems to me. Have you thought that idea out in full?

Lonesum: Yes I have. Already some twenty countries already have them with more to come. That is why we should all have them. If North Korea sends one over to us you can bet our government would chicken out and not send one back. The government of ours would say, "Oh diplomacy will solve the problem," as Los Angeles burns down to the ground. Thankfully a true Freedom Party member in Arizona would say, "nuts to that" and surely stand up and give North Korea one back. Then no more North Korea and the problem will be solved.

Editor: It seems now that our readers have clear views on your positions. Thank you for this interview.

Lonesum: Thank you for giving me this interview and allowing me to point out I will never lie to the American public. God bless America.

Post script: Two months later — Mr. Harry Lonesum did not win the election.

THE DREAM VACATION

"It's midnight in the Rockies. Time for the Jack Pine show on KSTPEE, broadcasting coast to coast and I am Jack Pine. Tonight the topic is UFOs so please call in with your observations, truths, experiences and concerns. While we wait for our first caller a word from our sponsor."

Aunt Phil's Bees Wax is the product every home should have. It will lubricate your sticky drawers and windows to cleaning out any and all stubborn stains. Made with all natural ingredients with no added chemicals, buy Aunt Phil's Bees Wax at your local grocery store. You'll be glad you did.

"This is Jack Pine on KSTPEE, go ahead."

"Yeah Jack, this is Harry from Iowa and out here we see lots of UFOs in our vast and dark skies. My question is why does the government keep covering up all the UFO sightings? What are they afraid of?"

"That's a good question Harry, perhaps our listeners have some answers? Our next caller, you're on the air."

"This is Bill from California and Jack I think the whole UFO subject is nothing but a bunch of bunk. If there was any truth to it where is just one spaceship or one little green man? It is imagination by a bunch of loonies, yes just ka-hului. There are no UFOs."

"Boy that caller has some strong opinions on the subject. He said there are no UFOs. What does our next caller think about that? Hello this is Jack Pine you're on the air with KSTPEE radio, coast to coast."

"Thanks Jack, the Bible says that God made the heavens and the earth. So God made all and if he wanted other people on other planets millions and millions of miles away then life could be there as he made us. If he did then certainly those people could come to earth. It really is all up to God."

"Well there's an opinion. Say folks have you put in for our Dream Vacation contest? You could win a ten-day Caribbean luxury cruise. To enter just send in a post card with your name and phone number to Dream Vacation, PO Box 100, Four Forks, Colorado, 80601. Say listeners only ten days remaining before the drawing so get your cards in soon. Do it today. More about the Dream Vacation later, now let's go back to our callers. You're on KSTPEE, go ahead."

"Yeah Jack, I'm Nick from Wisconsin and I was abducted by a UFO and taken into space. I recall them examining me. They were four feet high and gray in color. I don't know how long I was captured but there was one that gave the commands, as three of them looked me over. They returned me to my own backyard and I've had no after effects. Your caller that said we are loonies and there are no UFOs, well I hope someday he gets abducted that would change his mind."

"Wow, so spacemen took you to their ship. What was the ship

like?"

"It was a round disc with lots of colored lights. It flew at unknown fast speeds but inside it didn't even feel like you were moving. The inside had chairs or seats, windows, countless gauges and controls. I was strapped down to a table and that is what I could see. They examined me with a wand and took blood from me. Yes it was real and it did happen."

"Well let's think about that. Give us a call as we hear from a sponsor."

Did you wake up tired and jittery? Then you need a cup of Springer coffee to get your day going and to have a good one each and every day. Springer coffee is the one from the Columbian hills with special beans. It will get you going so try Springer coffee soon.

"Good evening to you all this is Jack Pine on KSTPEE broadcasting coast to coast. Right now I am having some Springer coffee and boy is it good. Before we get back to our callers I want to tell you about the Dream Vacation our station and sponsors are giving away in ten short days. We will select twenty lucky winners to join on a fabulous ten day cruise on the Caribbean with stops at many of the friendly islands. All you have to do is send in a post card with your name and phone number. The winners will be drawn and announced on my show Friday, November Thirteenth. The Dream Vacation cruise leaves December twenty eighth offering a gala New Year's Eve party aboard the ship. Wouldn't this be a great Christmas present to give yourself? The ship Heavenly Wave departs from Miami and you could be a winner. Get your cards in today. Now back to our callers. This is Jack Pine you are on the air."

"Jack, I think the IRS is ripping us all off. The new President said we were going to have a flat tax and all we got is the same 112 pages of tax laws. Only the big guys make out again."

"Well caller tonight the subject is UFOs and maybe on another night we will take up the IRS. So folks let's stick to UFOs tonight go ahead next caller."

"Jack this is John from Wyoming and I am a firm believer in UFOs but find it a stretch that anyone has been abducted by one. Maybe your last UFO caller was on too much whiskey and I do think our government hides the truth from us on UFOs. Even in Arizona the Governor saw UFOs and all the pictures of them proves they are real. Why the government hides the facts I don't know."

"This is Jack Pine on KSTPEE helping your night along. We sure have a lively discussion tonight on UFOs with lots of opinions. Call with yours at 818-050 -7676 and add to the discussion."

"Geese laweeze, hi Jack this is Louie from Delaware and I saw UFOs when I was in the Army. At nights in Vietnam we saw many that flew in an erratic motion that no planes could ever fly. Then a few years later my friends and I saw UFOs while in the Colorado Desert, I guess you call it the Plains. At night we would watch them go zigzag in the sky. Geese laweeze nobody will ever tell me there are no UFOs, I saw them."

"I'm Jack Pine and you're on the air."

"Hello Jack, my name is George Lonesum and I am a scientist with NASA when I'm not on my regular job as an animal control officer. In our research we have found many credible events of UFOs and have documented all of them. Under the Federal Information Freedom Act this information is available to all, so you can look it up. All our research was passed on to the Federal Intelligence Agents but they did nothing with it. It seems the government wants not a word of it to be studied or talked about. My conclusion is that UFOs have technology and weapons that all the world governments want. Therefore none of them say a word about them."

"Interesting George and one more caller before the break. Go ahead you're on KSTPEE."

"Thanks Jack, I'm Billy Bob from Alabama and I agree with your caller that said there are no UFOs. It's a hoax. We have no proof. It's just a bunch of maybes. Until I see proof its all about the hound that never caught a rabbit. That's what I think."

"Okay, more doubt on the subject. Now a few words from Soft Soap."

If you want the best we have the best and that is Soft Soap. The soap that will clean your body, your clothes, your car and everything you own. This is the space age miracle soap that does it all. Soft Soap is available in bar or liquid form at your local grocery store. Use it once and you will use it forever.

"It's getting into the early morning and you're on KSTPEE broadcasting coast to coast. I'm Jack Pine and glad you are with us. The topic tonight is UFOs and I hope you share your thoughts. Boy, tonight we have heard from one that was abducted to several that say they don't exist. Quite a range, so add to our conversation. With Christmas several weeks away I bet Santa will ride a UFO and remember the Dream Vacation starts on December 28th. The winners will be announced on this show on Friday, November thirteenth, so get your cards in today. This cruise offers a lot of fun, as you will live like kings and queens. I am ready for a caller, go ahead."

"Good morning Jack, my name is James from New York City and of course in the big city with all our lights we cannot ever see a star. But last summer on vacation in South Dakota we saw a billion stars. We viewed moving lights. I don't know if they were UFOs or satellites from earth? My question is how would anyone know the difference?"

"Good question James, I'm sure one of our listeners will help you out on that question. Next caller, go ahead you're on KSTPEE."

"Yes Jack, I am Hillary and I live on top of the Rockies in Montana. In the warm summer nights we view plenty of UFOs right from our yard. For the life of me I don't understand why our government goes to great lengths to not admit their existence. It just does not add up but I figure some day a hunter will shoot one of the

Martians and then the cat will be out of the bag. Do you think so Jack?"

"Maybe a caller will add to that. Now a word from Aunt Phil's Bees Wax the, wonder soap."

Aunt Phil's Bees Wax is the one to buy. It will fix windows that stick and clean stubborn stains off of any surface. Do yourself a favor today and buy some Aunt Phil's Bees Wax. You'll be glad you did.

"Well folks this is Jack Pine on KSTPEE radio closing for another night. Stay tuned for easy music with the Carl Banning program later today. Enjoy the music and may your day be a fine one."

With that sign off KSTPEE played easy music nonstop outside of the sponsor's ads until 6 AM when the Carl Banning program took to the air. Jack Pine would go back on the radio at midnight while all the other programs promoted the Dream Vacation to their listeners all day. The ten-day cruise was on the Heavenly Wave that was a World War II battleship converted into a not so much luxury liner. By all outside appearances it did look like a luxury liner with a paint job of white and aqua blue. Only inside the ship would voyagers learn the design remained as the sailors had it so many years ago. As examples there were no beds or private rooms. The sailors hanging bunks remained with sleeping in one large open room. These facts were not advertised and only once aboard would the cruise goers learn they were on a battleship with few design changes. The radio station was not aware of the primitive situation and booked on the Heavenly Wave only because it was the cheapest rate available. The ship appeared great to the station manager but he never went inside of it. The guns and other war functions were removed which did make it appear like one very large luxury liner. The truths would come once aboard and inside the ship. The nights and days continued with the Jack Pine program entertaining his listeners. Finally, November 13th arrived which was the night twenty fortunate listeners would learn they were the lucky ones to travel the Caribbean. Yes, they would be on the Heavenly Wave.

"Good evening and good night to our listeners on the East Coast.

This is Jack Pine on KSTPEE broadcasting coast to coast. Tonight is a special one on my program. Tonight is the one when twenty lucky people will be selected to go on the Heavenly Wave for the ten day Dream Vacation cruise. This Caribbean cruise will include a gala New Years Eve party to bring in your New Year in style. I will draw twenty post cards and you will be contacted by phone to learn the specifics of obtaining your tickets. If for any reason someone cannot go then a new card will be drawn. A representative of G and G Agency is with me tonight to verify the drawing fairness. His name is Forest Treeless and here is a word from him, Go ahead Forest."

"Hi folks, I am Forest Treeless and I am present to ensure the drawing is conducted in a fair manner. I represent the Good and Gracious Verifying agency with all our information available on the Internet. Tonight I will be drawing the lucky twenty post cards. I wish you all good luck."

"Thanks Forrest and our first winner is Captain Blackout from Greenland. Wow! A Captain from a cold country, he sure will enjoy the warm Caribbean. The Captain as well as all winners will be notified by phone as soon as possible. Here's a word from one of the great sponsors supporting the Dream Vacation cruise."

Folks have you used Aunt Phil's Bees Wax lately? If so you know what a wonderful cleaning product it is and I hope you have told your neighbors and friends all about it. Once you use it you will use it over and over for your lifetime. This is a promise. So tell your friends about Aunt Phil's Bees Wax. Buy some today and you'll be glad you did.

"This is Jack Pine and folks I do hope you support all the wonderful products our sponsors offer you. They are making the Dream Vacation possible along with our radio station. Okay, our second winner is Donny Hichcock from Rapid City, South Dakota and our next winner is Oly Nottestead from Three Rivers, Minnesota. Oly, is another winner from the cold country so I know he will love the Caribbean Sea. Time for one more winner before another supporting sponsor. That is Louise Dogman from Eau Claire, Wisconsin. Another winner from where the cold winter winds blow. So far our winners are from the north and they all will love the palm trees I am sure of that. Now a short word from Springer coffee."

Have you enjoyed a morning with a cup of Springer coffee? Then you know Springer does make you spring into life and makes your day a wonderful one. The flavor and aroma is the best possible just like those expensive designer ones only Springer comes with half the price. Now you can enjoy premium coffee anytime of day, that is Springer coffee indeed.

"This is Jack Pine and right now Forrest and I are enjoying a cup of Springer and it is great. Now for our next winner, who is Charles Seaman from Corpus Christi, Texas. At last we have a winner from the south. Charles will know winter's warmth I'm sure. Tonight we have many winners to select, so hold your calls for tomorrow night when the topic will be gay marriage. I'm sure that topic will have various views but tonight let's get back to finding out who goes on the Dream Vacation. Next is Elmer Hile from Hastings, Nebraska and our next winner is Jimmy Tiedown from Tulsa, Oklahoma. Forest we are moving right along. Next is Mary Ellen Shunneson from Taylor, Nebraska. Look at that, two winners from the same state. This is Jack Pine on KSTPEE and tonight we are drawing your postcards for the Dream Vacation. If you are just tuning in the Heavenly Wave cruise ship lifts anchor on December 28th for the fabulous Caribbean ten day cruise. Our next winner is Bill Hayling from Grass Lake, Illinois. Congratulations Bill and next is Louie Water from Rehoboth, Delaware. Wow! The last two winners are from water regions but the Caribbean sure will be warmer for them. Now another sponsor, making the Dream Vacation possible."

Say folks do you have trouble with your kids eating their vegetables? Your answer is here with Carrot Loops the cereal that kids love. The sweet taste is loaded with different vegetables packed with vitamins and essentials to make your children strong and healthy. The peas, beans, carrots, onions, tomatoes, garlic, celery and other vegetables along with lots of sugar will start your children off the right way every day. Good for adults too and remember this is the only cereal loaded with sugar. The whole family will love Carrot

Loops. So buy some today.

"This is Jack Pine on KSPTEE broadcasting coast to coast. We always bring you the best in easy music and talk radio. Tonight we are drawing for the lucky twenty people that will go on the Dream Vacation cruise leaving Miami, Florida on December 28th. Now let's pick another lucky winner and that is Harry Sharpshot from Ord, Nebraska. The Nebraska entries sure are lucky tonight and I think there's two or three from Nebraska all ready. Okay next is Slim Obeesitsy from Ogden, Utah. Slim knows about a salty sea and now he goes on a bigger and warmer one I am sure. Now our twelfth winner is Harry Lonesum from Two Points, New York. If my memory is correct I believe Mr. Lonesum ran for President in the last election. My guess is he will bring some politics to the cruise but I hope not too much. Our next winner is Opry Patchworth of Big Springs, Arkansas. Congratulations Opry. Our next ocean voyager is Bob Arneson of Davis, California. Bob is on or near the Pacific so I hope he brings a surfboard to use on the Caribbean. One more winner before a word from another cruise sponsor and that is Dr. Mudson from Moose Jaw, Alberta, Canada. That's great a Canadian listener and a Doctor at that. Now a word from our sponsor."

We have all you want and need. That is, Full Foods Grocery stores with one near you. Full Foods is what our name says. We have it all. Visit a Full Foods store today to have our friendly staff help you have it all. Once in our store you will fill out your list and find many specials you will love to take home. Let us provide you with all your Thanksgiving needs.

"This is Jack Pine with Forest Treeless drawing out the Dream Vacation winners tonight. We already are at number sixteen so let's learn who that is? It is Helen Campbell from Wall, South Dakota. Congratulations to you Helen. Our next winner is Tommy Lucky from Reno, Nevada. Well Mr. Lucky is lucky tonight. Now number nineteen is Johnny Burke of Boulder, Colorado. At last we have a winner from our state. Glad to see that and now our final winner. But first a word from our sponsor that is providing a surprise to this winner. Stay tuned to KSTPEE to see if you are the lucky winner?"

Soft Soap is the one for you and now available in the traditional bar or in the new liquid bottle style. Soft Soap cleans you and everything in your life. Our natural ingredients are as soft on your body as any soap can be. Plus it is so soft you may use it on your baby. We guarantee you will find none to compare. So buy some today to clean your world. You'll be happy you did!

"This is Jack Pine on KSTPEE, the radio station you love. Well folks we are at number twenty, the last lucky number of the Dream Vacation cruise. Our sponsor, Soft Soap is giving away a bonus prize to this winner. That is one thousand dollars in cash. Now won't that be nice to go traveling with? So Forest who is the lucky voyager? It is Perry Thomas from Thommivile, Indiana. Congratulations Perry, you have one Lucky Star tonight giving you the voyage plus one thousand dollars. Well my time is up for this evening and I want to thank Forest for doing the drawing tonight. Stay tuned to KSTPEE for easy music and then the Carl Banning program coming up soon. This is Jack Pine saying good night and good morning to you all from the Rockies. Have a fine day."

With that the twenty listeners were selected and would be notified by the telephone number they had put on their card. It was learned all twenty were able and willing to go so no other cards needed to be drawn. Thanksgiving and Christmas would come and go with December 28th the day all would arrive at the Florida dock. They would board the Heavenly Wave along with eight hundred and fifty other paying passengers to take the Caribbean cruise. This low number of passengers on a ship that could hold thousands must have meant the word was out regarding the Heavenly Wave. Only the unexpected would book on an old battleship that appeared to be a luxury liner. There were no other ten-day cruises at the low rate offered on this ship. The Heavenly Wave must have earned its reputation from all honest travel agents with only the crooked ones signing up newcomers to a World War II battleship. KSTPEE listeners would be newcomers.

The passengers all started to board the Heavenly Wave at 9 AM and were instructed to gather on the main deck. Folding chairs and Springer coffee was available to the crowd as excitement filled the air.

However the coffee costs three dollars and twenty-five cents per cup with no free refills. The ship had a crew of fifty but none of them could to be found to help in any manner. Older passengers had a difficult time with their luggage and it was only the younger passengers that helped them. Louie had a large black trunk that he hauled aboard dragging it most of the way. He went right past the sign that read, "No Animals Beyond This Point" and he hoped his contents would not bark. Of course the literature he had received weeks earlier told him the same but somehow he didn't read that part. He struggled up to the main deck with the huge black trunk and sat in the last row of the folding chairs. There was another older lady with a huge black hat that brought on board a box with air holes in it. Then another couple had what appeared to be a birdcage but all thought the seagulls certainly were singing a nice tune today. Or maybe it was the pelicans of Florida that sounded like canaries? This all meant Louie was not alone in a small infraction plus the sign did read animals not birds.

Finally after an hour or so all the passengers gathered on the top main deck with the ship's horns blowing. The horns had the familiar sounds of a World War II Battle Station cry. They did not sound at all like the other luxury liner ships, which was for certain to all. In fact some retired Navy men looked around to take their old battle stations. Luckily the stations and guns were removed or perhaps a war might have started right then and there. The sounds did mean they were out to sea moving away from the docks. The happy passengers were on their way to their Dream Vacation headed for the Caribbean Sea. It was a pleasant sunny day with the Atlantic calm as the ship picked up speed and the Captain took center stage. He spoke into microphones that transmitted to large speakers positioned so all could hear. "Welcome aboard the Heavenly Wave. I'm Captain Alfred E. Newman and my first mate is Otto Leakman. He is now at the wheel so we are in safe hands as I address you today. First, I hope you know you are on the most unique cruise ship in the world? The Heavenly Wave is actually a vintage World War II battleship converted into the most modern luxury liner possible (a lie). We have maintained certain features that the sailors of seventy-five years ago lived by to offer you ten days of fantastic travel only available on this ship. Our crew of fifty will assist you in any and all your needs (a lie).

We will be stopping at four different islands in the Caribbean where no passports are required, so unpack your swimming suits. On the ship we offer three different mess halls for your dining pleasure that are open 24 hours a day (another lie). We hope you will find the meals at the mess hall named Captain Jack's on level one to be a delightful experience. This Hall offers the food the seamen had seventy-five years ago. Don't worry, as it is fresh and not that old coming from the Full Food Grocery store. Then on level two is the mess hall Hook and Line which offers up fresh seafood of the Caribbean. Finally on level three is the Holy Cow providing good old tender meat and potatoes fit for a king or queen. The tender steaks are indeed mouth watering and the best money can buy (yet another lie). We guarantee you none will go hungry on the Heavenly Way."

With the Captain's announcement regarding food many passengers were indeed becoming hungry. Not a word was said about breakfast or for that matter any breakfast type of food available. They later would learn breakfast food on this ship was like finding a palm tree in the Arctic. Not even Carrot Loop's cereal was aboard this ship. The Captain continued, "For your entertainment we have plenty to offer you as you all enjoy this cruise. On level number two we have a slot machine casino and on level three we have both a slot machine casino and a casino offering you table games and even more fun slot machines. I also almost forgot [a lie] on level one there is also a slot machine casino. All of the casinos are open 24-hours a day for your enjoyment and our friendly staff will assist you in locating the fun rooms (not a lie). I assure you that all of our slot machines have liberal payouts (another lie) so have fun in our casinos and good luck in them. In that we are at sea any age may play in the casinos (meaning get your kids playing too). Then for even more entertainment on level one we offer you: shuffleboard, badminton fun and a fitness area with a weight room to work off your huge meals. On level number two is a bowling alley and a large swimming pool. Also enjoy the Comedy Club offering nightly shows on this second level. I must advise you some of the shows may not be suitable for our younger voyagers, as some shows are a bit off-color. Then naturally you are always free to come onto this deck to watch the sea and the world go by."

The entertainment segment of the Captain's talk was now over. It seemed to most that the casinos are where they wanted you unless of course you loved shuffleboard? This was a low cost cruise and they were going to fleece your pockets with slot machines some thought and they were right. With no mention of breakfast the next shock was to come from Captain Newman. "Well ladies and gentlemen as for your rooms. I know you were all advised you would be living just like the brave sailors on this ship did at the time of war (not true). You will enjoy the bunks just as they did as one big happy family. Single women will be in the area marked SW, single men in area marked SM with married couples in MC. All the quarters are located on level one and you may now go there to set yourself up. Myself and the entire crew do hope you have a wonderful Dream Vacation."

The eight hundred and seventy lucky passengers next went step-by-step down to level one with no assistance from the vanishing crew. Many of the elderly simply threw some of their suitcases into the ocean, as they knew they could not carry more than their essentials down the many steps. It was indeed a pity that this ship had no elevators as all the other cruise liners had. The sailors didn't have one so why would the passengers need one? The people that had booked on this voyage were slowly becoming aware of just why this one was at such a bargain fare. When they arrived at their rooms the truth really sunk in. There were no rooms and there were no beds. Instead each quarters was exactly as the sailors had left them seventy-five years ago. Each quarters was one large room with swinging bunks allowing for no privacy whatsoever. This situation in the MC quarters would certainly curtail any romance by the married. This was not a place for those on their honeymoon either. Each bunk did have new bedding but outside of that fact this was not a luxury liner but a battleship with no war. The bathrooms had stalls with of course no doors and the shower room was just that, a room for twenty-five passengers to take showers together. The full figured passengers never took showers, as they were embarrassed to have others see their plump bodies. In days to come bars of soap did show up at the swimming pool. Since the voyagers had no options they placed their belongings by the swinging bunks to make the best of it. Several said that when they stopped at the first island they were going to buy an airline ticket back home as soon as possible. Especially the plump ones wanted out of this madness. Louie from Delaware was in the SM quarters with his huge black trunk. He opened it and out popped his dog Sparky. The dog was an eighty-five pound Black Labrador that immediately ran around looking for a fire hydrant and since there were none he was happy to lift his leg on traveler's suitcases. This event did not make Louie or Sparky favorable with the residents but fortunately Louie had baby wipes to clean off the dog's necessity. Then Sparky ran around the large room seeking something not known after being cooped up for hours. Louie thought all of the events were humorous but his fellow travelers had different thoughts indeed. With well over three hundred people in the SM quarters' and even more in the other quarters allowed for no privacy in any of them. A dog running around in the SM quarters' which was both the men's living and sleeping area naturally did not make many of the voyagers very happy. Some wondered what would take place when the dog had to poop? This indeed brought about very unhappy thoughts, which added to the discomfort of being on level one of the ship. It happened that on this level was the engine room that let off diesel fumes into all of the quarters. The added smell of dog poop could make living in the SM unbearable. This was not a luxury cruise given the surprises of this very first day.

Once all the voyagers had settled into the three swinging bunk areas it was close to noon. Having had no breakfast they were eager to have a lunch when a few of the friendly staff members provided them with the current news. That was food was only available at Captain Jack's mess hall on level one. The other two mess halls that were to be open on a 24-hour basis were closed for maintenance. That meant eight hundred and seventy voyagers had to somehow eat in a mess hall designed for three hundred and fifty people. That was impossible and resulted in complete chaos. Once the first three hundred and fifty were seated the helpful staff told the other travelers they could eat in shifts once the first had completed their lunch. Lunch was served all right. It was hot dogs, potato chips and Kool-Aid to drink. Voyagers were allowed seconds which ended up to be cold hot dogs. The second and third shifts would get to enjoy the cold hot dogs as well but Louise Dogman of Wisconsin was the first to discover the casinos had hot food offerings. In all of the casinos there were vending machines that had hot beef sandwiches and corn beef ones on rye you could buy. The food prices were high as $8.25 for a sandwich, $6.25 for a beer and $5.25 for a shot of whiskey. The lines to the food machines were long but at least you could buy a hot sandwich over a cold hot dog. Twenty of the ship's crew was constantly cooking to keep the vending machines full making this the only place where twenty-four hour food was really available. Then another twenty staff workers helped in the three casinos to assist the slot machine players with their needs. This accounted for why there were very few of the crew remaining to help on any of the passenger's other needs. The casinos took priority over anything else on this ship at all times. The goal of keeping you in one was the top priority of the ship's mates. The Captain also hoped all would go ker-plonk, ker-plonk with their quarters into the hungry slot machines.

Louise had met Mary Ellen from Nebraska in the SW quarters' even though both women were married. They had elected to travel alone and leave their husbands at home and were taking the cruise they both had won from the Jack Pine radio program. While enjoying the high priced sandwiches on the second level casino Louise said, "Look at those fools putting their hard earned money into slot machines that never can be beat. When they go broke they go over to one of the ATM's for even more money to throw away. People are sure dumb to believe they will ever become rich playing a slot machine. Look at them, they are like zombies in a trance." Mary Ellen loved playing the slot machines but for obvious reasons never said a word about that to Louise. She would sneak into a casino in the very early morning when she knew Louise was fast asleep. Once at a casino she would cash the limited $200 check and proceed to lose all that money. Then she would go to another casino on a different level and do the same thing. Night after night she would continue this process as a duck goes to water. At some point her duck hunting husband would learn of the money spent which would result in them eating over three hundred ducks for meals as they had done in earlier years. Worst, now they would surely be eating mud hens too!

Aside from the casinos with the hot food there were other forms of entertainment on the Heavenly Wave. Level one had both the badminton court along with the shuffleboard area. The engine room on this level unfortunately produced an excess of both diesel and exhaust fumes that would go into both entertainment areas. Actually the fumes went everywhere on level one including into the sleeping rooms. No doubt this design would have the voyagers eventually go into the casinos where the Captain wanted them and the air was clean. The badminton court seemingly was always available for this sport or activity had lost its charm years ago. It's location closest to the engine room only found the brave picking up a racket. If you wanted to play this game it was the only one with no waiting lines. Shuffleboard was another matter as this game area was packed all day. During the day the ten lanes were laid out on concrete with long lines of spectators waiting for their turn. That area had no chairs so they would stand for hours until the fumes would overtake them. Then they would take to the casinos for air and perhaps a beer. Since level one had the two activities, the sleeping areas, a casino with clean air and Captain Jack's meals along with Kool-Aid it may have been that some old timers spent their entire ten day Dream Vacation on it. They just did not want to climb the many stairs to go beyond level one. Then the fitness and weight rooms were on this level too with more of the polluted atmosphere. Voyagers could work out to be healthy and trim in the air that would destroy their lungs. Only a few took advantage of these rooms for those that did certainly had grey matter missing from their brains. How could you be healthy and ruin your lungs at the same time?

The second level had better air and more entertainment. The swimming pool was here with the full figure folks in the pool along with three feet of soapsuds around them. There were bars of Ivory soap floating around but the sponsor's Soft Soap was not to be seen. The large size pool the Captain told about was not to be found on this ship. Only two-dozen voyagers at a time would fill the pool and it was only four foot in depth at any one place in it. The pool was more like a wading pool with no room for swimming and not enough depth to allow for any diving. That is unless you wanted a knot on your noggin? Maybe the Captain meant to say large size bathtub? More entertainment on this level was the bowling alley and that is what it was, a one-lane alley. Eight hundred and seventy travelers with a one-lane bowling alley did not make for a good sight. People waited in line for their turn and it was a long line. If any bowler took more than ten frames a fight would develop with more knots on the noggin possible. A major fight like a heavy weight one would occur if the full figure travelers were part of the fights. Eventually, a crew worker would come to end the fights with the Captain unable to understand why fights would happen at all? He thought such a fun activity would have all happy. If you got a turn on the alley or just there to watch the fights develop you ended up with two entertainment venues. Then in the evening the Comedy Club was here as well. The Captain had warned there might be some off color parts during the shows. He was right and the shows were not for the younger travelers. Rumor had it there was a ten dollar and twenty-five cent cover charge and beer was six dollars and twenty-five cents for a small cup. Then the show room was kept at ninety degrees in an attempt to sell plenty of the beer it was said. You might say on this voyage there were no bargains if any of this was true.

On the third level there were two more large beautiful casinos that did make the voyagers feel that they were on a luxury liner, which the rooms were designed to do. With the sleeping quarters down on level one it seemed these casinos had to be special to attract people up to them. It offered hot food in the vending machines with a dollar discount and one free beverage to the players. These casinos needed to have voyagers climb the many steps up to them and the dollar off actually helped attract players. The casinos were the most spacious and beautiful ones indeed always having many players in them with the sound of quarters going in being music to the Captain's ears. He apparently received a cut for he pushed the casinos constantly to those that would listen. The Quarter Step Dance Hall also was here where in two nights the Gala New Year's Eve party would take place. Unfortunately until then it was closed for decorating purposes

Day two of the Dream Vacation found the passengers adjusting to the battleship. They had learned about the limited fun activities, the hungry slot machines, the crummy restaurants and their deplorable sleeping arrangements. Many were having hopes and dreams of leaving the next day when the Heavenly Wave would visit the first island stop. Most of the travelers spent their entire day visiting with each other on the top deck. They had the folding chairs, the fresh sea air and each other on this level. When hungry they went down the many steps to find Captain Jack's was closed for repairs. On the third level the Holy Cow mess hall was serving steaks and finally was open. That menu was fried round steaks, potatoes, with corn and of course Kool-Aid. The steaks were as tough as leather so Sparky received most of them. It took him two or three days to chew up one meaning he would have over a ten-year supply. Many of the voyagers gave in and bought the $8.25 sandwiches and brought them up to the top deck. They were on the Caribbean with a soft south breeze making for tranquil travel. However, there were some that had developed seasickness. Those poor souls were on the top deck away from the others hanging onto the rails emptying their stomachs into the sea. One of them was Charles from Corpus Christi and healthy voyagers asked if they could help him? He only replied, "Oh God." Then later others ask him if they could get him a drink or some food? Charles once again only replied, "Oh God," as he puked over the railings. Others were in this poor condition as well and they too cared for nothing to eat or drink. This group only wanted land. On this day with the majority on the top deck there were some at the swimming pool and other venues as well. The wealthy were going Ka-ching, Ka-ching with their quarters into the slots enjoying the pleasant atmosphere of the casinos. The Captain came on the PA system to announce, "Ladies and gentlemen smoking is only allowed in the casinos and on the top deck. Please refrain from smoking beyond those areas. A fine of $300 will be for smoking outside of the designated areas. Thank you and have a nice day." This meant the old timers on the first level would have to put away their pipes and other smokes. They would have to leave their exhaust filled entertainment areas and enter a casino to enjoy one of their pleasures. Of course this was just one more ploy to get casino players. It seemed this ship wanted to suck every quarter out of everyone's pockets before it would be happy.

As nightfall came to the voyagers many brought up their beddings to the top deck. They would sleep on a hard flat surface under the millions of December stars. This was an improvement over the swinging Navy bunks that put an arch and pain in their backs. Plus the sea air was free of engine fumes and the three hundred odors people made in a confined area. On the huge open deck even the honeymooners found private areas for their romance as long as they kept their distance from the seasick ones. With the warm night many decided that they would sleep on the hard deck every night of their Dream Vacation. Outside of the twenty that had won their vacation from Jack Pine all of the others had paid for this cruise. Sleeping on a hard deck or sleeping in an exhaust filled room with three hundred strangers was not a romantic luxury winter cruise they learned. How this had happened to them they did not understand but they did know on the next day they were going to buy an airline ticket back to Miami. Tonight they could watch the stars and fall asleep to the sounds of Charles going, "Oh God," all through the night along with a chorus of his seasick fellow travelers. This was just a part of adjusting to a cruise on a World War II battleship they all had also learned.

The next morning attitudes had improved because the voyagers knew the great ship was to dock at Barbuda today. Plus on the top deck where most were news spread that coffee was available in the top casino for a mere $4.25 a cup with no refills of course. Most had their coffee in the open air awaiting their next pleasure when the Captain gave an announcement, "Ladies and gentlemen we will be docking at the Island of Barbuda at 10:30 this morning. If you go ashore we advise you to check in your valuables with the ship's purser at the second level casino. You may visit the island until 8 PM this evening. At 7 o'clock we will sound the ship's horns to notify you of our departure in one hour. May you all have a wonderful day." This news was their real pleasure as the ship docked on time and only a handful remained along with the old timers on the first level. They did not want to tackle the countless stairs and were content to play shuffleboard and sneak a smoke on their level. Louie stayed on the ship, as he did not want to leave Sparky alone on the Heavenly Wave. He met the cooks from the Hook and Line and the Holy Cow to tell them what an expert potato peeler he was. He said he could peel any type of potatoes and brown ones too. The cooks took an interest as they never had heard of brown ones and gave Louie a job in the ship's potato department. Aside from peeling potatoes he could cook them baked, boiled and fried. Louie was given the keys to all three mess halls and went to work peeling potatoes while the others were on the island. Over eight hundred of the voyagers headed directly to the Barbuda Airport. All wanted a one-way ticket to Miami or for that matter anywhere in the United States. In the next 48 hours there were four flights to Miami and since only smaller Jets could use the airport only sixty passengers could be on each flight. Within one hour's time all but one of the tickets were sold out. The last ticket was sold to a newly married couple on their honeymoon. At first it appeared they could not decide which would be using the ticket and who was to stay on the Heavenly Wave. Everyone watched this spectacle unfold when she hit him with her purse as they both screamed obscenities at each other. He then knocked her to the ground as she kicked and yelled. At this point her high-heeled shoes went flying off her feet. They continued tossing around and she ended up on top where she proceeded to knock out his two front teeth. She did this by pounding his face mercilessly with a high heel shoe until his face was bloody. The fighting seemingly went on forever until Airport Security guards came and broke up the fight. She somehow had the ticket so the guards took him off to jail and as he was led away in handcuffs she cried out to him, "I am going to mothers' and I never want to see you again." As all of this was going on one businessman with his wife offered $2,000 each for two tickets. There were no sellers, which indicated on just how bad a Dream Vacation was on the Heavenly Wave. The honeymooner's fighting did add some entertainment value to the cruise as some thought about how grand love could be.

Poor Charles along with a line of sick ones lagged behind in their condition to the airport. All the tickets were sold long before they arrived there so they all would just have to enjoy this day on land until the next island. At the airport two hundred and forty tickets were sold which meant now only six hundred and thirty voyagers would remain on the Heavenly Wave when it sailed on. Maybe some of the crew jumped ship too by getting some of the tickets? If so then more voyagers would have to return to the ship. The unfortunate non-air ticket holders would have to make the best of it on Barbuda. As luck would have it their ship was the only cruise ship to visit Barbuda on this day. They had the entire island to themselves and to the many tourist restaurants they went. Some ordered two or three meals at one time after having lived on vending machine sandwiches the past two days. Here beer was only two dollars so they could have plenty of that too. The really smart travelers had taxis take them to the grocery stores where they stocked up for the next leg of their journey. Then there were the tourist shops and the sandy beaches to enjoy. This island was the very best part of the journey even if they weren't able to buy a ticket to Miami. Then the battle cry horns of the Heavenly Wave sounded and all knew it was time to return to the ship. Earlier during the voyage Louie had made friends with Oly from Minnesota. Oly had gone ashore and returned at 8 o'clock along with all the others. Louie had a special nostalgic yearning for Spam and had asked his new friend to buy some on the island for him. Oly came to tell Louie, "Vel Loies, I cood onlys gets yous sex cans of der spams tas others byes tit too, tis tat okey dokey ten?" Louie answered, "Geese laweeze Oly, that is great! I'm going to fix you up a meal of it better than anything you've had on this old bucket of bolts." Oly's eyes lit up and he responded, "Okey dokey ten, vill ave a feast wit tit." "So, Geese laweeze you could not buy a ticket, Oly?" "No, tey sells outs for I coulds buys one. Tey must ave been ones hundreds wanting tos gos ome." "I am sorry Oly, but why would you want to go home in frigid January where it is so damn cold?" "Vell Loies, I gots some de Mrs. Butts hots chili ups tere that wood bes hotter ten tis ocean plus I puts alls me moneys in de machines that goes Ka-ching Ka-ching. I's gots good noose, on de island I's makes a news friend. Captain Blackout and he's a real ships Captan, kan we's ave him fer spams too?" "Sure Oly, you got enough for you, the Captain, me and Sparky too, plus I'll cook up some potatoes with it. We will have a huge feast."

At dark most of the six hundred and thirty voyagers once again took their beddings up to the top deck. Charles and his crowd were already up there hanging onto the rails with no beddings. After the long day the healthy watched the clear sky as they rested on the hard deck and soon they fell asleep as the ship sailed south. Very early in the morning a light mist and drizzle started sending the healthy ones to their dry Navy bunks. They would finish their sleep there while the sick remained outside come what may. At nine o'clock in the morning Captain Newman made an announcement, "Ladies and gentlemen happy last day of the year. Tonight we will have the Gala New Year's celebration at the Quarter Step Dance Hall. I hope to see you all there." Word had reached him that many of the voyagers had purchased beer and whiskey on the island to his displeasure and then he continued, "Tonight all will be given complementary champagne to bring in the New Year, plus a cash bar will be available. I must remind you it is against ship rules to possess any private alcoholic beverages, so please enjoy the cash bar. Thank you and have a nice day." The ships rules where in the small print no one read in the glossy brochure mailed weeks prior to the cruise. Of course the rules were designated to have the travelers spend as much money as possible only on the ship's goods. Toothpaste was included as well. On this last day of the year by noon the mist had turned into hard rain with dark skies. Captain Newman made another announcement, "Ladies and gentlemen it appears the sea may become a little rough today as we are heading into a small storm. This old battleship will have no trouble dealing with it but I must advise all to not go onto the top deck today. This is for your safety and I look forward to seeing you all tonight at the Quarter Step Dance Hall. Have a nice day." The ship rocked very little as the waves increased and the voyagers went to enjoy their lunch. The Hook and Line was closed for maintenance, as always, the steaks at the Holy Cow were too tough to eat, which left Captain Jack's or vending machines as choices. The majority went for the hot dogs, with mostly cold hot dogs being served to enjoy along with the diesel smell filling the air. As they were eating the sea became rougher and the great ship started to sway side to side. Once in the storm's center it tilted in a violent fashion tossing everything loose flying through the air. The passengers could hardly stand upright, as the great ship could not handle the angry sea. They were in a major storm making those that had eaten very sick. The ship going violently side to side sent many to the restrooms to vomit up their hot dogs. Even the $8.25 hot beef sandwiches could not be spared. Regardless of the Captain's orders many were so ill they did take to the top deck to send their meals into the sea. Charles was on the deck repeating the only two words he knew, "Oh God." As the masses hung onto the rails with grips of iron, it was a miracle none went overboard. The huge waves sent mist and water over the top deck making all soaking wet in their misery. The storm continued all day and into the night having those with empty stomachs returning to their bunks. Once in them they would swing side by side giving them terrible dry heaves. Given their deplorable condition they wanted nothing to eat, drink or anything to do with any New Year's gala party.

With the storm continuing a few healthy ones did go to the Quarter Step Dance Hall to hear the band and bring in the New Year. As the ship continued it's rocking motions they would be disappointed once again. There was no band but rather the disc jockey, Harry Snapshot playing records from the World War II era. Songs like 'Kiss Me Once, Kiss Me Twice' and Bing Crosby singing old songs no one could relate to played. By midnight only a handful remained listening to Big Band music that they didn't know how to dance to. Outside the five-foot waves with huge whitecaps pounded the ship. At one o'clock Harry stopped playing records to bid all a good night and a Happy New Year. The not so Gala Party was over.

The first day of the New Year had the Caribbean storm gone and now there was a calm sea. The sun brought temperatures into the pleasant 80's as the Heavenly Wave continued its southern journey. The ideal conditions brought cheer and recovery to all that were sick the prior day although none were eager to have more then a cup of tea or coffee. The mess halls never served any breakfast food what so ever during the entire cruise unlike all other cruise ships. On the Heavenly Wave at ten AM Captain Jack's open for hot dogs or the voyagers could buy an egg and sausage sandwich out of the vending machines for a mere $8.25. It was always hoped the three quarters in change would find their way into a slot machine. This ship never missed a trick and another would come later in the day. For now all was restful outside of in the SM quarters' where Sparky was running around retrieving a ball. He had gained favor and laughs by practically all the men and laughs were rare on this ship given the overall bleak conditions. Louie with Oly's help always took care of Sparky's duty by flushing it down a toilet so that smell was promptly taken care of. Sparky's high energy was the only energy on this day of recovery and Louie helped him up the many stairs to the top deck where he could run around the huge deck area. Louie and Oly threw the ball a good number of times and then Sparky went over to a group of men visiting.

The politician Harry Lonesum, Bill from Grass Lake and Captain Blackout seemed to be enjoying the day. Mr. Lonesum was talking about all his ideas of everyone having a nuke and his big ASS involvement. The outlaw type Bill found the idea of everyone having a nuke very interesting as the Captain drank whiskey from his flask breaking the ship's rules. Bill asked Lonesum, "How far would I need to be from a nuke to be safe? I'd like to have one to blow up every duck and Game Warden back home on Grass Lake? It would be fun to see all the feathers fly and Game Warden's badges blown up to pieces with one push of the button." The politician answered, "Bill if you could see the feathers fly it would be the last thing you would see on this green earth. I don't think a nuke is the right way to blow up a lake; you just need a tank or two. Why do you find it necessary to shoot a poor duck anyways? There is no need to kill any birds what so ever in this day and age, you can buy a clean chicken in any grocery store." "Ah, you are a pansy Lonesum. I'll shoot any duck anytime and anywhere I want. People like you would be target practice back home, no wonder you lost the election." "Bill I'm against the shooting of all birds, remember I'm a big ASS member. That is Association to Save the Sparrow." As they continued arguing the flock of seagulls that followed the ship were milling around and Bill pulled out his six-gun. BAM, BAM one bird fell dead into the sea as everyone on the deck immediately turned to the shots. Sparky ran over to look at the dead seagull but did not jump over the railings. Lonesum in shock said, "My God you are crazy, those birds were doing absolutely nothing to harm us. People like you should never be allowed to have a gun or a nuke either." Bill replied, "Cheer up, I am a felon and not supposed to have a gun, but I say screw em."

Louie and Oly went over to Sparky and the three men, as they too were concerned about the shooting. Charles in the background could be heard saying, "Oh God!" Bill had put his gun away and Oly introduced Louie to Captain Blackout that was yet drinking from his flask. Eventually all got to know each other and then they talked about this and that. Louie said, "Geese laweeze there is little fun on this ship, if I wasn't peeling potatoes I'd be bored to death. This ship only stopped at one island and that wasn't all day so I never even got to visit it." Oly added, "Yeah an tose spinnin machenes gots alls me monee cept for a few dollors." The Captain said, "You know mateys I know how to run this ship, I say we do a mutiny and I'll stop at any island for as long as we want. Yes siree mateys mutiny is what we need." Lonesum reflected on the idea, "Mutiny hum, then an Island. We could set up a government where everyone is free and nobody could kill anything except maybe each other. I have good ideas on how to run a country." Bill then drew out his six-gun again and said, "I got Sweet 44 here and she is always itching to shoot anything that moves. Maybe you Lonesum would make good target practice in your new government? Well Sweet 44 could take over the ship, but who's going to run it?" The Captain drinking from his flask answered, "Well Mateys I am a full fledged Captain I told you and I could run this tub with one eye closed. I say mutiny." Oly said, "Okey dokey ten, I say mutiny ta gets me quarters back." Louie was unable to think on how to get the mad crazy talk back to rational thinking. He took Sparky and climbed down the many steps to his quarters' and he figured he would just wait for the shots of Sweet 44 and the politician starting his brave new world. He wondered on how Oly was doing and then did get an idea. So he climbed back up the many steps to the main deck. He approached the mad group, "Geese laweeze guys I have a great idea. Let's have that feast of special Spam and potato pancakes. I have the keys to the mess hall so let's go there and have a great meal for a change." Louie even asked the man hanging over the railings if he would like to join them. The man only muttered, "Oh God." The rest agreed that it was a good plan so all climbed down to level one and Captain Jack's mess hall. Louie then cooked potato pancakes and fried up the Spam in his special sauce. The men ate until their bellies were more then full and the talk of mutiny was no more.

Later in the afternoon the cruise ship would have another trick designed to take more of the voyager's money. Captain Newman came on the PA system, "Ladies and gentlemen, at four o'clock on the second level casino we are having a free tournament with prizes, a free drink and a gift for all. This is for your pleasure with the first two hundred lucky voyagers getting to play, so hurry over to the second level casino now. Have a nice day." With most of the passengers recovering from yesterday's storm and their stomach illness only about one hundred and fifty showed up to the tournament. Their free drink was the champagne left over from the gala party and the gift was a cheap plastic key chain having the Heavenly Waves logo on it. The tournament was fixed having the cruise worker's friends win all the prizes with the competition over in a very short time. The entire event was just to get players back into the casino, which it did. The

ATM and the slot machines were the real winners.

It was January 2nd and the sixth day of the cruise when attitudes brightened. On this day the ship would dock once more visiting the second island scheduled on the cruise. Many of the voyagers wanted their Dream Vacation over and they would go to the airport hoping for a Miami flight. Others just wanted to be on land, especially Charles. At ten o'clock the ship docked with Captain Newman announcing that all should return by eight o'clock and have a nice day. Once on the small Caribbean Island it was learned that there wasn't a major airport and there were no flights going to Miami. There was not even a sandy beach but a rocky one for this island was made up totally out of rocks. Here there wasn't any dirt or vegetation except for what was placed in man made boxes arranged in a pattern that held palm trees. There was a downtown restaurant strip with over a dozen and even a McDonalds'. The island's only employment appeared to be restaurants, bars, and tourist gift shops. In fact there were plenty of drinking establishments and restaurants making it appear on this rocky island people only ate and drank so maybe that is why the locals called home the PIG? The stores and homes were all constructed out of rocks and concrete with even the golden arches made out of rocks. The Island's name was Palm Island Gardens and that is why the local people said they lived on the 'PIG'. The Island's long name was years ago established to fool tourists but once here they found the only trees were the ones planted in the boxes. The voyagers packed the restaurants for great meals while enjoying two dollar beers and also were delighted to go swimming in water deeper than four feet. A Canadian professor, Doctor Mudson found this to be a strange island. It was one he had never seen or even had heard about. Here was a place with no dirt, which happen to be his main study back in Canada. He struck up a conversation with a fellow young voyager, Donnie Hickock from Rapid City, South Dakota. "Well young man what do you think about this Caribbean Island, one with no dirt except for what is in the tree boxes? I wonder how much rain falls here? How would you like to live on such a place as this, `eh?" Donnie answered, "Holy macaroni molly, I never thought about any of it, I am just happy to get off that rocky boat and be on solid ground. I won this trip but it sure is a far cry from what I expected." "Son this is not ground, this is volcanic rock only, eh.

Ground has dirt, mud and muck for that matter, `eh." Donnie answered, "Holy macaroni molly rocks or dirt what's the difference? Where I live we have lots of rocks and in fact I am an idiot in a rock band." "A rock band, `eh, I wonder why there are no dirt and roll bands, `eh?" Donnie answered again, "Well rock and roll makes more sense than dirt and roll I guess unless you're a dog. Look at those clouds I'll bet it will be raining here soon." The Professor nodded his head back and forth while saying, "What a shame rainfall with no dirt, `eh." Danny now had heard enough from this strange man concerned about dirt, rocks and rain so he drifted off to the salt-water ocean leaving the Canadian looking into a box of dirt.

Palm Island Gardens had slot machines and ATM machines in its drinking establishments. Mary Ellen from Nebraska and Tommy Lucky from Reno were playing them in a bar called the Last Chance Red Eyed Saloon. The slot machines were the type that took three quarters per play and offered a big jackpot. Sitting next to each other Tommy said to Mary Ellen, "Well at least these machines let you play with them giving you back a little here and there. The ones on the ship just eat money and I never seem to get a penny back from them. I've seen you playing them, how did you ever do on them?" Mary Ellen answered, "Yes these are fun and the ship ones are a disaster for me. I've blown more money there than I can afford. My husband will kill me when he sees our credit card bill next month as what I spent on Christmas plus the ship's machines won't make him very happy." "What does your husband do?" "He hunts ducks mostly but he thinks he's a writer of sorts and does short stories. He's never made a dime at that so he hunts ducks." "Hunts ducks, can't be much money in that? Hey, I met a guy on the ship that hunts ducks too. I think his name was Bill. So he hunts ducks?" "Yep, that's what he does, so we eat more of them then Carter has pills. I have two jobs to keep us going, what do you do?" "I live in Reno and am the Executive Director for ASS, you might say I am the biggest ASS." Tommy enjoyed the humor of answering his employment in that manner and then explained, "ASS is the Association to Save the Sparrows. It is a group for the protection of all birds really. The members are all fanatics so I get to direct a group of crazy people that are a bunch of ASS's. That's my job so it is funny that I am sitting on a Caribbean Island next to a lady that eats many birds.

What are your two jobs?" Mary Ellen now wondering about this man said, "My jobs are not much compared to yours'. I check out at a Full Foods grocery store full time standing on my feet all day and then work twenty hours at Hanabees where they make ammunition. I don't have much free time so enjoying this cruise even though it is far from perfect. Sleeping in a hammock is not very good on my back so I am going to try sleeping on the top deck with a lot of the others." Their conversation continued as their slot machines took quarters and gave some back unlike the Heavenly Wave machines. Then Mary Ellen's machine made an explosion of sounds with all looking at it and her. Tommy said, "You did it! You hit the super jackpot you lucky girl!" The machine she was playing was one connected to the thirty ones throughout the town offering a huge jackpot. She had won the grand prize of $50,000 from her three quarters. She was in shock with the jackpot but had no idea on just how much she had won. The saloon manager came to her giving her some paperwork and then explained, "Congratulations young lady, you have just won $50,000! You need to take this authorization to the bank two blocks down and they will pay you, as we don't have that kind of money here. This machine is linked with thirty others so the bank has the money." The winning machine continued its loud sounds and would until the bank shut it off. Tommy said he would stay with the machine while Mary Ellen went to collect her money, which would insure no one could fool with her winning slot machine.

After given exact directions in her excited condition she went to the bank. Once there the bank manager asked her, "Do you want your money in American currency or Palm Island Garden's currency called rockers." Naturally she preferred American money so the bank put all the currency in a locked suitcase except for ten $100 bills she kept out. Returning to Tommy at the Last Chance Red Eyed Saloon with her new suitcase in hand she told him, "Here's $500 for you watching things and now I am going back to the ship to lock this money up." He replied, "You don't have to do that and I'm going to walk back with you to make sure you are safe." Mary Ellen insisted that he keep the money she gave him and then they went back to the Heavenly Wave. She gave the suitcase to the purser and then went up to the top deck to walk around in her continuing excitement. Tommy went back to the PIG with his $500 and at seven o'clock the ships' battle cries sounded telling all it was time to return shipside and leave Palm Island Gardens.

The following day was the seventh day with another island stop scheduled. The voyagers were happy about this event as the food and lack of the ships' real entertainment would make any Caribbean Island a pleasure. In the day's early hours a few hundred were on the top deck awaiting the landing. As an island came into full view the Heavenly Wave continued past it with no announcement concerning it. The travelers concluded that island was not the right island and soon they would be on a different correct one. Almost all of the voyagers had given up on flying back to Miami for they felt since they had endured to this point a couple of more days would be bearable. They eagerly were waiting for the correct island to come along with sandy beaches and good food. They hung onto those ideas for hours but no other island appeared. Finally in the late afternoon Captain Newman informed the voyagers that due to the New Year's storm they were behind schedule and would not be stopping on this day. However, tomorrow they would be visiting an Island. The news made for an angry ship once more. Sparky was not angry as he had over one hundred men to play with and give him attention in the SM quarters'. There most of the older men and some younger ones took down their personal hanging hammocks and made beds with them on the floor. The hanging hammock beds gave them arched backs, which resulted in painful backaches. It made them wonder on how the sailors survived both the war and their beds? Sparkly cared less about that for he had a new game to play with the men. He would take a bedroll, tear it apart and then proceed to chew a hole or two in the blanket. The voyagers learning this would take their holed bedroll and exchange it for someone else's on the floor that was not chewed up. Over and over both Sparky and the men played hard at this game. Basically the men thought this was all in fun for it broke up playing shuffleboard and badminton that they were truly bored with. The bowling alley only offered heavyweight fights and the swimming pool always had three feet of soapsuds. The slot machines very seldom paid off so all in all entertainment on the Heavenly Wave was at an all time low. Sparky chasing a ball or ripping up bedrolls was welcomed entertainment for the men. Besides if you found and asked a crew worker he would always give you a new blanket. The real trick in the game was to find a crew worker.

At super time the options were Captain Jack's or the Hook and Line. The Holy Cow ceased operation for the Dream Vacation's remaining cruise. Word was the left over round steaks no one could eat anyways were dumped overboard for the seagulls or the sharks. Sparky had a cooked pile of them too. The angry voyagers ate more hot dogs, minute orders of fish or vending machine foods. Following their meals over two hundred went to the ship's second level where the Comedy Club was located in search of some nightly entertainment. Once there they really learned there was a ten dollar and twenty-five cent cover charge that they had heard about along with the $6.25 beer. This was the show the Captain had noted would have some off-color parts. He was right about that except it wasn't parts but rather every sentence was nothing but filthy language. After 15 minutes most all had heard more than enough and left the show. Some wanted and others demanded their money back and those persistent were given vouchers. Later they would discover the vouchers were only good at the slot machines to their disgust. Then once again the majority took their bedrolls to the top deck and slept where Charles was presently saying the only two words he was known for.

Day eight of the Dream Vacation started out good by all accounts. On this day the great ship docked at the island called Flowering Island based on the sweet and beautiful fragrances produced by its thousands of tropical flowers. With two days remaining the voyagers planned on enjoying the beautiful Caribbean Island with none interested in going to the airport. For the first time nothing could get in the way of the voyagers having a fun and great day. Well almost nothing. Another cruise liner with five times as many passengers had docked at the Island one hour prior to the Heavenly Wave. Usually not a problem but on that liner a stomach virus had run ramped with six hundred or more deathly sick. The ill ones were quarantined at one section of their ship but of course the virus still made it to the Flowering Island. Many of the sick snuck off to go to the airport and boarded every flight back to the U.S. that was possible. Remaining on the island were plenty of sick ones to create an epidemic and that is what they would do. By one o'clock in the afternoon the virus had spread everywhere on the island affecting travelers and natives alike. The flowering aroma of this Island would be no more with hundreds of people puking all over. Now it smelled just like puke on every square inch of the Island. Most voyagers returned to their ships believing they would be safe there but of course they were not.

Upon boarding there was Charles hanging onto the railing. No one talked to him as by now everyone knew his two words by heart. Some went to the ship's casinos to drink beer and whiskey believing that alcohol would protect them from the virus. All it really did was make them walk funny and do stupid things. One guy went nut-so in the head and staggered around going quack, quack with no other words. He thought he was a duck and with his blurred vision he thought the others in the barroom were big geese. His actions were mild in comparison to all the insanity going on by the drinkers. In the end the booze did nothing to stop the virus so most of them staggered up to the top deck and railings. As they traveled up the steps they puked on them as fifty others already had. It was all just one sloppy mess now on the entire Heavenly Wave plus the sickening smell mixing in with the diesel fumes made it unbearable. Some old timers probably stayed at level one with shuffleboard but most of the drinking voyagers headed up the sloppy steps to the top deck. There they would grab onto a railing to hang their heads over the ship only thinking about what Charles had many times said. Maybe some said his two words too? Once their stomachs were empty they slipped and fell onto the steps going down to their sleeping quarters'. They would be falling down into the disgusting slop and then covered in the puke they crawled into their bedrolls or hanging hammocks. Actually the diesel fumes now smelled good compared to the puke stench in each quarters'. Only the casinos were disinfected, cleaned and sprayed with flowering odors, which was supposed to be the island's experience. At seven o'clock the battleship disguised as a luxury liner sounded the battle cry with only a handful returning to the ship as most already were on it. By eight o'clock, six hundred and thirty voyagers, fifty crewmembers and one Captain sailed off to the north. Day number eight of the Dream Vacation resulted in one wet dream for most.

The Heavenly Wave was scheduled to visit four islands and had docked at three. In Barbuda there was an exodus to the airport, at the second Island it was just rocks and the last offered an epidemic virus. This was not a story you would be telling the grandkids about. No one would be saying, "in the good old days" regarding this voyage either. This was a voyage now of the sick only wanting to go home. On this nice day at full throttle Captain Newman was heading the ship north to Miami. There would be no fourth island stop, as he knew the passengers conditions. To protect himself he sealed off the wheelhouse where he would stay. Things were so bad he could not even come up with a scheme to get his voyagers back into the casinos. He gave thoughts about a game where the sickest would win but dropped the idea. Practically all on the top deck were hanging their heads over the railings. The very unfortunate ones had diarrhea as well creating big problems for them. Some did try to hang both ends of themselves over the railings and given the awkward positions it was indeed a miracle that no one went overboard. Louie was one of the few to escape the virus and he did what he could to keep his distance from the ill. He locked himself and Sparky in the Hook and Line where he peeled a mountain of potatoes. He wondered why he had remained virus free? When yet on the Flowering Island he had overheard native people talking about the virus. One had said it was a harmless virus but in his local dialect it sounded to Louie that he had said it was a 'houndless' virus. Accordingly, Louie gave it his close association with Sparky as the reason he was protected from the virus. He decided to sleep with Sparky and even snuggle up with him on the night remaining. If he ended up with fleas that would be minor compared to the virus. The cook came into the kitchen to tell Louie, "You have a pile of potatoes ready for five days, but hardly a soul will be here to eat them. People are too sick to eat and the cruise will be over in a day. Don't do anymore and Louie I'm going to tell you to leave here now with your dog. It does not look very good to have a dog here in the kitchen even though he doesn't eat fish. You probably have done enough potatoes for the next five days as I've said but if I am wrong I'll send for you. Sorry, but that's the way it is unless you put the dog out without you?" Louie answered the cook, "Geese laweeze I got to be with Sparky now more than ever. This is a houndless virus so he's saving me. I think I'll go over to the swimming pool if you need me." The cook had no idea what he was talking about as Louie and his dog left the Hook and Line. He went to the pool where he met up with his friend Oly. His Minnesota friend said, "Uff-da, tere sures ones sick boats wee's on. I's had soms Mrs. Butts chili I's founds in mee stuff, ates tit n God's knows I's no sick so I's okey dokey ten, what abouts yous?" Louie was real happy to see Oly had escaped the virus and told him, "Geese laweeze it sure is good to see you not sick Oly. I see there's about twenty here and they all look okay too, hope the virus is not here?" Oly answered, "No alls ere tis okay as dey nots up-chuckin at alls. We's safes ere butts nothin ta eats ere." Louie said, "I can go make potato pancakes and French fries then everyone here could eat, but I have no Spam left. Geese laweeze, I can fry up some fish too and you can help me carry it all over here. That will make everyone here happy." Then Louie announced to the crowd what he and Oly we're going to do at the Hook and Line. The bunch applauded and yelled out "Thank You!"

It was ironic that on a Caribbean cruise the healthy group would be confined to a swimming pool of four feet of water with nothing to look at but aqua colored brick walls. They could have done that in New York City. Naturally many of the paying customers would want their money back but that would never happen. On the brochure in small print by the no animals allowed part was the, 'All Sales Are Final, No Refunds' clause. They would get to grumble about this trip so the lucky ones were the radio show voyagers, as they did not have to pay for this nightmare trip. They're recourse was to get back on the talk radio program to tell listeners that whatever they do, don't send in any postcards. It was a sure bet that none on this cruise would ever set foot on the Heavenly Wave once off it in Miami.

Oly and Louie returned with the hot food for the hungry healthy crowd. Sparky was happy to see his master too as he had waited by the pool being banned from the kitchen. He especially enjoyed the French fries along with plenty of fish the cook didn't think he would eat. In fact the dog had second helpings of the fish and fries. Sparky then retrieved a ball thrown into the pool countless times. Next he peed in a corner and no one cared. His master had fed them all and for that they were most grateful. Louie told his friend, "Geese laweeze, Oly go over there and rub that pee all over you. We are up against a houndless virus and that is the only real medicine on this ship. That will protect you from the virus. I learned this back on the island and the pee has saved me. Do it Oly!" Oly walking over to the corner replied, "Uff-da, yous tinks dog pee tis medicane? Vel tit won't hurts nutin sew's I's dos tit buts tit vill smells mes alls over." Louie assured him, "Oly compared to the puke or chlorine and diesel fumes it will smell like perfume." Oly went to the pee and rubbed it all over his hands, face and clothing. One other fellow hearing their conversation went to the corner to do the same. Louie only wished there was enough pee for everyone in the pool area.

The big clock on the aqua wall said it was eight o'clock and with swimming done during the day most of the healthy men and women would attempt to sleep. A joint was passed around to assist in sleeping but that backfired and most just got the munchies. They gobbled down all the cold French fries with cold cod on crackers. They had Kool-Aid spiked with someone's forbidden whiskey not fearing the three hundred dollar fine. No one would own up to having banded whiskey on this supposedly luxury cruise anyways. All they had to do was make it through the night so cared less about any stupid ship rules. Most finally went to sleep while others stayed awake in anticipation of having this past disasters' trip and ten days behind them. Accordingly, they drank more whiskey. Louie made a huge bedroll on the floor with many dry towels. Then Oly, he and the dog would sleep the night away. He even convinced Oly to snuggle up with Sparky for more protection from the houndless virus.

The next morning would conclude the Dream Vacation nightmare but not the virus. That they would get to take home with them and the suffering at both ends would be theirs. This condition would extend their vacation memories for weeks. Upon docking in Miami goodbyes were said between new friendships. However, all were in a stampede to get off the ship. Louie invited Oly to visit him in Delaware promising him he could catch a big fish there and they could eat Spam too. With all rushing off, the Captain came on the P A system, "Ladies and gentlemen thank you for choosing the Heavenly Wave for your Caribbean cruise. We hope you have enjoyed your time as much as the crew and myself have enjoyed serving you [a lie]. We hope to see you all again in the future and may you all have a healthy new year." With that the Dream Vacation was over. Louie had driven down to Miami so was driving home to Delaware to face the harsh realities of normal life. Later that night he had the car radio on.

"Hello you're on the air with Jack Pine on KSTPEE radio broadcasting coast-to-coast. You're on the air, go ahead."

"Thanks Jack, concerning tonight's topic of having sex before marriage. I am Billy from Kentucky. My friends call me Hill Billy and I'm a Baptist so we are forbidden to make love til we're hitched. But have you ever seen a good Baptist family? Boy, it's full gear once we're married. I've got six kids and we're not done yet. Will have more soon as my wife ever gets rid of her darn headaches. So, I say everybody should wait till they are married before having sex and find a woman that don't have headaches."

"Well thanks Hill Billy. By the way folks our station and sponsors gave away twenty lucky cruise vacations last January and will be doing the same this year. Many of the January voyagers called in asking that some night cruises be our topic. We will do that as they all had such a wonderful time. Won't it be fun to hear about the great times and fabulous food the cruises offer people away from their normal living? But, now a word from our sponsor."

Louie turned his radio off, gave Sparky a bone and thought about peeling potatoes.

ABOUT THE AUTHORS

John Shunneson

John grew up to enjoy the great outdoors at Grass Lake, Illinois which is on the Wisconsin border. There his mother, Vi raised his older brother, Arlad and John with all the outdoor activities one could imagine. Hunting, fishing and camping the three would enjoy in Illinois and Wisconsin. After high school John attended Wisconsin State University–Whitewater through his junior year. He attended one summer term in Paris, France during his sophomore year and he also went to the Bahamas that same year. Then in 1967 he transferred to the University of South Dakota where he earned a BFA degree in 1968. In 1969 he went to the University of California–Davis and earned a MFA degree in 1971. His employment history is wide and varied. He worked at his father's fishing resort during summers and after his BFA degree was employed as a commercial artist in Milwaukee, Wisconsin. At the University of California-Davis he taught a summer ceramic's class following his MFA degree and then moved to Minneapolis, Minnesota where he was employed by the Walker Art Center in their A–V department. Next moving to

Colorado he worked as a commercial carpenter. Returning to education in 1979–80 he taught on the High School level at Greeley, Nebraska. In 1981 he returned to school to earn a MA degree in Education at the National College of Education in Evanston, Illinois. During the period of 1981 through early 1984 he also was an instructor at the College of DuPage in Glen Ellyn, Illinois. The National College of Education during 1982 and 1983 employed him to instruct graduate courses in adult education. In 1984 John returned to Nebraska with his wife, Mary Ellen and went to work for the State of Nebraska's Elk's Association program of assisting disabled people into employment. That was a grant program that expired in two years. He and his wife then opened up a retail store and outfitting business in Central Nebraska and South Dakota. In 2004 John was the comedian in the Deadwood, South Dakota Chamber of Commerce's Christmas production rounding out his employment years. The couple then returned to their Nebraska home where unfortunately in 2006 John had his right leg amputated above his knee. During his lifetime John was always connected to the outdoors. Growing up on a rural lake offered a wide knowledge of the great outdoors along with being a Boy Scout and Explorer Scout. In adult life he worked as a big game guide in Wyoming and an outfitter in Nebraska. All the years of guiding and outfitting offered an abundance of humor it must be said. During 2011 John wrote the humorous newsletter, "Musky News" that was distributed to fishermen headed to Maine. Presently he offers his fun and humor in the stories of, "Humor In The Great Outdoors."

Mary Ellen Shunneson

Mary Ellen is John's wife and has been the guiding light of John for the past 34 years. Her laugh and humor is contagious as one will experience in her true story included in this book. Her many years of working in their retail stores seemingly offered all her customers a laugh or two. The long hours of 4 AM until 10 PM during the hunting seasons working in the outfitting business had Mary Ellen giving the hunters countless laughs as well. Having no formal college degree she has a PhD in love, laughter and joy. She is a remarkable person with an inner beauty known to all that know her. Along with offering her story within, Mary Ellen has spent hundreds of hours editing this book making it a reality. She also has spent hundreds of hours fishing, a sport she loves.

Jim O'Connor

Jim and John started this book in the early 1980s only to have Jim pass away in 1998. One of his true stories included in this book is a tribute to him. His dry humor is remarkable and he is greatly missed by all that knew Jim. He grew up in the Nebraska Sandhills with a love of the outdoors along with a great understanding of nature. He was a hunter, fisherman and a trapper. He attended Kearny State College studying literature, which he continued to do throughout his lifetime. His massive personal book collection contained the classics to modern fiction with all in-between. Jim served in the US Army during the Korean War era. Following his service he worked primarily in sales, which he excelled at. All that dealt with Jim knew he was honest and extremely likable. We hope you enjoy his story and humor.

Contact Information:

John or Mary Ellen Shunneson
Box 204
Taylor, Ne 68879

john@shunneson.com